THE
BOOK OF
MURDER

THE BOOK OF MURDER

A PROSECUTOR'S JOURNEY THROUGH LOVE AND DEATH

MATT MURPHY

HYPERION
AVENUE

First Edition, September 2024
10 9 8 7 6 5 4 3 2 1
FAC-004510-24185
Printed in the United States of America

This book is set in TT Bluescreens, DIN Condensed, and Chronicle Text
Designed by Amy C. King

Library of Congress Control Number: 2024934919
ISBN 978-1-368-10406-7
Reinforced binding
www.HyperionAvenueBooks.com

SUSTAINABLE FORESTRY INITIATIVE
Certified Sourcing
www.forests.org
SFI-01681

Logo Applies to Text Stock Only

DEDICATED TO THE VICTIMS OF VIOLENT CRIME

CONTENTS

NOTE TO THE READER

The cases I discuss in the pages ahead are based on a careful review of the available record, but also my personal recollection of events. While I have tried to be as accurate as possible, many of these trials happened years or even decades ago. If I recount anything that diverges from the official record, I humbly submit that the record is correct.

I wrote this book with the intent of educating the public and honoring the victims of violent crime. Nothing I say should be considered an attempt to add anything substantive to any of these cases on appeal, advance any political agendas, or offend anyone (with the exception, perhaps, of a murderer or two).

I should also add a trigger warning:

This book contains detailed descriptions of bad people murdering (mostly) good ones. Out of respect for the reader, I have removed some details too graphic to share. Out of respect for the victims, I have tried to include everything else.

INTRODUCTION

THERE IS NOTHING like the feel of a rounded pintail.

That extra bit of fiberglass and foam on the trailing end of a surf-board gives you just a little more hold on the face of a wave. Perhaps a tad less maneuverable than other tail designs, but add a late drop, an offshore breeze, and the rising sun of an early morning surf session, and that additional hold can make all the difference in the world. Especially for a journeyman surf talent like me.

As with so many things in life, that one tiny yet distinguishing detail can often mean the difference between success and failure, between riding the wave to the beach and floundering in the icy cold water. It was February, a few weeks before my thirty-fourth birthday, and I was floundering like a champ. The brilliant young woman I thought I would marry had just become engaged to someone else. I couldn't eat, I couldn't sleep, and I couldn't stop thinking about her. Like a bad country song stuck on repeat, my mind was an endless loop of regret and self-loathing, only temporarily soothed by the pounding surf of a Southern California winter.

Between the resident pod of bottlenose dolphins that swam through the lineup most mornings and the perfectly triangulated bomber squadrons of California brown pelicans gliding just over the glassy surface, I could sometimes grab a few precious moments of mental calm, at least until the questions came rushing back: Did she really love this guy? Was there truly no chance? How did I ever manage to screw it all up? I was trying to drown demons, but no matter how long I stayed in the water, they always seemed to be waiting for me back on the beach. My personal life was an unquestionable mess.

Professionally, on the other hand, my career was on an absolute tear. I was a young Deputy District Attorney in the Orange County DA's Office, in the midst of a yearslong winning streak, and I had just been promoted to the Homicide Unit. The youngest addition to an elite team of trial lawyers, I was spending my first week on assignment in a place that would become my professional home for the next seventeen years. But on that morning, as I made my way back over the chilly sand to my car, all I could think about was her.

It was a classic winter day in Southern California, with blue skies and a Santa Ana breeze blowing through the trees. I was standing there, in the parking lot of the Manhattan Beach Library, peeling off my wetsuit, starting my quick change into another, more tailored kind of suit that I wore on most weekdays. I rinsed myself off while standing in the five-gallon plastic storage container that often functioned as my shower on the best surf mornings. I poured warm water from a red gasoline jug over my head. Wash the salt off, towel dry my feet, a little deodorant, and I was usually good to go. That morning would be different. My phone had blown up with messages while I was still in the water. It rang once again as I held it.

Someone had been murdered in Newport Beach, and I was about to walk through my first homicide scene.

////Λ\\\

I threw my still-dripping wetsuit into the back of my old Nissan Pathfinder, balanced my surfboard on the reclined passenger seat, and headed directly to Orange County. About an hour south of Los

Angeles on the 405 Freeway, Newport Beach is one of the wealthiest and prettiest cities in California, if not the world. Like a Beverly Hills by the sea, it has all the palm trees and couture, with the added bonus of bikinis. The harbor is ringed with opulent waterfront homes equipped with private docks hosting multimillion-dollar yachts. It is a place where murders are rare, and the residents certainly want to keep it that way.

Morning traffic gave me time to get caught back up in my swirling head: Would my lack of sleep be obvious? Would my brand-new colleagues—the detectives I hoped to be working with for years to come—realize I had been surfing when they tried to call me? Given that I still looked like I was twelve years old, would they even believe who I was? And, of course, the question I couldn't escape: Was my ex really going to marry that guy?

But sunscreen, insomnia, and an aching heart were far from my biggest fears as I navigated traffic that sunny morning. We have all seen the moment on TV or in the movies when the new guy shows up and sees a dead body for the first time. The reaction is so common among rookies at a crime scene, at least as portrayed in pop culture, that it has its own entry on the TV Tropes website. I was so green in the Unit that I hadn't even thought to ask anyone if it was really a thing. Was I about to make a fool of myself? Would I contaminate the scene, lose the respect of my detectives, and be subject to endless hazing for years? "Murphy," I told myself, "in the name of all things holy: Please. Do. Not. Puke."

After talking my way past a perimeter officer assigned to the yellow tape, I met the detective at the door and was escorted into the well-appointed Newport Beach town house, trying not to embarrass myself with my utter lack of experience. Detective Sergeant Dave Byington walked me into the middle of a beehive of activity—police officers, forensic scientists, photographers, and CSI technicians of every stripe—and the air was electric. It was like some huge emotional charge had gone off and the reverberations were still echoing around the room. You could just feel that something terrible had happened.

There were scented candles burning in the entryway and on the bar-style counter that separated the wood flooring of the kitchen from the white Berber carpet of the living room. I tried to take it all in as Byington walked me to the kitchen, which, like everything else in the place, appeared new, neat, and perfect . . . except for the dead guy on the wooden floor at my feet. My moment of truth. I took a deep breath and looked down: He was no older than forty, with a plaid shirt, blond surfer locks, and brown tennis shoes, sprawled out on his back at the bottom of a staircase, eyes half-open, staring at the ceiling with the uneven gaze of the dead.

It was his stillness that struck me first—as if he had been frozen in time. There was motion all around him—from the trees blowing in the wind outside, to all of the technicians, cops, and crime lab personnel—and yet there he was, in the middle of it all, perfectly still. He had a small folding knife in his partially open left hand and a wallet chain leading to his right back pocket. I noticed it instantly: Why would a lefty carry his wallet in his right pocket, or a righty hold a knife in his left hand? That didn't seem right. Then I looked at his shoes, of all things, and wondered if he'd had any idea those would be the last shoelaces he would ever tie.

I had no mysterious urge to vomit—and, no small feat, I had forgotten all about my ex-girlfriend.

/////\\\\\

I say this now, more than twenty years later, after attending perhaps a hundred similar homicide investigations, all unique in their own way: Every entrance into a murder scene is like walking into the center of a three-dimensional puzzle (albeit a puzzle with a dark emotional energy sometimes still lingering in the air). In murder cases like these, figuring out the truth often boils down to the smallest things: The direction of a single drop of blood. A tuft of lint on the floor. A wedding invitation that seems out of place.

Evidentiary details don't forget, they're not biased, and you don't have to work around their schedules. In the simplest terms, a prosecutor's attention to detail will often mean the difference between winning—achieving justice—or a murderer going free. And that scene in particular was full of memorable details.

The victim had been shot once in the back, twice in the chest, once in the temple, and once in his mouth. In the words of Detective Byington, who was standing to my right, our suspect had "killed the shit out of him." In fact, as Byington lifted the left shoulder of the victim to show me two bullets embedded in the hardwood, directly under the two holes in the man's chest, he said, "She pretty much stapled him to the floor." Two handguns had been placed on the white carpet, very close to the body. One had recently been fired, and one had not. The six-shot revolver at my feet, therefore, seemed to have been the murder weapon, and yet we ultimately accounted for no fewer than nine holes. The shooter, quite significantly, had taken the time to reload.

We walked to an upstairs office, past a semicircular smear of blood on the wall of the stairwell. There was broken glass, three more bullet holes in the wall of the office, and another in the wall above the stair-case banister. It was clear that the shooting had started upstairs, and the shooter scored at least one hit before the man got to the kitchen. Probably the shot in the back, meaning he rolled down the lower steps, smeared blood on the wall in the process, and . . . still held on to the knife? Could the shooter have planted it? There were more candles upstairs and rose petals on the floor leading to a perfectly made bed in the primary bedroom.

One more detail I will never forget: propped up all over the interior of the townhome, a series of Polaroid photos depicting an erect penis in various stages of arousal. Dead guy, two guns, one knife, and a house full of Polaroid boners. Super weird, for sure, but also strangely comforting. Having just spent four years in the Sexual Assault Unit, no crime felt complete without some sort of weird sexual element. After those dark and twisted days of my previous assignment, I could certainly handle weird, especially in the context of a sexually motivated crime. Strange as it may sound, in that moment, I felt an odd sense of belonging. But, as I stood there, trying to absorb everything going on around me, I was struck by something else: the realization that while horribly gruesome, that poor, bullet-riddled man at my feet was perhaps the most fascinating thing I had ever seen. Someone had killed him, brutally, and it was our job to figure out exactly how, who, and why. The *how* was pretty obvious, and the rest was about to get even more interesting.

As with every murder, detectives immediately went to work putting together the missing pieces. As details emerged over the next couple of days, they seemed salacious to me, though I'd see much more soon enough. It wasn't the victim's home, but our suspect's. The dead guy had apparently been stepping out on his wife with the pretty, forty-one-year-old financial planner who had lived there with another man, her ex-boyfriend, who had recently ended their relationship by telling her that he was gay. Fresh off that heartbreak, she began her affair with the victim, who had likely shown up that night to tell our suspect that he was breaking things off and going back to his wife. This wasn't what she wanted to hear, not at all. A second breakup was apparently too much for her to take—or so we believed.

We don't know exactly how the conversation went—the unique

feature of all homicide cases is that your best witness is always dead—but it ended with our victim peppered with bullets on that kitchen floor. I charged the scorned financial planner with murder, and it would have been an engrossing trial . . . but what happened next took the story to the next level. The financial planner bailed herself out of jail, found her ex-boyfriend (the one who had told her he was gay) at a local hotel, waited for him to fall asleep, and then bludgeoned him to death with a tire iron she brought in from her car. In fact, she did such a thorough job that we could only identify him via his fingerprints. She then drove to a local gun range, rented a handgun, and blasted all that rage and betrayal right out of her skull. No trial needed; she took care of it all herself on a quiet Friday afternoon. This was the end of my first week in the Unit.

"Welcome to Homicide" was the reaction of my supervisor, and soon-to-become mentor, the immensely talented Lew Rosenblum, whose unbeaten streak as a prosecutor was the stuff of legend. Lew said, with a wry smile: "If you think that was crazy, just you wait. . . ."

Quite a welcome it ended up being. For the next seventeen years, if a murder was committed in the cities of Newport Beach, Costa Mesa, Irvine, or Laguna Beach, California, I was there, behind the yellow tape, often shivering in the cold with my detectives and my team. Whenever there is a big crime story, and we read about how "they" charged a criminal defendant with this, or "they" arrested him for that, "they" is really a reference to the prosecutor behind the scenes. In those cities, for those years, "they" was actually just . . . me. Looking back on that long-ago day in Newport Beach, I entered that townhome a young man with a broken heart. Seventeen years and a lifetime later, I exited my final murder scene as an older man with a troubled, but still hopeful, soul. This book is the story of that journey.

//////\\\\\

Before we go further, I think it would be helpful to provide a little background on the Homicide Unit, or really on the life of a prosecutor in general. The Orange County District Attorney's Office, where I worked, oversees a population of approximately three million people, the fifth largest District Attorney's Office in the United States, with a broad range of the very, very poor to the very, very rich. There are nearly three hundred prosecutors in the office—but only eight or nine of us in the Homicide Unit, a very specialized place to be.

Orange County utilizes a relatively unique system known as *vertical prosecution* for specialized units like Gangs, Sexual Assault, and Homicide. Individual prosecutors are assigned to cover specified areas of the county, and they follow their cases from the beginning all the way up through the system—from the crime scene to the investigation through to the trial and sentencing. The idea is that a prosecutor will be more effective if they have been there from the start, working with the local detectives, getting to know the families and the witnesses, every detail imprinted in their minds before they ever stand up in front of a jury. When you see the body of a murdered human being in a ditch, on a kitchen floor, or on an autopsy table, it is an image you will never, ever forget. I might have been juggling two dozen cases at the same time—murders often take years to proceed through all the way to sentencing—but I still got to know some of my victims' families quite well.

There is a ritual of sorts that takes place whenever a prosecutor rotates into a new unit. You have two orientations upon your arrival. The first is the official one. Your supervisor welcomes you, explains your responsibilities, assigns your cities, and tells you who your investigator is going to be. Your job during that conversation is to smile, nod, and thank them for the opportunity.

The second orientation is the real one. If you're lucky, you have a buddy in the Unit who has been there a while and can give you the true breakdown. This is when you learn the essentials for survival: who can be trusted and who can't, where to park, what happens if you're late, and how to actually do the job. If your buddy is a genuine friend, they might also tell you some of the ways the new assignment may affect your personal life.

When I finished my time in Misdemeanors and rotated onto the Felony Panel, where we worked on everything from felony DUI cases to attempted murders, I was warned by a friend, "Forget about having a social life while you're here." He was right. I tried twenty-four felony jury trials in twelve months and despite my maddening penchant for self-sabotage, I managed to win them all. Awesome for my career; not so great for my relationship (yes, the one who got away).

When I rotated into Sexual Assault a year later, a loyal pal walked me through the basics: "Chuck's a great boss; never file a case without good corroboration; try not to miss Taco Tuesdays; your cases will ruin your sex life for at least six months; don't be late for Friday meetings or you have to buy doughnuts for the whole team; use the yellow form when you file a case—"

"Back up," I interrupted.

"Taco Tuesday?"

"No, the other thing."

"Yep, this Unit will mess with your head like nothing you have ever seen before."

I scoffed. I was twenty-eight years old with an amazing girlfriend and figured I was Superman. Sure enough, in the end he was right. In the Sexual Assault Unit, you spend ten hours a day exposed to some of the sickest material you can possibly imagine. Eighty percent of the caseload involves the sexual abuse of children, and the rest consists of rape, child pornography, and, for a change of pace, the occasional sexual abuse of an animal. It doesn't take long to recognize that, with a few notable exceptions, almost every defendant is a man. You end up immersed in the very worst of male sexuality, and it inevitably takes a toll. Deviant, abnormal, and very, very hard to get out of your head when you get home.

The warning I should have heeded on my first day in Homicide was far more subtle. As is customary, I met with my predecessor, the person whose caseload would become mine. I had big shoes to fill. Debbie Lloyd was a legend. Smart and unrelenting, she was rotating out after twelve years of prosecuting murder cases at the highest level. I actually used to go watch her in action when I was a baby Law Clerk. Debbie was an absolute badass.

Unlike my previous introductions, Debbie's lessons were unspoken and far more profound. Though even if she had shouted them into my ear, I doubt I would have listened. Debbie had never been married and had no kids. She came into Homicide as a young, unmarried ass-kicker. A dozen years later, she was leaving the Unit with an impressive list of professional accomplishments, but still with no husband and no family.

I didn't even think about it.

And even if it *had* crossed my mind, I'm not sure that I would have cared. I wanted to be in the top spot. I wanted to hone the craft of trial work and perfect my skills. I wanted to be the person in the middle of the toughest case, against the greatest defense lawyers. I wanted the sense of professional accomplishment, to be mentioned among the greats. I wanted the big win . . . pretty much for the sake of the big win.

I cringe today when I think back to the naivete of the kid I was back then. Having grown increasingly confident with each trial victory in Sexual Assault, I was young, hungry, and more than a little brash. Heavy caseload? Good. Long hours? Good. Tough trial? Great.

Moving to Homicide, I had made it to the top. At one point or another, every young Deputy DA aspires to be promoted to Homicide.

From the outside, you see the stars of the office going after the worst defendants, against the best defense lawyers, in trials presided over by the most experienced judges. The cases are gripping, the detectives are dedicated, and the resources available are almost limitless. From the gallery, you can see the good guys fighting the bad guys in the very purest sense.

As a newbie, you can only hope to one day become one of the eight or nine senior deputies doing this work. Except that as you watch from a distance, you fail to appreciate what the work could mean for the rest of your life. A Homicide prosecutor, when doing the job right, is completely immersed in all things brutal death. To be any good at the job, you must spend long days, and even longer nights, completely dedicated to legal theory, trial tactics, causation, forensics, bloody crime scenes, bodily decomposition, late-night phone calls, search warrants, autopsies, grieving family members, and the often-crushing weight of internal politics, media attention, and profound responsibility. Most rational people would much prefer to spend their time with family and friends and not dive headfirst into grisly trials that take months to complete, where a single mistake could mean media scorn, career death, and, worst of all, a murderer going free. And yet, even understanding all of that, and now having lived it, I couldn't get enough. Truth be told, I still miss it every day.

I'm asked sometimes, "Did you ever prosecute someone you thought might be innocent?" It's actually one of the most common questions I'm approached with, and it's often asked in a whisper, as if to invite me to reveal a just-between-us secret.

The answer is easy: No.

But the well-intended inquiry underscores a common fallacy many people hold regarding the role of a prosecutor in the American system of justice. The prosecutor, for lack of a better term, is the *good guy*. Before the case is even filed, the prosecutor acts as a sort of mini judge—not a rubber stamp for the police, but a totally independent decision-maker objectively and skeptically reviewing the evidence and moving forward only if they are totally and without a doubt convinced that the suspect did it, as well as that the admissible evidence is persuasive enough to convince a jury. In the 1935 Supreme Court case *Berger v. United States*, Justice George Sutherland wrote regarding the role of the prosecutor:

> The United States Attorney is the representative not of an ordinary party to a controversy, but of a sovereignty whose obligation to govern impartially is as compelling as its obligation to govern at all; and whose interest, therefore, in a criminal prosecution is not that it shall win a case, but that justice shall be done. As such, he is in a peculiar and very definite sense the servant of the law, the twofold aim of which is that guilt shall not escape or innocence suffer. He may prosecute with earnestness and vigor—indeed, he should do so. But, while he may strike hard blows, he is not at liberty to strike foul ones. It is as much his duty to refrain from improper methods calculated to produce a wrongful conviction as it is to use every legitimate means to bring about a just one.

What this means, in plainer language: The prosecutor is not paid by conviction or the number of people charged. We are supposed to be totally unmotivated by financial incentives or politics. In reality, being a prosecutor is one of the only practices of law where you never actually meet your client. The prosecutor represents the "people" of whatever state in which we are sworn. Our client is literally everyone and yet no one at the same time. The job, in its purest sense, is to serve the ethereal concept of justice, and, long before we zealously advocate for the imposition of a criminal sentence, that means we must pursue the truth, fairness, and, above all else, justice.

Indeed, when I was going through training at the beginning of my career, Chris Evans, then a co-supervisor in the Homicide Unit, and now a Superior Court Judge, told us: "Make sure the defense has everything. Then beat them with it." With that in mind, I would invite the defense to come to my office and go through my boxes of discovery themselves to make sure they had access to absolutely everything. Then I would arrange for them to visit the police department and be given a chance to examine every piece of physical evidence collected during the investigation. I believe every prosecutor in America should do the same thing. It is clean, aboveboard, and, in the end, you will never regret it. Give them everything, and then beat them with it.

Unlike virtually every other form of law, the prosecutor should never have a client who is wrong, or unreasonable, or who pays based on success. The job is simply to do the right thing. We must act as a bulwark against overzealous police, dishonest "victims," unfair judges, underzealous colleagues, and a hundred other pitfalls where a criminal case can go awry. Countless times, I had no choice but to disappoint detectives or the families of victims because I couldn't ethically file charges. Other times, I picked up cold cases that had been discarded years before (some of those ahead in the pages of this book) and realized that new evidence, new technology (DNA, footprint analysis, and more), or just a fresh set of experienced eyes had changed the equation.

Sometimes, you can find gems in those dusty old boxes that make it possible to overcome previous doubts and effectively convince a jury. Sometimes, once again, it can be the smallest detail. In all circumstances, even after a case is filed (or, as my old supervisor Rick King used to put it, "after the missile has been launched"), if a prosecutor learns something that makes them entertain even the smallest doubt regarding guilt or the propriety of a particular charge, enhancement, or anything else on the criminal complaint, they have a sacrosanct, ethical obligation to dismiss that charge immediately.

Humans can be wrong, of course. Well-intentioned prosecutors are wrong all the time. But we must always subjectively believe we are doing the right thing. If a prosecutor doesn't, and proceeds anyway, that is a huge problem. This is actually the one type of law where, ethically, you have to subjectively believe everything you say in the courtroom. Defense lawyers have the obligation to zealously advance a client's position, and their subjective opinion of whether or not their client is guilty is irrelevant. This is not true for a prosecutor. In a strange way, the good prosecutor is a kind of rebel embedded in the system itself. Although you are hired and literally "sworn in and deputized" by the elected District Attorney, the ethical rules apply to you as an individual. If you think something is wrong, it is wrong. You can't simply go along with it out of nicety or some misplaced sense of subordinate obedience.

That principle applies across the board—even when politically inconvenient. For example, when the famous "Three Strikes" was enacted by the California State Legislature—a widely misunderstood law—we got an edict from the top. Three Strikes allowed for a sentence of up to twenty-five years to life in state prison for a defendant convicted of a felony who had two prior violent felony convictions. A lot of people incorrectly believe that the law is automatic, and that great injustices have occurred as a result. The truth is that the prosecutor and the Court have complete discretion to "strike" (or dismiss) the enhancement based on a variety of mitigating factors. Virtually every case that came through the system back then resulted in something far less than twenty-five years to life, based on the unique equities of each case. But it was a good option for judges when dealing with the most violent and scary criminal defendants.

I actually only had one case (of literally hundreds) where a non-violent third felony resulted in a life sentence. This was a vicious sexual predator who kidnapped, raped, sodomized, and attempted to murder a young woman in the early 1980s. He was released from prison and promptly molested a six-year-old girl in the back seat of a car. Unfortunately, the case was incredibly difficult, because there was no DNA and it boiled down to the little girl's word against his. The prior crime, given the horrific violence involved, had been ruled inadmissible—that is, we couldn't tell the jury about it. But the rapist had also failed to properly register as a sex offender, which is a nonviolent felony. That was a crime we could certainly prove, and so I did. That was the only nonviolent third strike I ever prosecuted through trial, and I would do it again. The defendant received twenty-five years to life, and we should all pray that man never gets out again. For the others, we virtually always reduced the sentence. In other words, "striking strikes" was almost always the right thing to do.

Despite this, as line prosecutors we were directed by our "tough on crime" elected DA to object on the record each and every time a judge dismissed a strike. The political decision had been made to tie our discretionary hands as prosecutors, leaving common sense and fairness up to the Court. By objecting on the record, the idea was that the DA's Office would look tough on crime while the judge would be out on a limb if the defendant went out and did something awful after being released.

As a young prosecutor, what do you do with that? The only way I can accurately, if somewhat crassly, describe my feelings about that policy is that I thought it was bullshit. Not to mention, I also thought it would hurt our relationships with the judges—with whom we needed to build trust so they would back us on the cases that were most critical and ultimately get the worst offenders off the streets.

Long before I got to Homicide, on my first day of Felony Panel, I was assigned to Judge Mike McCartin in Westminster, California. He is a great guy and still a great judge. I went in with maybe twenty cases, and the public defender and I proceeded through them with McCartin in chambers. I then watched as my new judge made the right call on every single one of them. He gave breaks to the people who deserved them, second chances when merited, and backed me on the few cases where the defendant really needed a stiffer sentence. When we went back out into the courtroom, and onto the record, he began taking the guilty pleas. After the first one, he turned to me as an automatic part of his routine and said: "Regarding the Court exercising its power [to dismiss a strike] pursuant to *People v. Romero*, I know Mr. Murphy has something he wants to put on the record."

I looked at him and without a second thought said, "No, I don't." He looked back with a slight pause and a knowing glance. It was a minor rebellion against a ridiculous policy, my ethical obligation to do the right thing being far more important than some memo drafted by someone who knew nothing about the merits of the cases we discussed. I don't think Judge McCartin undercut me on a single case after that, and neither did any of the other judges in that courthouse. Looking back, it was a pretty cocky move for a young prosecutor, but it felt like the right thing to do at the time and I have no regrets. Besides, it's far too late to fire me now.

Years later, the motto of the Homicide Unit became *"Fiat Justitia, Ruat Caelum*—Let Justice Be Done, though the Heavens May Fall." I always liked that. It meant that regardless of the political consequences, opportunities for promotion, or fallout in the media, our job was always to do the right thing. That may seem obvious, or quaint, or easy—but trust me, with elected District Attorneys, especially in the modern era, it is not. To me, it meant that my job—my sworn duty—was to execute justice on a purely case-by-case basis. As a prosecutor, you do not defer to "the greater good," nor choose the "lesser of two evils." There is no quaint euphemism to properly rationalize the potential for horrific abuses of prosecutorial power. As a prosecutor you must seek to do right by every single victim and every single criminal defendant who lands on your caseload. If that means the world burns, so be it. Your tools are honesty, hard work, and the truth. My job was to make the call, take the heat, and to the flaming walls of hell with everything else. I liked that.

Of course, like I said, sometimes prosecutors are wrong. They are human. We can and do miss things. But I was never, ever, less than 100 percent convinced of the guilt of every defendant I took to trial.

///////\\\\\\

Every day in the Homicide Unit was just a little different from the day before, from assisting detectives in generating search warrants, to meeting with families, to deciding when we had enough evidence, who to charge with what crime, and when to charge them. And while you might imagine you need the most polished, presentable lawyers handling the cases inevitably getting the most media attention, no matter what you're wearing or how you look, there was only one skill that ultimately mattered in the job: If you can't persuade a jury, you are useless when it comes to actually achieving justice.

Counterintuitively, the best trial lawyers are often quite rough around the edges. There is an old saying you sometimes hear in law school: "A students become professors, B students become judges, and C students become trial lawyers." In other words, in the specialized world of jury trials, the person who barely made it through law school is often the opponent you have to worry about the most. With no disrespect to the Ivy Leaguers, the most impressive academics often fall by the wayside long before they get anywhere near the truly heavy cases.

The people in Homicide were a very special group, and I was

privileged to be among them. There was Lew, a former Marine Corps officer who spent twelve years as a Line Deputy in Homicide before becoming a manager and had just come in to replace the former head and real architect of the Unit, Rick King. Rick was a decorated war hero in Vietnam who saw real combat and lost real friends. When the new DA was elected, Rick was sent to Sexual Assault, where he became my boss—and one of my first true mentors—before I got to Homicide.

Many of my colleagues in the Unit were also often former military. Howard Gundy was a marine, Mike Murray was a graduate of West Point, and Jim Mendelson was a lieutenant colonel in the Marines who commanded a squadron of F/18 Super Hornets before retiring and going to law school. And then there were the investigators, all sworn police officers, who formed a critical part of the Unit and an indispensable part of our team. Many of them were also former military, and more than one had either been wounded in combat or shot while working the streets on patrol. I was surrounded by people who had quite literally trained to sacrifice their lives in service of the community. (My own educational pedigree, on the other hand, had been determined with an eye toward which schools had access to the best surf spots.)

Lew had been tasked by our DA—an alum of the Homicide Unit himself—with building Homicide into the most effective unit he could. Lew wanted combat soldiers, fighters, mutants. At our level of trial competence, Senior Deputy District Attorneys have virtually all received lucrative offers to go into private practice. In the world of lawyers, actual trial experience, especially when complemented by a little talent, is rare and valuable. As a result, the Homicide Unit was composed entirely of attorneys who had turned down money in exchange for something else. Lew's growing team was gifted, steadfast, and, unlike most lawyers, entirely unmotivated by financial enrichment.

From the outside, we may have appeared to be a collection of spirited misfits, some of whom swore too much, drank too much, and often had difficult personal relationships outside of work. We were perceived as a loud, brash, sharp-elbowed, inappropriate, and argumentative collection who had no problem standing up to police officers, judges, and especially defense lawyers. But my colleagues were also brilliant, fearless, immensely talented, and utterly dedicated to the victims they served. In my eyes, they were superheroes, albeit flawed ones, and remain among the finest human beings I have ever known. I was and remain profoundly humbled and honored to have been a part of that group.

Because our average tenure was measured in decades, not just years, we built confidence and improved our trial skill as time went on. Competitive as our crew was, we also learned from, supported, and even pushed one another. Young prosecutors—and, for a long time, I was one—can be timid about the calls they make and decide not to file cases that seem too hard to prove. In the context of homicide cases, that means murderers go free. Whether to file charges is a subjective decision that every prosecutor has to make. As confidence grows, and as skill improves, the answer to that question naturally evolves with the prosecutor's ability. Before too long, the nickname for the revamped Homicide Unit became "Murderers' Row." I have always thought the label was far more a reference to the individual attorneys who worked there than the defendants we were prosecuting.

////I\\\\

There is a sense of dark fascination that draws us into these kinds of cases. Not just detectives or prosecutors, but *all* of us. There is also a voyeuristic element to many homicides, especially those that are committed indoors. When you walk into one of those scenes, it's like a time capsule of the very last seconds of someone's life. To preserve the crime scene, everything is frozen in time. The TV is still on, the dinner half eaten; I had one case where a woman was killed in her kitchen while she had a disco CD playing on repeat. So it was still playing when we walked in to survey the scene. The happiest music imaginable, and a woman face down with a screwdriver sticking out of her back. Dark, surreal, incredibly sad, but simultaneously impossible to look away.

As a result, many people are utterly compelled by murder—look at the crowds at the annual CrimeCon convention, or the multitudes of television programs, podcasts, and books on the subject. We all—prosecutors certainly included—want to figure it out. We desperately want to know what happened, who did it, and "why." The public's interest in true crime is booming, and I think part of the reason is that these cases are reflections of our own lives.

Most murders involve real relationships between real human beings. No rational person can truly understand the motivations of a child molester, but a murder involving husbands and wives, business partners, or neighbors is very different. And although forensic technology has advanced wonderfully over the past couple of decades, the motives of most murder cases remain completely unchanged: anger, jealousy, lust, greed. The methods of committing and solving these crimes have become far more sophisticated, but the fundamentals of why murders are committed have not changed in two hundred thousand years.

In these cases, simply put, we see ourselves. We all get knocked down from time to time. We experience loss, jealousy, and longing, and we have all suffered relationship woes where we just can't seem to find our footing. We can't sleep, can't eat, and can't concentrate. We understand some of the passions that accompany many of those who kill, and yet we would never do it ourselves. But we must also remember that the most cunning and ruthless predators the earth has ever produced are not sharks, lions, or the Tyrannosaurus Rex;

they are us. We are smarter, far more devious, and have a capacity for evil that other predators simply don't. A T-Rex would not befriend a Triceratops before devouring it, and no shark has ever been driven by twisted sexual fantasy when it attacks. Animals kill for food, but people—sometimes—kill for fun. Human beings are the preeminent apex predator. Nothing hunts us ... except ... us. In life, sometimes we become that limping gazelle on the savanna, and anyone who has ever watched a nature documentary knows what happens next. But instead of a lion jumping out of a bush, it's a guy like Rodney Alcala, the "Dating Game Killer" (whose story I'll come back to later), Ted Bundy, or a woman like Kathleen Turner in the movie *Body Heat*.

These cases involve living, loving human beings with dreams and hopes and humor who were almost all loved by someone. And they were taken away, on purpose, by someone else. Often for the dumbest and most banal reasons imaginable. The criminal prosecution is, in many ways, a reckoning for the crime committed. Closing arguments, if done right, are a requiem to the individual whose life was cut far too short, far too soon. They can't say it anymore, so as a prosecutor, you say it for them.

Each murder also offers us the opportunity to reflect on our lives, how fortunate we are to still have them, and what a miracle it is that we are given however much time we get on earth. As a prosecutor, when you stare at a dead body, perfect in every way but for the bullet hole in their head, it forces you to ponder some very deep philosophical questions. In the simplest terms: Where did they go? Are we really all just electrical impulses coursing through sacks of meat? If so, I have some serious questions. Over time, I have careened from the existentialism of Camus to stoic philosophy, religion, cold physics, and back again, all in the service of trying to figure it out. Where I ended up landing: When surrounded by death, you quickly develop a desire—a screaming, pulsating need—to actually live.

You also develop a respect for just how many people in this world are *not* out there committing these horrible acts but are here to do good. For every murder you see as a prosecutor, many incredible people enter the picture and dedicate themselves to seeking justice. From the first police officers to arrive, to the crime lab personnel processing the scene, to the jury, and ultimately to the sentencing judge, my faith in humanity was restored just a little more with each case. To contribute to making it right, all it takes is careful, diligent thinking, an open mind, and a commitment to bringing justice to families who have suffered the ultimate loss.

The cases I'll describe in these pages each have their own lessons, relatable components, and details that may very well give you nightmares this evening. Each of them, in my mind anyway, is absorbing in its own unique way. It has not been easy, and I have paid a price. Some of that price I'm still figuring out today, even as I write this book. But I hope that coming along for the ride will help you better understand humanity, restore a little faith, and perhaps even inspire you to give an extra hug to your loved ones.

I would often tell my juries that I fully expected them to find things that my team and I had missed. I may have been living a particular case day and night for years, but that jury box contained twenty-four eyes and five hundred combined years of common-sense life experience.

"You'll see things we didn't, I'm sure," I would say, "but I guarantee that everything you find will only add to all of the evidence pointing toward guilt. And I can't wait until we can sit down together at the end of this, and you can tell me what we missed."

So let's get into some more cases. And at the end, you can tell me exactly what I missed.

Welcome to the book of murder.

CHAPTER

1

WHAT EXACTLY IS MURDER?

AFTER THE SCORNED financial planner, the next investigation to land on my desk involved an incident that took place at a "doper motel" in the city of Costa Mesa—a location that existed almost entirely for the purpose of consummating drug deals. A twenty-year-old addict had apparently ripped off another young user, with maybe twenty bucks at stake. This was my first real "victim" from the fringe. Like many American cities, Costa Mesa has a depressing stretch of road where the outcasts congregate, where homeless people mix with sex workers and drug addicts on the wrong side of the tracks. Methamphetamine in Southern California has had a huge impact on the edges of society, and its association with causing manic and often violent behavior has earned it the informal moniker "the devil's drug." As a general rule, where there is meth, there is also high drama and plenty of violent crime.

After the perceived rip-off, the aggrieved party soon returned with two of his friends, and the twenty-year-old ran for it. A chase ensued around the motel. The entire ridiculous scene would have fit nicely in an old episode of the British slapstick comedy *The Benny Hill Show* as the men circled around and around, right up to the point when the fleeing young man decided to elude his pursuers by running directly into six lanes of traffic on a busy boulevard. He was immediately flattened by a truck. Killed instantly.

Once again, I was looking at a dead body. But this one was different. In the Newport Beach town house, it was pretty clear there had been a murder. But was there a murder here, too? As a prosecutor, what do you do with something like this? Were the young men chasing after the dead guy legally at fault? The causation necessary to file criminal charges requires what is known as *reasonable foreseeability*. In other words, was it reasonably foreseeable that the deceased would have run into traffic to escape a twenty-dollar drug debt? It was not an academic question; we could have sought life in prison, and, honestly, these were unsympathetic characters. A jury might well have convicted them, and a judge might well have sentenced them to life in prison. But they were still young men. And beyond legal standards, my real task was to figure out the right thing to do.

As a prosecutor, the job is always to address the paramount question: What's right, and what's wrong? On the one hand, I had the death of a young man, technically "caused" by the three idiots who were chasing him. On the other hand, was their conduct worthy of life sentences? I wrestled with the question for about a day, and decided that it was not. I went to Lew Rosenblum's office to report my conclusion. I told Lew that I "felt awful" but just didn't think we should file against the chasers.

"You feel awful?" he asked me. "Let me give you a piece of advice:

Sympathy is like money in the bank. No matter how rich you are, it is always finite. Think carefully before you make a withdrawal. Victims in this Unit are not all the same.

"That young man died because of a long series of very bad decisions," Lew continued. "If you spend too much sympathy on him, or others like him, you won't have any left for the truly innocent. And rather than hitting your stride in a few years, you will burn out and be gone in a flash."

The story begs a larger question: If that wasn't murder, what is? I was fourteen when I saw an elderly woman get hit by a bus when she was crossing the street. That was tragic, absolutely—but no one was morally at fault. Murder is different. Murders aren't tragedies. A human being intentionally taking someone else's life in cold blood is evil, not tragic. Tragedies happen; murders are committed.

We all have some quintessential image in our minds of the classic murder. Sonny getting ambushed in *The Godfather*, something out of a Sherlock Holmes novel, Colonel Mustard in the library with the lead pipe . . . but *murder* is actually a very broad term that covers a wide variety of circumstances. Depending on the case, sometimes an intentional killing isn't a murder at all. So, more broadly, perhaps a better question is: What is homicide?

A homicide, put simply, is the killing of one human being by another. But homicides come in many different forms. When Terra Newell, the stepdaughter of con artist "Dirty John" Meehan—the subject of a podcast with over twenty million downloads and a TV series on Bravo—plunged a knife into her stepfather's body thirteen times as he attempted to kidnap and kill her, that was a homicide, but it was no murder: It was self-defense. In fact, it was *awesome* self-defense. I later found Terra to be a lovely human being, certainly not a murderer, and gladly guided the case through the system to clear her of any and all wrongdoing.

Unfortunately, the vast majority of women in Terra's situation don't end up as the heroes in a Bravo miniseries; too often, they end up dead in a ditch. People like Dirty John almost never end up as "victims," but instead as defendants. So, if Terra's actions don't qualify as murder, then what does?

Murder is the intentional killing of another human being with what is known as *malice aforethought*. Those ancient words essentially just mean that the killer decided to kill before committing the deed. Terra took a life from someone who deserved it, *richly* so, and when she plunged that knife into that terrible man's eye, her actions were completely justified. Murder is when someone kills under circumstances where the act *cannot* legally be justified. There is always a reason why one person kills another (jealousy, revenge, anger, stupidity), but to boil the law down to its most essential elements, if you want to avoid spending the rest of your life in prison, the reason better be pretty good. If not, the ancient legal concept of murder will descend upon the killer. Going back to the first written set of laws—the cuneiform of the Code of Hammurabi—we can see that the rules governing criminal behavior are not entirely unlike those we use today. In fact, they are remarkably similar. No, it's not still an eye for an eye, but the underlying common sense is still there. Do wrong and pay a price; do more wrong and pay a higher price.

When I first came into the Unit, Lew sat me down with a chart that he used to explain homicide analysis—the degrees of "badness" of a killing—to a jury. And there was nothing terribly mysterious about it: From best to worst, the killing of another human being can be good (*self-defense*), accidental (*involuntary manslaughter*), bad-but-we-understand (*voluntary manslaughter*), bad (*second-degree murder*), really bad (*first-degree murder*), and horrific (*capital murder*).

To put it more concretely, I like to use the example of two cowboys in a bar, whether in a saloon a century and a half ago or a honky-tonk last week in Texas. Horses or pickup trucks, six-shooters or semi-automatics, the human components—and the law—are exactly the same. Let's call our guys Billy and Wyatt, and let's start with a generic second-degree murder. They're leaning against the bar, drinking whiskey, when Billy insults Wyatt's hat. Wyatt reacts with his ego, and immediately decides, "I'm going to shoot this SOB." He grabs the six-shooter on his hip and fires, killing Billy instantly.

We can unpack that. There was an unjustified intent to kill followed by a deliberate action to do so. A reasonable person wouldn't have done this, of course—and yet we also have to acknowledge that there was no time to contemplate, no careful thinking that preceded the act. Wyatt never weighed the reasons for or against pulling the trigger. That's a second-degree murder, by definition.

But imagine that instead of having the gun on his hip, Wyatt had to walk out of the saloon, over to his horse or pickup truck, and rummage through his saddlebag, find the gun, and then walk back through the door, through the smoke and the music and the dance floor, search out Billy in the crowd, find him, aim, and then shoot. That's unambiguously worse than the first scenario. Shooting someone out of anger is bad. Shooting them when you've had a chance to reconsider is worse. Wyatt had all the time in the world to consider the consequences of what he was about to do, and yet he did it anyway. That is a classic example of murder committed with *premeditation and deliberation*, or *murder in the first degree*.

We can change it up again. Same two cowboys, same saloon, but this time Wyatt is showing off his new six-shooter with a specially modified hair trigger. He has had a couple of shots of whiskey and starts playing quick draw, pointing the gun right at Billy. He opens the wheel and dumps the cartridges out onto the bar, thinking he has emptied the gun of the full six but failing to take the time to realize there's only five there. One cartridge inadvertently left in the gun, Wyatt goes quick draw—*click*; quick draw—*click*; quick draw—*bang*. He shoots Billy dead. Here, there was no intent to kill Billy, no malice toward the victim, but Wyatt was acting like such an idiot that it could surely be said he was operating with a *conscious disregard for human life*. This is also known as an *implied malice murder*. There was no desire to kill, but there *was* an intent to act like such a jackass that it can be said that he consciously disregarded the safety of everyone else in the saloon. As a society, we recognize that this was an accident, but under the *implied malice theory*, we don't really care. When someone is a big enough fool, and they utterly disregarded the safety of the person they killed, the accidental perpetrator can still be held accountable for a second-degree murder.

Bear with me as I continue to nerd out on this: As you see, the analysis is a mixture of subjective state of mind and objective circumstances, and it is fundamentally based on common sense. Now, suppose that instead of uttering a stupid insult, or playing a game of quick draw, Billy says something far worse. Imagine Wyatt's wife had just been raped by an unknown assailant the night before. And then Billy reveals to Wyatt that he is the rapist and he has no regrets. Wyatt reacts instantly out of anger and kills him on the spot. Same cowboys, same bar, same six-shooter, but entirely different circumstances. The killing is technically still unlawful—there's no self-defense here, or defense of another—but it was performed under such extreme circumstances that we recognize what is known as *legally adequate provocation*. In other words, he shouldn't have done it, but, for lack of a better way to put it, we understand. When a reasonable person in the position of the defendant might have done it, too, we call that *voluntary manslaughter*. This is a second-degree murder in every respect, but the mitigating circumstances are so extreme that we reduce it to a lesser offense—as we should.

These are the basic concepts. Where murder cases get really interesting is when we go beyond mere words to circumstances where the motives and methods are truly diabolical. Or when, if not for the hard work of dedicated people, the killer would get away with it. This is where the good guys come in—the place where individual detectives and prosecutors can make a real difference.

Say we have the same bar, and the same two cowboys, but we learn that Wyatt has secretly been sleeping with Billy's wife, who, coincidentally, stands to gain a million dollars in life insurance if Billy were to die. When Wyatt comes into the bar, starts an argument with Billy, and shoots him dead, suddenly we have a whole new dimension to our analysis. Wyatt *claims* that Billy went for his gun and that the killing was in self-defense. Convince a jury that it wasn't self-defense, and Wyatt's on the hook for first-degree murder with the *special circumstance* of financial gain.

Special circumstances—which include things like murder committed during the course of a kidnapping, robbery, arson, a drive-by, poisoning, torture, sexual assault, or perpetrated for financial gain, to name a few of the most notable possibilities—elevate a murder to a potential death penalty case, also known as *capital murder*. These are tough cases, because the legal, ethical, and procedural burdens are all on the prosecutor. Fail to convince the jury, and a ruthless killer goes free.

Or try this one: Wyatt and Billy are in business together, and suddenly Billy disappears without a trace. There is no body. Wyatt shows up with a bill of sale, signed by Billy, deeding him full ownership of the cattle ranch where they were previously partners. He also spins a yarn about Billy leaving to buy property somewhere else. The story is dubious, but Wyatt then produces witnesses claiming they saw the transaction take place, and Billy was last seen with a saddlebag of cash riding in the direction of his purported new ranch. Is it legit, or a financially motivated conspiracy? Can you be sure until you've talked to Wyatt, interviewed the witnesses, done some on-the-ground investigation? Had Wyatt and Billy been arguing over the future of the business? Did Wyatt have gambling debts on the side? Had Billy warned his brother that Wyatt was out to get him? These are the juicy ones, where the skill and dedication of the prosecution team can make or break the case, and where a dogged detective can mean the difference between justice being served and a killer getting rich. As far as I am concerned, these are the cases that represent nothing short of good versus evil.

Lew used to say that it took a minimum of five years in Homicide before someone became truly comfortable with the breadth of what "murder" can really mean. Yes, every case involves a dead body, but they are all so unique. A case about a bar fight is such a different legal animal from prosecuting a serial killer. It's not that there's a hierarchy—these are all situations where a life has been taken, they're all as consequential as anything can possibly be to the victims and their families, and it's impossible to argue that there's a better or worse way for someone's life to be cut short by the actions of another—but there are differences, and we can categorize them in certain ways.

Broadly speaking, there are child abuse cases, robberies-gone-wrong, domestic violence murders, gang murders, implied malice murders, provocative act killings, sexual assault, serial killers, and conspiracies to murder for financial gain—to give you the big headline labels—but they each draw on different motives, different actions, and different flaws within the plan and within the people who commit them. And while I say there's no hierarchy, at the same time I do feel compelled to acknowledge that, politically, of course there are differences, and many victims are far more innocent than others. A child abducted and killed, or a celebrity, or a crime that happens in some unusual or surprising way—those are the cases that make headlines, and then of course once the media gets involved, the pressures, on the elected officials, at least, are different from when the victim is a sex worker or a homeless drifter without a family.

(For the good prosecutor, of course, none of that should matter, and in a perfect world, it doesn't. Your number one priority has to be whatever case you're working on at that moment, and I felt very much obligated as a human being to make things right no matter the status of the victim. In fact, in cases of "low-status" victims with no loving family or friends in Court, I would remind the jury that it was even more important that, through the process of deliberation, they ensured the victim be treated fairly.)

When you work on enough cases, you come to see patterns that repeat themselves within the different categories. After a few years, you begin to look for specific tells during an investigation. Serial killers, for instance, love to collect trophies—mementos of their victims—and also can't seem to resist representing themselves at trial (though it never goes well for them). Couples who conspire to kill for money usually can't wait to spend it and will often plan large purchases before they've even done the deed. Gangsters have a habit of bragging about what they did, sometimes even immortalizing it on tattoos—and, yes, it's hard to erase that evidence.

After enough trials, you learn to predict how a jury is going to react to each defendant. You realize how powerful a particular type of evidence is, because you have seen the impact in trials before. The learning curve is steep, and it takes a while to hit your stride. But once you do, you can feel it—you're in the zone.

Ultimately, the motive and methods often make the difference as to why certain murders capture our interest and some escape public attention. Often, there is nothing more interesting than a good old-fashioned whodunit. But the truth is, figuring out the killer's identity is usually only part of the battle. The "why" is often the most important part. There are certainly compelling cases that do not involve homicide, but when it comes to crimes like robbery or sexual assault, figuring out a defendant's subjective reason for acting often leads to a big "who cares?" In four years prosecuting sex crimes, it simply didn't matter that I still had no idea what drove child molesters to act. If they did it, then they did it. But from a prosecutor's perspective, without having to figure out the why, the cases become somewhat formulaic and two-dimensional.

Murder is different. Murder requires an answer. The jury must ultimately make a call as to what was going on in the mind of the accused killer, and as a prosecutor, you must figure that out long before they do. Of course, going down the rabbit hole of a murderer's thoughts can be as disturbing as it is compelling. Few suspects confess their motives, even when caught. Once the "who" has been figured out—you know they did it, and they know you know—they move quickly and passionately into lying about the "why," whether claiming that it was to defend themselves, or that they were provoked, or that a carefully planned first-degree murder was actually a spontaneous crime of passion. It shouldn't shock anyone to learn that those willing to take a human life will typically have few moral compunctions when it comes to lying about it. Especially when they come to understand the legal advantages.

On the other hand, sometimes the murderers are just too stupid to come up with much of a story. Like Spencer Fox and Travis Frazier, two white supremacist skinheads who, needing money to support their meth habit, decided to rob a 7-Eleven store, both wearing full face masks to conceal their identities. If not for the sheer brutality of the crime, these two clowns would have appeared more comedic performance artists than criminals. They stormed into the 7-Eleven and Frazier hit the clerk—an immigrant from India taking on extra shifts to send money back home to cover the care of his son with disabilities—over the head seven times with a heavy metal Maglite flashlight, fracturing his skull. Simultaneously, Fox climbed over the counter and stabbed him in the heart with a giant Rambo-style hunting knife.

Only then, after they had killed the poor man, did they think to ask him to open the cash register. Of course, he couldn't help them by then, and so Fox—who forgot to cut eyeholes in his face mask—pawed around in an attempt to do it himself, and, finally, in the midst of frustrated failure, lifted up his mask to see if that would make things easier. It didn't, and Frazier and Fox left the store empty-handed, laughing as they ran out. In a move only making sense to them, they then started stripping themselves of their masks, jackets, bloody weapons, and even their pants as they ran over the parking lot planter and into an adjacent apartment complex. It was like the Yellow Brick Road of evidence, but with swastikas.

This was a case from early on in my time in Homicide, and it was, to put it mildly, not a challenging one to prove. We had everything on tape, in high fidelity—it was, after all, a 7-Eleven, with security cameras absolutely everywhere. Which made it hard for the unmasked—and instantly recognized by the local police detective—Spencer Fox to deny his guilt. He did anyway. As for Frazier, he got separated from Fox during their escape and ended up hiding in the bushes. (Fox got back to the car first and actually drove off without him.) A tattooed skinhead found in the weeds at three a.m. near a murder scene is what some people might call "suspicious." He was found by a police dog, and came up with the worst story ever: He was on his way home from a party. In his underwear. On one of the coldest nights I had ever experienced in Southern California.

Q: *So . . . who had the underwear party?*

A: *Um . . .*

Frazier was arrested, and Fox was found hiding out a few hours later at a friend's place a dozen or so miles away. Then, in a truly awesome bit of police work, the officers pretended they'd gotten their signals crossed and needed to wait for a second car to transport the two of them separately to jail. In the meantime, they told them to wait together in the back seat of a fully miked-up squad car and sternly told them, "Do not talk to each other until we figure this out!" Did they listen to that instruction? You already know the answer.

"I was fucking clean. I was doing fucking Rambo shit crawling through the goddamn bushes and shit," Fox said to Frazier.

"Our bail's probably high as shit," Frazier said to Fox. "I'm never going to see my fucking kids again."

Articulate skinheads, both of them.

The clerk's DNA was all over them, on their clothing, on the murder weapons, and it was not a hard case to prove. Frazier went to state prison . . . where he murdered another inmate and then laughed when he was sentenced to death. Utterly senseless. Cases like these might have made me cynical about humanity, hardened and numb to it all—but the honest truth is that I think they actually did the opposite. First, they reminded me that no matter how bad our lives seem to be, at least we get to wake up in the morning and try to make it better. We can be in the most toxic relationship, desperate for money, for companionship, for anything—and yet we still have pizza, we still have Netflix, we can still enjoy something. We still have a chance. Maybe murder cases are so compelling, in part, because sometimes we need to remember that.

There is also a refreshing purity to the work. The right and wrong of murder cases transcends political parties and divisive domestic politics. The legal concepts you work with predate not only Democrats and Republicans but also the age of monarchies and empires. When it comes to murder, wrong is wrong, and a mother's grief is the same today as it always has been. In a time of increasingly vitriolic national division, when every time we turn on the TV someone seems to be yelling at us about the virtues of their "side," these cases are a refuge. A rare zone of agreement, where bad is still bad, and good is still good. Juries in Southern California will virtually always represent a broad cross section of demographics, economics, and political beliefs. With the right judge, and good jurors, politics should mean exactly nothing. I am very proud of the apolitical nature of the work I did. Your job as a prosecutor is to bring diverse people together and get them to agree, in a time when ideological disagreement seems to infect everything. Working murder cases for the better part of two decades, you learn pretty quickly that the vast majority of people in our communities, at least those who show up for jury duty, are good. It doesn't matter if they are Democrats, Republicans, Independents, or other, jurors are motivated by good, they want to do the right thing, and no political party has a monopoly on justice. It may sound a little corny, but these cases really are all about human beings, fairness, and the fundamentals of right and wrong.

So, that covers murder from a simplified legal perspective. Hopefully these concepts are interesting and the way I have explained them makes sense. But there are a couple of additional viewpoints on murder that are worth a brief exploration. There is a comedian I follow on Instagram named Rodney Norman. He once posted his perspective on enduring hardship, saying: "You're either a child of God or a cosmic miracle, either way you're pretty friggin' awesome." I loved that, and from either a religious or a scientific standpoint, Rodney is not wrong.

All of the world's major religions agree that murder is bad. In the Judeo-Christian tradition, "Thou Shalt Not Kill" is of course one of God's commandments. In an interesting article published in the *Chicago Tribune* in 2012, Rabbi Marc Gellman noted that the Hebrew word *ratzah* (to murder) in the commandment had long ago been translated incorrectly into English as "to kill." In Biblical Hebrew, there is an entirely different word with that meaning (*harag*). Rabbi Gellman calls the translation "profoundly and radically incorrect." "Thou Shalt Not Kill," though it sounds catchy, has actually always been "Thou Shalt Not Murder." And there is a difference.

Every other major religious tradition on earth concurs whole-heartedly, Hinduism, Islam, and Buddhism among them. Regarding murder, from a religious standpoint we are all very much aligned.

From a purely scientific perspective, the great astronomer Carl Sagan pointed out, in 1980, that "the nitrogen in our DNA, the calcium in our teeth, the iron in our blood, the carbon in our apple pies were made in the interiors of collapsing stars. We are made of starstuff."

This awesome scientific truth means that we, when you really think about it, are accumulated bits of stardust, which over the evolution of eons became sentient. We are, each of us, aggregated bits of the universe literally contemplating itself. And if that isn't a cosmic miracle, then I cannot imagine what is. With more than eight billion of us on the planet, we may be ubiquitous and common to one another, but when you consider the incomprehensible size and age of the universe, an individual human being might just be among the rarest and most remarkable things in all of creation. A clump of stardust, gazing back into the heavens, with love and humor, hope and joy. By any measure, dousing that beautiful light, especially one that brings delight to others, in a fit of rage, to gain resources, or for sexual fun, is a terrible scientific outcome.

So, what is murder? From a legal, religious, or purely scientific viewpoint, the murder of an innocent human being is simply the very worst thing.

CHAPTER 2

GANGS, AND WHY YOU SHOULDN'T JOIN ONE

MY VERY FIRST jury trial in the Homicide Unit was a Russian mafia case. Very interesting—but only to a point. When people think about organized crime, their minds often conjure up television shows like *The Sopranos*, or movies like *The Godfather* or *Casino*. When we hear the word *gangster* in the context of crime, we might think of rap videos, or perhaps envision an antihero like Joe Pesci's character in *Goodfellas* or Michael Corleone in *The Godfather*. Outlaws like Al Capone and John Gotti occupy significant real estate in our collective imagination, and it is easy to understand the fascination. They have money and power and sex, without following all the conventional rules that the rest of us have to live by. They don't work in cubicles or spend their lives mindlessly commuting. We imagine them existing in a completely different universe, day-to-day, than we do. And, perhaps, sometimes, we romanticize it a bit.

The reality, of course, is in stark contrast to the movies. The truth is that most gangsters are just thugs who steal—and eventually they get what's coming to them. In the end, the law, or the lifestyle itself, will catch up to them. Many of them, especially on the street level, are simply semiorganized bullies. They threaten innocent people, intimidate for convenience, and hurt for fun. Their victims (usually) don't deserve it, and quite often they are not just violent but, like my 7-Eleven neo-Nazis, also pretty dumb. My grim takeaway from years in the trenches is that active gangsters, no matter who they are, are often not that bright, do stupid things, and either wind up getting caught or getting killed.

True to form, the Russian mafia thugs from my first trial were *very* bad people, doing *very* bad things. Ramadan Dokovic had come to the US from Serbia ten years earlier, and met up with a cousin, Mike, in New York City. Mike was involved in a bank fraud scheme with some fellow Eastern European bad guys and brought Ramadan in on it. Eventually, they were caught, and Ramadan ratted out the gang to the authorities in exchange for probation. He was immediately labeled a *dousnik* or a *stukach*—Serbian and Russian, respectively, for snitch—and kicked out of the crew. With no legitimate prospects in New York, Ramadan moved to Southern California.

Cousin Mike spent a little time in prison, then got deported back home across the Atlantic—but eventually made his way back to the US, to Southern California just like his cousin, and back into a life of crime. Mike rejoined his ring of Eastern European thugs, who amassed a collection of private ATMs from which they would pull banking information—account numbers and PIN codes—of the people who used them. They purchased a card-making machine from Germany, which allowed them to manufacture their own debit cards, put any name they wanted on them, and gain access to accounts, draining their victims of money like parasites sucking blood. And these guys were killing it.

Thanks to unlimited access to cash, Mike and his crew were surrounded by hot women, expensive cars, Cristal champagne, and all the gaudy trappings of success you would expect from a gang of nouveau riche criminals from the former Communist bloc. But Ramadan was still on the outside, having burned the relationship years earlier. And he was getting desperate. He had been working at a pizza joint and got a young woman pregnant. He owed child support, but then he lost his job. He had nothing—and nowhere to turn. He found out that Cousin Mike was running a side hustle, in addition to the ATM scheme, selling stolen Rolex watches that belonged to a local jeweler in Newport Beach. So Ramadan reached out to the jeweler and offered to get the watches back—for $20,000.

The jeweler agreed—bad move—and Ramadan met up with Mike's associate Miroslav Maric, demanding the watches. Miroslav rolled up to the meeting in a new convertible Mercedes 500SL. (As I said, the ATM scam was really working for them.) Like something out of a movie, Maric was sporting a half-buttoned Italian shirt, gold chains, and expensive designer sunglasses perched on his bald head. Ramadan, on the other hand, was wearing a dirty hoodie, an outfit befitting an unemployed pizza guy. Albeit an unemployed pizza guy with a gun.

Ramadan and Maric ended up inside Maric's convertible Mercedes, "negotiating." When Miroslav refused to return the watches, Ramadan played his ace. He pulled the pistol and pointed it at Miroslav, who looked at the gun and again refused to budge. Now what? Legally, this was already an armed robbery on Ramadan's part, even if the property he was trying to steal was stolen in the first place. But Maric, nobody's *suka* (bitch), made a play for the weapon, and the two wound up fighting over it in the crowded parking lot of a Jack in the Box in Costa Mesa—right in front of a bunch of horrified soccer moms picking up lunch for their kids. The first shot may well have been an accident, hitting Maric in the lower abdomen. It was survivable. The second shot, also likely survivable, was in his chest. But Ramadan, long on bravado but short on brains, decided to finish the job—"doming" him, as the gangster slang goes, shooting Maric execution-style in the head. Ramadan then lit a cigarette, put the weapon on the trunk of the car, and waited for police.

Ramadan figured he could pull the same move he had a decade earlier, cooperating with the cops, telling them about the ATM scam, and ultimately going free. Except that this was murder. He confessed everything and then asked for his deal. But no one ever promised him a deal. Given the fact that he confessed, my first murder trial wasn't exactly tough. Not to mention I also had about a dozen eyewitnesses, plus loads of forensics, and he was caught at the scene with the gun. It was a little like riding your first bike with training wheels. Dokovic ended up sentenced to fifty years to life in state prison. We ultimately recovered a roll of undeveloped film from Maric's car that showed just how much cash they were dealing with—a life of luxury, women, and expensive booze. Awesome, of course . . . until you get shot in the head.

Is it wrong for me to feel like the world became a better place the instant Maric slumped over the steering wheel of his Mercedes? I'm sure he had moments of being a decent human being at some point, but, at the time of his death, cosmic miracle or not, my victim was living a parasitic lifestyle. These guys weren't just stealing from banks but from the actual people who used their machines. Even Maric's family didn't seem too upset. They came swarming in, never asked to meet the prosecutor, and I felt like they were more interested in the watches and the car than justice for Maric's killer. We made clear we weren't giving up the Mercedes—it was our crime scene, after all. Before long, they packed up and left town.

I don't want to be too harsh on them. They may have been perfectly decent people who just happened to know what a lowlife Maric really was. But this actually points to one of the fundamental reasons why gang cases were never the most rewarding to work. It's difficult to garner much empathy for a thief who hurts the innocent, a gangster-victim who took pride in terrorizing the hardworking and honest people living in his neighborhood.

That's not to say gang culture can't be interesting, or that the cases didn't often involve some complex legal theories of attenuated criminal liability, like conspiracy, aiding and abetting, and natural and probable consequences. But ultimately the philosophy of gangs, if we can call it that, is fatalistic, and doesn't provide much hope for the gangsters themselves, or people like me dealing with the aftermath. One of the most popular tattoos of Hispanic street gangs, for example, has been co-opted from the theater, of all places. The sad mask/happy mask image that some might associate with Shakespeare is actually ubiquitous in gang culture and has been inked on literally thousands of California gangsters. They call it "Laugh Now, Cry Later," and it reflects the idea that they will have their fun in the moment but know they'll eventually either die or go to prison. It's sad, really, until you stop and think about what they go out and do to earn those prison sentences.

Any temptation to feel bad for them exposes another common misunderstanding held by those who don't know the gang world: the well-intentioned naivete of psychological projection. When thinking about worst-case scenarios for our own lives, spending years in prison surrounded by convicted gangsters is pretty high on the list. We naturally imagine it to be pretty high on anyone's list, and so we feel for the gang members doing serious time. But in doing so, we place our own fears and feelings on people who have chosen a very different life. For many of them, if they had the capacity to think like the rest of us do, they wouldn't be gangsters in the first place. Prison is already an accepted part of their plan. They know the rules of the game, and arrive in "the joint" to find a ready-made political structure in which they have a waiting role. They are reunited with older members of their gang who have been sentenced for earlier crimes, and will soon welcome more of their gang buddies who are about to commit future ones. When it comes to the murder of another gangster, these guys will literally laugh about it. To them, the killing is justice. Genuine remorse, as we know it, simply does not exist in their mental or verbal lexicons. Most of these people (compared to the innocents they hurt) are not worthy of much sympathy.

Sure, the culture can capture one's attention, and organized crime scams can certainly be intriguing, but at the end of the day, especially after you have prosecuted a few, most of the associated murders are just . . . not that interesting. With some notable exceptions, there is no great matching of wits in gang investigations. Most of them are stupid killings, of unsympathetic victims, where dumb mistakes are made and they easily get caught. And, if police are slow to figure it out, the aggrieved gang almost never is, and will usually exact some form of justice anyway.

Going further, it is almost impossible to relate to a "victim" like Miroslav Maric on a human level, or to the motive of some knuckle-head "putting in work" for a gang by committing a drive-by or "representing" the gang by picking a deadly confrontation with a stranger. Human psychology is an interesting thing. Many of us possess an almost primal instinct—self-preservation, perhaps—to look at a violent crime and try to rationalize it in an effort to convince ourselves that it could never happen to us. If we feel like the victim was using poor judgment or exhibiting some kind of moral failing, then we are reassured that as long as we make the right choices, we'll be okay. It's why the news media gives so little attention to gang murders—and maybe why I couldn't get as emotionally invested in them. We can all tell ourselves: *I'm not in a gang; it wouldn't happen to me; he probably deserved it.*

Back when I was in Sexual Assault, we would encounter this same primal instinct to rationalize. Somewhere in the unspoken recesses of a juror's mind, especially with adult female victims, they often wonder, Did she do anything to bring it on herself? Did she drink too much? Leave her friends too early? Walk into an unsafe area? Trust the wrong man? The answers to those questions can be complicated. Of course, whether a victim ever *deserved it* is simple: Nothing a victim does should ever justify a sexual assault, and almost no one deserves to be murdered. (There are certainly some gangsters who push that principle.) Still, people want to find a reason. They want to find a way to go on with their day and not have to worry that they could be next.

But my own lack of overwhelming empathy was part of why I was quite happy that in Homicide we had the option to leave most gang murders to the Gang Unit. When the suspect and the victim were both gang members, we almost always opted to let the Gang Unit handle it. I much preferred to work on cases where the victims were people I could relate to, and their families were people I liked. Rather than prosecuting gang cases, I got to experience them through my colleagues' stories. There are some great ones. Gallows humor, given the absurdities of the gang world, was a common feature of the Gang Unit.

One story that always comes to mind is a case that my colleague Howard Gundy brought with him when he was promoted to Homicide. As Howard explained it to the Unit one day, a trio of gang members pulled up to a quinceañera party. There was a driver, a shooter in the right-front passenger seat, and a seventeen-year-old gangster in the back, along for the ride or perhaps for emotional support. The shooter shot into the crowd of teenagers and family members on the birthday girl's front lawn, eight or nine rounds from a distance almost impossible to miss, and yet . . . he missed entirely. The driver then started to speed off into the night—so far so good. According to Howard, the kid in the back seat then decided to contribute. He stuck his head out of the right-rear passenger seat window and, while throwing gang signs with both arms, proclaimed to the "pussy motherfuckers" at the party exactly which gang had just tried to murder them all.

One of the party guests—from a rival gang—had heard the shots, ran outside, pulled out his own firearm, and started blasting away. Firing blindly and sideways in the direction of the speeding car, he somehow managed to hit the seventeen-year-old cheerleader still hanging out the back window—right between his eyes, killing him instantly. An impossible shot. (Lew, listening carefully, paused and then, with a soft voice and a straight face, said, "Well, at least he died doing something he loved." And then he walked into his office.)

From a legal perspective, the story gets a little more interesting. Howard didn't prosecute the gangster who actually killed the "victim." That guy, gang member or not, had been substantially provoked—he was shot at! Rather, Howard charged both the driver and the failed shooter with the murder of their confederate under what is known as the *provocative act doctrine*. (See, I told you the legal theories can sometimes be the fun part.)

What this means: If a bad guy does something during the commission of a crime (in this case, the attempted murder of everyone on the lawn) that provokes a legally justified use of deadly force in response to his actions (here, the rival gang member shooting back), and that response results in the death of one of the bad guy's partners in crime (the smack talker in the back seat), then the bad guys who started the whole thing are on the hook for the murder of their friend. Some people bristle at this result at first glance. After all, why should the kid on the lawn be allowed to shoot at a fleeing vehicle? Is it really self-defense when the car is driving away?

The answer to this is a combination of legal reasoning and common sense. Do you prosecute an innocent homeowner for shooting an armed assailant in the back? In law school, the answer might be "yes," but in real life, a jury is unlikely to convict, and a good prosecutor must think about justice above all else. The drive-by was not a provoked shooting. Returning fire at someone who just tried to kill you and your family and friends is a morally defensible act. Who's to say the car wasn't going to circle around the block, with the shooters coming back to try again? The guy on the lawn was reacting to someone trying to take his life, and there's just no way a good prosecutor would charge him rather than the people who started the whole incident to begin with.

Of course, imagine the conversation as the public defender attempted to explain this complex legal concept to a client who had just learned he was about to go down for the murder of his own homeboy after picking a fight that they had so spectacularly lost.

Gun safety, as it turns out, is not a high priority among most gang members, as this story illustrates. Another incident: Two gangsters in Santa Ana decided to do a drive-by on a slow Saturday night. They had gas in the tank, selected the right house, and thought they had a plan. They drove up so that the target house was on the left side of the street. Rather than having the driver turn the car around so that the passenger-side shooter would have an unobstructed field of fire, the guy with the gun decided to instead blast away out the open driver's-side window. However, instead of leaning over the driver and firing out the driver's-side window, he just shot . . . from the passenger seat. Not the best tactic, but also not necessarily fatal to the plan.

As long as they have done a little pre-game coordination, or at least have the ability to count—*one shot, two shots, three shots*. In this case, the driver hit the accelerator before his passenger was done, which meant the car was moving forward, but the gun certainly wasn't. A valuable lesson in physics, perhaps. The final bullet ended up blasted into the right side of the driver's skull, killing him instantly. The car then crashed into a nearby tree, leaving the shooter injured and the murder weapon sitting next to him in the wreck when the police arrived. Detectives call that a "clue."

Under the doctrine of *transferred intent*—when someone intends to harm a particular victim, but unintentionally kills someone else instead—the shooter's actions amounted to first-degree murder of the driver, with an additional twenty-five years for the use of a firearm. The issue is a matter of degree. Without the doctrine of transferred intent, he might be liable for only second-degree murder—shooting in a reckless way, an accidental death. But he premeditated his intent to kill—first-degree murder—and so that's what he ended up with. No discount for killing the wrong person. Incidentally, no one inside the house was hit.

On another case, I dealt with a gangster, just paroled, who decided that the first thing he wanted to do with his freedom . . . was shoot someone. His buddy had rented a car, he hopped in, and they met up with a couple of friends, including a woman who ended up in the back seat. They drove around the neighborhood and got approached by a different woman, who assumed they were either buying or selling drugs. Our hero asked her where she was from—the classic gang challenge—and she said she wasn't in a gang but named one she had friends in.

Wrong gang, wrong answer. He shot her in the head. The woman in the back seat started screaming. Our shooter turned around and told her to shut up or he'd shoot her, too. She didn't stop screaming, so . . . he shot her in the chest. She then bled out all over the back seat of the rental car. This was not a part of his buddy's plan when he drove out of the parking lot at Enterprise. So, our gangsters decided they needed to get rid of the body. They drove to Newport Beach and chose to dump her into the ocean. Good thought. The problem is they drove to a bridge over the Newport Back Bay (not the ocean), and it was a foggy night. They stopped on the bridge, threw her over the railing, but instead of a splash, they heard a thump. They literally missed the Pacific Ocean, and she landed in the ice plant below. (Note that the Pacific Ocean is the largest geographical feature on earth.)

Meanwhile, they still had the car. The parolee told his buddy to burn it, but his friend reminded him, "Hey, cabrón, it's a rental car!" So he dropped off the shooter, drove all the way to San Diego, found a car wash with one of those big self-service hoses, and sprayed down the interior. However, in trying to get rid of that much blood, he ended up flooding the car and simply caused the stain to spread. The vehicle was now completely waterlogged, and an electrical component shorted out on his way back to Orange County. This caused the vehicle to break down on a deserted stretch of the 5 Freeway, which runs through the middle of Camp Pendleton Marine Corps Base. It was dark, it was three o'clock in the morning, and our hero was stranded.

Luckily, he was a member of AAA—gang members can sometimes make responsible choices!—and called for a tow truck. Unluckily, he was still a gangster, so when the tow truck driver was slow to arrive, he called back and threatened him, promising to "fuck him up" if he didn't come faster. The tow truck driver explained that he didn't want to "get fucked up," but he was the only truck assigned to that stretch of the highway . . . and rather than deal with threats, he would simply call the police instead. When officers arrived, they found an agitated gang member, in the middle of the night, with diluted blood all over the back seat and floorboards of his rental car. Then they noticed a bullet hole right in the middle of the whole mess. Police considered that a bit suspicious. Arrests were made, and everyone went right back to prison. Miraculously, the young woman who originally approached the car and was shot in the head actually survived.

In case that's not enough, I have one final bit of gang-related hijinks to share. When they aren't arrested immediately after the killing, gangsters often can't resist commemorating their actions with new ink somewhere on their bodies. Tattoos are a common way of proudly proclaiming that they have committed a murder. Of course, any previous arrests or photographs make it pretty easy to figure out when the new tattoo was added, and thus it becomes a pretty strong piece of evidence connecting them to the crime. Perhaps you want to make the case that a new tattoo could mean just about anything? The standard image these gangsters choose for their new piece of body art is a gun pointing outward. Impossible to decipher the meaning of that one. . . .

Similar to the tattoo of the gun pointing outward, there's the one of the knife with blood dripping from it. Again, not so cryptic. But it's important to put yourself in the mindset of the gang member. These are badges of honor. They are proud of what they've done, and having killed someone is a big deal in their world. There's actually nothing worse in the gang community than claiming you've done something when you haven't. There are prison tattoos that are very common: a star on top of your elbow if you've spent a year in county jail, or a stone tower if you've done time in Folsom, or a spiderweb on your elbow if you've been to state prison (as opposed to the local jail). If you get one of those tattoos and then people find out you didn't actually do the time—you did thirty days instead of a year, say—then you're going to take a beating, or worse. And if you're not in the gang and you have one of their tattoos, well, that will almost certainly be a death sentence.

I admit that I'm making light of some of this, and perhaps I shouldn't be. These are vicious people doing terrible things, and I don't mean to minimize the damage they cause. These cases are certainly not always easy to prosecute. From a legal perspective, there is a challenge in educating the jury about gang culture. After all, it is very difficult for a rational person to believe there are those among us who will literally kill over a look, or noticing a stranger on the wrong street in the wrong neighborhood. But, just like my Russian/Rolex/Mercedes murder, the "victims" of the homicides in this world are often, if not usually, other gangsters. It's not about social standing—an innocent homeless person is often just as sympathetic as anyone else—but gang members have affirmatively chosen a life that embraces thuggish criminality, including murder. I don't want to sound callous, but for the decent, hardworking people around them, those deaths are often win-wins.

All of that said, there are many reasons why someone may choose to "jump in"—that is, join—a gang, and not every gang member turns out to be a hopeless psychopath. Part of the job in Homicide requires you to attend "BPT Lifer Hearings," where you travel to prisons across the state and participate in parole hearings for convicted murderers. You enter the facilities and get escorted by guards to the hearing rooms. For some of the older gangsters, it felt as if many of them reached a point, usually sometime after the age of forty, when they realized the lifestyle they embraced as a young man had led them absolutely nowhere good. Some of them were even smart enough to harbor genuine remorse as they looked back on their lives. For some, their highest ambition now would be to sit on a couch after a long workday, drink a beer, and watch a Lakers game.

I believe that guys like that are no more dangerous than a white-collar embezzler paroled from Federal prison, and perhaps even significantly less so. They must be old enough for the juice to have drained out of them, to be genuinely done with gang life, and wise enough to never want to go back. I have sat across the table from a few of them. With those guys, I believed they had done their time, justice was satisfied, and they had earned the privilege to again taste freedom.

Nevertheless, as a prosecutor, I liked to save my energy for true victims, and the gang cases I did take on were almost exclusively those where the victims weren't gang members but people who should never have been in harm's way. After that first trial, with Ramadan Dokovic put away for a few decades, I was eager to move beyond gangs and on to something a little more emotionally rewarding. Then again, as the old saying goes, "Be careful what you wish for."

CHAPTER

3

THE POLITICS OF DEATH

LEW'S EARLY-ON ADVICE about saving my sympathy for the innocent stuck with me. And no one is more innocent than a five-year-old child. After the Ramadan Dokovic trial, it wasn't long before Lew was back in my office with something really horrifying. If you follow true crime news, Samantha Runnion's name might ring a bell. She was a five-year-old girl, two weeks from her sixth birthday, when she was abducted in broad daylight from her yard—fifteen feet from the open front door to her house—where she was playing with a friend. A man in a light-green sedan stopped his car and asked for help finding a lost dog. Samantha's friend backed away, but Samantha didn't—and the man grabbed her, forced her into the passenger seat, and drove off. Neighbors heard her screaming. "Help me! Tell my grandmother," she shouted. The whole thing took maybe twenty seconds—and Samantha was never seen alive again. It was every parent's worst nightmare.

Media attention on the kidnapping was instant and overwhelming, as anyone would expect. Orange County Sheriff Mike Carona held a press conference. The FBI sent in a team of criminal profilers and studied satellite images. It seemed like the entire world was looking for Samantha.

I had been in the Homicide Unit for less than three months at this point. Lew walked into my office and handed me the file. "Here's the deal," he said. "As horrible as it is, this little girl is going to be found, and she is likely going to be dead. The sheriffs will need someone to work with during the investigation, to be their guy for warrants, late-night phone calls, and whatever else we can help with. This case is yours, and it's going to be big, so wear a nice suit."

Sure enough, the next day, Samantha's body was found by a hiker climbing up a twisted mountain pass, in a dry patch of dirt next to the Ortega Highway, fifty miles from where she'd been abducted. She was just there on the ground, unburied, naked, on her back with her legs spread apart, and her brown eyes staring lifelessly into the sky. The hiker begged the police dispatcher to send help quickly: "Please hurry. I'm scared, and I want to get out of here," he said.

Mike Carona made a public statement directly addressing the kidnapper: "Don't eat, don't sleep, because we are coming after you." An anonymous tip led to a suspect, Alejandro Avila, who had a car that roughly matched the description. Investigators checked his criminal background and learned that two years earlier he had been accused of molesting two children, one of them his ex-girlfriend's daughter—who lived in the very same complex as Samantha, with her father. Avila had been arrested, charged, tried, and (incredibly) acquitted. What he certainly would have learned during that experience was that the criminal justice system sometimes fails. And now his next victim was dead. I would hope the lesson for jurors would be that if you let a child molester go free, this, sadly, is what can happen.

There are images in my mind from the autopsy of that little girl that I will never be able to unsee, and the existence of the previous acquittal added a terrible new layer to the case. Had the prosecution not failed in their trial, Avila would have been in state prison and Samantha would still be alive. The world was outraged, and the amount of global attention that fell on Orange County is hard to describe. We had inquiries from everywhere, there were rows of cameras waiting for us outside the courtroom, and even President George W. Bush weighed in and called Mike Carona "America's sheriff."

As the elected officials fought for camera time and credit for the arrest, it fell on me to explain to Erin Runnion, Samantha's grieving mother, how the system had failed her little girl. I had to tell that poor woman why the monster who had defiled and murdered her young daughter was free, instead of in state prison where he clearly belonged.

I went to her modest apartment with my investigator to introduce myself in person and walk her through the process. Even today it is hard to articulate what I experienced. I had seen anguish before. I had a very close friend who was killed in a car accident when I was seventeen, and I had spent some time with his mother as we both processed the loss. But up to that point, I had never experienced anything like the day I met with Samantha's mother. I walked in with my investigator and a yellow pad as if I expected to take notes, and immediately found myself in the presence of pure, apoplectic grief. I think until that very moment, I had failed to truly appreciate the role of a prosecutor. I had been hoping for the big case and the big win. But seeing Erin's face, I realized how much I still had to learn, and how small the competitive dreams of a young prosecutor really were, in the big picture. This, I realized, was the enormity of the prosecutor's true responsibility. I had been a fool to think the job was just about catching bad guys. It was also about devastated family members, suffering in a way few can imagine. My job was to help them through this brutal process.

In the Homicide Unit, there are people depending on you in ways that nobody teaches about in law school. Your responsibility in a case like this—and really, any murder case, because everyone has parents, everyone has someone who cares, or at least once cared, about them—is first and foremost to obtain justice for the horribly wronged mothers, fathers, husbands, wives, children, brothers, sisters, aunts, uncles, friends, and lovers. You learn very quickly that they are far more important than the person who committed the crime. Not legally, but morally. Your purpose when dealing with the kind of suffering that Erin Runnion was experiencing should have nothing to do with ego, or the "big win." The most important part of my job, fundamentally, was about empathy and compassion. I needed to help that poor woman and her family through the worst thing a parent can possibly endure.

The whole thing absolutely broke my heart, of course, but there was another profound lesson that emerged as I began to work the case: Screw up a trial at this level, especially when dealing with a truly predatory defendant, and innocent people will die. Sometimes, that innocent person will be a five-year-old girl just playing outside with a friend. The weight of responsibility was immense.

We issued a warrant for Avila's cell phone records, which often provide powerful evidence of location. Cell phones are engineered to seek out the nearest tower to find reception, maybe the next nearest if it's a busy time of day. Someone on their phone, driving in a car, will often ping multiple cell phone towers even on short trips to the market. A longer drive will leave an undeniable electronic trail, much like footprints on a beach. Investigators can calculate direction, time, and even speed of travel. The day of Samantha's abduction, the picture Avila's cell records painted was clear and chilling. He had been arguing on the phone with his girlfriend as he drove out of Lake Elsinore—where he lived—and pinged on quite possibly every single cell phone tower going north on the 15 Freeway. He then traveled west on the 91 Freeway and directly into the city of Stanton, the location of Samantha's condo complex. The timing lined up perfectly.

We put together another warrant for Avila's vehicle, and it was carefully processed for fibers, hairs, fingerprints, and DNA. Within twenty-four hours, Samantha Runnion's DNA was identified on the passenger's-side door handle. Between his history, the cell phone records, and the DNA, Alejandro Avila was more than done. I absolutely understood how to prosecute this case; what I didn't yet understand was how to deal with national media attention while navigating big-time politics.

I filed the murder with special circumstances—and the elected DA quickly announced that we were going to seek the death penalty. Avila was arraigned the following day. Walking out of Court with our District Attorney and his entourage, we were mobbed by the media. There were perhaps fifty cameras outside the courthouse, each with a reporter and sound technician, so many that they were lined up in rows. There were trucks with cranes shooting out the top and more cameras. The lights felt brighter and hotter than the sun. "Don't screw it up" just kept echoing in my head.

It was apparent from the very beginning there were two distinct dramas going on in the investigation. First, there were the dedicated professionals grinding through the stress and long hours in a noble effort to catch and punish a very, very bad guy. There was a purity to their work, and they did their jobs well. But then there were the political aspects, and the involvement of other people not necessarily motivated by goals so noble. A promising lead would be followed by a suspiciously fast news story. No sooner would investigators find a new piece of the puzzle than someone in the sheriff's office would leak it to the press and we'd see it on the nightly news. The investigators weren't shy about expressing their frustration.

I talked to Lew about the leaks, and again he hit me with a gem I will never forget: "Chasing leaks is like chasing ghosts," he said. "Scary at first, but the reporters will never burn a source, and you will never catch one on video. They're frustrating and annoying, but just like a ghost, in the end, they will never really hurt you." Sage advice, but the distraction was hard to ignore. Beyond the leaks, it was tough not to notice the people uninvolved in the day-to-day of the case jostling for credit. At Samantha's funeral, Erin Runnion was flanked by her husband on one side and Sheriff Michael Carona on the other. Samantha's grandmother was displaced to the second row by a stranger putting himself right up there with the grieving family. Law enforcement doesn't typically go to funerals unless they are hoping for the killer to show up. Funerals are for family. It seemed like an invasion to me. And for what?

Using grief as a photo opportunity was pretty cringey. I tried to reason it through: Perhaps it was a part of some bigger strategy. Maybe Carona wanted to bring more attention to the fine work of law enforcement, for the entire nation to see? Maybe the family had asked him to come? If any of that was going on behind the scenes, I certainly didn't know about it. Meanwhile, Carona went on CNN's *Larry King Live*, with the host echoing the president's "America's sheriff" comment. It seemed more like a personal victory lap on the national stage than for some greater good.

I don't want to judge him too harshly, but as the assigned prosecutor—who Carona never consulted—I absolutely hated it. As my first experience on a case with national media attention, I can admit now that I handled it poorly. Not the media, but the internal politics of it all. And it cost me, professionally and personally. When our media relations representative "informed" me that she planned to take some of our most important witnesses on the national talk show circuit, I protested. In fact, I was downright pissed. And she overruled me in a fashion I thought was rather dismissive.

Lew was incensed; I was naive; and the shoe was about to drop. I liked our DA, my boss Tony Rackauckas. He had always struck me as a pretty rational guy. I figured I could simply explain my concerns to him and he'd understand. I went to his office and told him that I thought parading witnesses on talk shows was a terrible idea. Why should we unnecessarily hand the defense an opportunity to get an inconsistent statement from a witness? The slightest detail, if innocently misremembered, could damage the witness's credibility and hurt our case. And for what? Right as I finished my pitch, the media representative walked into his office. No knock. She must have seen me go in. He excused me to talk to her alone. I knew that wasn't good.

An hour later, Lew's boss, Bryan Brown, came to my office. Bryan was a legendary prosecutor in his own right, and beloved by the troops. He bore a striking resemblance to the actor Gary Cooper, with a devilish gleam in his eye. He had always supported and promoted me. I knew Bryan had my back, and I knew he was on my side. I had just presented a rational objection to something that, even to this day, I believe was an incredibly dumb idea. But I was an unproven rookie in the big leagues. I had never done a death penalty case, and I could sense what was coming.

Bryan closed the door. "You are off the case, but I promise it's the best possible thing for your career."

Ouch. In my hopeless naivete, I was more than a little shocked, but Bryan was absolutely right. To this day, I feel nothing but gratitude for the wisdom and guidance of Bryan and Lew. And I learned how to navigate the system, even when politics intruded. I never had another case taken away from me.

Alejandro Avila was eventually tried and convicted by my colleague (and eventual boss) Dave Brent. He had decades more experience at the time and put on a tremendous case. He even brought the courtroom to silence by persuasively arguing that Samantha's DNA found inside Avila's car may very well have come from her tears. Avila was sentenced to death and lingers now, twenty years later, on death row. Meanwhile, Mike Carona eventually ended up indicted on federal corruption charges—alleging that he used his office for personal financial gain—and served five and a half years in prison. As frustrated as I may have been with Carona and the undersheriffs directly beneath him, I didn't see that one coming.

//////\\\\\

Before the Samantha Runnion case was reassigned, I was feeling pretty invincible as a prosecutor. I was riding high on my Dokovic win, had a load of good cases stacked up behind it, and felt like I had arrived. In Lew, I had a boss I loved. My friends in the Unit used to joke that if Yoda and *The Karate Kid*'s Mr. Miyagi had a baby, it would turn out to be something like Lew. He was slight in stature, soft-spoken, wise, fair, and an absolute badass when the chips were down. He wanted to teach, and I desperately wanted to learn. I had been handed arguably the biggest murder case in the country, which even the president was talking about on national television. I was walking out of Court to banks of cameras, and friends I had not spoken to in years were reaching out, saying they had seen me on the news. I felt like the world was watching me, and cheering me on.

Until suddenly it wasn't. My professional future was still beyond bright—I had Lew, I had my colleagues, my investigators, my assigned cities, and I was very much still a prosecutor on the rise. But I had just lost a pretty meaningful internal political battle. It was big media, a big case, and the loss felt like a big hit. Lessons in life, especially important ones, tend to sting.

On the personal side, I was still reeling from my ex-girlfriend's engagement—I was still only a few months past that moment in the parking lot when I got the call to check out my first murder scene, and still surfing as many mornings as I could to try to forget those impossible-to-get-past feelings. But hey...maybe they could still break up? Maybe she would decide to come back? Maybe it wasn't really over?

In the words of my good friend Dennis Conway—who had just been promoted to Homicide with me—I was very much still "suffering the hope."

Until suddenly, again, I wasn't. In a laughable coincidence you simply can't make up, the very same day the Runnion case got reassigned, the invitations to my ex-girlfriend's wedding started to arrive at the homes of some of our mutual friends. In the ebb and flow of life, we all have good days and bad days...and that one felt like a very bad day. So much for hope. One of my good friends, and an invitee to the wedding, knew I would be pretty down. He dragged me out with a bunch of our buddies, figuring it would do me some good. And it worked, at least for a while. We had some food, some laughs, and then, as had happened countless times before, one of the more extroverted guys in our crew began chatting up a group of women sitting together at a local sushi bar. They were friends from college, we were friends from high school, and our two groups matched up almost cosmically well. I soon found myself in a conversation with a beautiful woman—and suddenly things were looking up. By the end of the evening, couples started pairing off, numbers were exchanged, and, bizarrely, three of my closest friends would wind up marrying the women we met on that night. They are all still married today.

I was already starting to see how this job might be difficult to reconcile with a healthy personal life. I was working sixteen-hour days and loving almost every minute of it, but also starting to wake up to dreams of dead children. I began having nightmares that my defendants had escaped justice and were free to kill again because I had failed. I had a recurring dream where I was giving a closing argument and the jury just wouldn't listen. (Truth be told, I still have that one.) I was being jarred awake to cold sweats in the middle of the night.

The job, of course, can certainly affect your personal life and romantic relationships. But I was about to learn how poignantly the reverse can also be true. I would soon receive a big lesson in how romantic relationships can also significantly impact the work. To explain, I need to go a little bit deeper into some embarrassing aspects of my love life. I promise this brief sojourn will end up connecting to one of the most notorious murders of the past thirty years.

/////\\\\\

To begin, when it comes to matters of the heart, I am far and away the biggest fool I know. The pain I felt over the loss of my ex-girlfriend was not the first time I experienced a broken heart, nor would it be the last. Dennis Conway used to joke, "You have two talents, dude: closing arguments, and screwing up relationships with nice women." He was kidding, but not really. He was certainly right that most of the people I have been with over the years were very nice, some far nicer to me than perhaps I deserved. But not all. There was one, in particular, who was just plain awful, and in retrospect—thank God for that.

I didn't know what I was getting into that night at Rock n' Sushi, but it certainly seemed like fun at the time. In hindsight, I was in no state to start any kind of serious relationship, not two hours after learning my ex was actually going to get married. But right at the beginning (like with many disastrous relationships), it felt like this woman was different. Articulate and striking, with big brown eyes containing just a hint of sadness, I was drawn to her immediately, even if some of that was surely about being distracted from my stupid broken heart. Just like the other three couples who met that night, we began dating. And just like the others, it got pretty intense pretty quickly. Soon enough, we were all getting together as a giant group almost every weekend.

Like the heartsick fool I was, I stumbled blindly into a serious relationship with a woman I barely knew. The rush was partly from my own misjudgment about who she really was as a person. I tend to have a maddening blind spot where I perceive mundane acts of kindness as actual human connection. This exasperating ability to misjudge potential romantic partners only gets worse when I'm emotionally vulnerable. And on the night we met, I was about as down as it gets.

I should have seen the red flags right away. She was often late, but usually with a good excuse. Dinner reservations have limits, though, and I had more than one uncomfortable moment of staring at an empty chair across a candlelit dinner table. She was busy, but then again so was I. She'd apologize the next morning, but it always seemed to happen again.

As time went on, I started to notice a meaner edge. Half jokes she made to baristas and waiters calling them out for minor mistakes soon swung my way. She started to drop little digs in front of other people. I smiled and tried to laugh them off but was finding myself in a situation I had not encountered before. We all want to be seen, understood, and supported by our romantic partners, and I had just been with someone who was wonderful in those ways, but my new relationship seemed to be missing some intangible gear. On the surface, it looked perfect. Physically, we were a good match, and it was a bonus that three of her good friends were getting serious with three of mine. All six of them were well on their way to marriage, starter homes, children—the works. She seemed to enjoy showing me off to her other friends (at least at first), but also had way more enthusiasm when talking about her weekend parties—or even her ex-boyfriend—than hearing about murder cases. My work is certainly not for everyone, I get that. But there is a point when some degree of understanding becomes important if a relationship is going to succeed.

When I would wake up with those cold sweats, the woman next to me seemed far more concerned about the wet sheets than the nightmares causing them. She was increasingly disinterested in what was going on in my head. And then there were her friends. Not the ones who would eventually marry my buddies, but another small group to which she was very much devoted. They were nice enough, at least in the beginning. They were well-meaning and highly educated, but ideologically... rather set in their beliefs. It wasn't so much about politics—people like this can be all over the spectrum—but about whether my profession was good enough for their friend. They were the kind of people who would brag about getting out of jury duty and then lecture me about their perceived failings of the criminal justice system. All without a hint of irony. A couple of them had family money, high-paying jobs, and degrees from places like Harvard and Stanford—and very much considered themselves to be intellectual elites. One of them even liked to remind me that my beloved alma mater, UCSB, had a reputation as "a bit of a party school." Sure, maybe it did, and I certainly had more fun than they did in college, but I never saw a single keg party in the victim/witness room of the DA's Office.

In the end, I think they saw me as a government lawyer with a couple of interesting stories, but without the financial power and prestige they envisioned for their friend. Their strange snobbery really made me love my team, my cops, and my jurors all the more. It's hard to know how much their opinion of me influenced what happened next, but it contributed to my growing unease with the relationship.

I just didn't have the emotional bandwidth at the time to realize that if her friends thought like this, then she probably did, too. Oh, how I cringe when I look back on it now.

Years later, it's so easy to see. I staggered into that relationship emotionally wounded and didn't want to admit I was with the wrong person. The more I tried to convince her of who I was, and the importance of what I was doing, the weaker I felt and the worse it got. I think when we find ourselves trying to explain who we are to a romantic partner who fundamentally doesn't get it, the battle is already lost. Our friends were starting to take big steps, but I couldn't seem to find my feet. Like the old adage says: "The way you feel about someone and the way they make you feel can be two totally different things." Looking back, I am ashamed to say that I put up with it for far too long.

About eight months in, she invited me to the Bay Area for a wedding. Two of her good friends had chosen a quaint little hotel in the rolling hills and vineyards of Napa as the place they'd get married. In retrospect, perhaps Wine Country wasn't the best place for us to be. When we arrived at the hotel, I learned that my girlfriend used to hook up with one of the groomsmen when they were back in college. An ex at a wedding is not unusual, and I am not a jealous person, but sometimes you can just tell when there is a lingering spark between two people. I did my best to fake a smile and be a good guest in a room full of people I mostly didn't know—except, of course, for her opinionated friends, who all seemed to be there. It was going to be a long night. I'm sorry if you see the rest of the story coming—I'm embarrassed to say I didn't.

At some point after the ceremony, the toasts, and the cutting of the cake, I snuck over to the hotel bar to catch a bit of the UCLA football game in their season opener against Alabama. I was joined by some other plus-ones—we didn't think anyone would miss us at the reception. Besides, by this point pretty much the entire wedding was drunk, and I figured I would let her have fun with her friends. After a while, I headed to the bathroom, down a long dark hallway in the old hotel. I passed an amorous couple making out against the wall—and did a double take. *It was my girlfriend and the groomsman.* My eyes and brain couldn't seem to reconcile what I was looking at. It set in like a kick to the stomach.

Between Misdemeanors, the Gang Unit, Sexual Assault, and my early work in Homicide, I had completed perhaps eighty jury trials by that point in my career. I could speak English, language was my currency, and I knew how to talk. And yet, in that moment, I had nothing. I managed exactly two sounds, and one of them is barely even a real word: "Um . . . dude . . . ?"

Her eyes went wide as she looked up, and as he removed his tongue from her mouth. The groomsman scurried away, muttering something like, "I'm sorry, I didn't know."

I was stunned. Through the fog I found a full sentence: "So . . . you understand that means we're . . . done, right?" I walked away. Her drama turned on like a switch as she followed me back to our room. She cried, tried to blame the guy, and kept saying she loved me. I told her I was done. I packed my bag and explained that I was leaving first thing in the morning. She collapsed onto the bed, still wearing her dress, and it didn't take long before she was out cold and snoring. I counted the hours, wide awake, until the sun came up and I could get out of Napa. I squared my shoulders and tried to walk out of that hotel with as much dignity as I could muster, but the truth is that I was crushed. I entered that ridiculous relationship as an emotional wreck in the first place . . . so where would this leave me? Fifteen months earlier I had been with a smart and fiercely loyal woman who desperately wanted to marry me. How, in God's name, had it all come to this?

But life is a funny thing, and it is amazing how some of our lowest moments often spawn our highest achievements. Sometimes this is because we dig in and become better versions of ourselves, sometimes it is because these low moments open a door to something better, and sometimes it is due to pure, dumb, serendipitous luck.

Driving back to the Oakland airport in my cheap rental car, I immediately called my friend Sean, who organizes an annual surf charter with a bunch of my friends. I had already told him I couldn't go that year. I had work to do, I hadn't trained a bit, and, after all, I'd had a wedding to attend at the same time as the trip. As soon as he answered, he could tell I needed a buddy. "Please tell me there is still an opening. I need to go surfing . . . *badly*."

The news was good, and I was packing boards as soon as I got home. I was on my way to Eastern Indonesia for eleven days on the sailboat *Mahalo*, which, quite appropriately, means "thank you" in Hawaiian. Unbeknownst to me at the time, that trip was going to be profoundly important in ways I never could have imagined.

////Λ\\\

Indonesia is a unique, incredible place for surfers. Bands of energy from the storms off the southern coast of Africa, one of the angriest stretches of ocean in the world, travel thousands of miles over the Indian Ocean, organizing themselves along the way, before reaching the shores of the Indonesian archipelago. Perfectly groomed, they stack up on the coral reefs of "Indo" as some of the best waves in the world. It's also a great place to get your head together, and nothing felt like more of an escape than Roti Island.

One of my favorite surf spots on Roti is a place called "Sucky Mamas." The break is what Australians refer to as a right-hander, which dredges up over the shallow reef and barrels into a deep channel about one hundred yards down the line. It's brilliant when the conditions are right, but very dangerous when the tide gets too low; I loved it for the peace of mind I found there. The takeoff requires full commitment, and you need all the skill you have as a surfer to make it safely to the deep water of the channel. For me, that meant applying whatever mental focus I could muster. Concentration and success on one wave led to increased confidence on the next. And the view from inside the barrel, especially when framed by the deep blue of the tropical ocean, is an image that every true surfer lives to see.

Years later, I would break a rib surfing that very spot, and come as close to drowning as I ever have. But on that trip, fresh off the disaster in Napa, I just couldn't get enough. One glassy afternoon, when the conditions were perfect, a giant yellow sea snake swam right through the lineup. Five feet long, with the thickness and color of a grapefruit, it frightened just about everyone out of the water. Sea snakes are generally pretty docile, but when one of the most venomous animals on the planet swims right by you, it definitely commands your full attention. Scary as it was, it was also hard not to marvel at its grace. Much like the surf spot itself, the snake was both terrifying and awesome. Besides, when everyone else saw it as their cue to go back to the boat, it meant more waves for me. A dangerous creature, at a dangerous wave, and far, far away from engagements, weddings, and cheating girlfriends, I was suddenly in the water by myself, and my mind drifted toward a minor epiphany.

The love of my life (at least to that point) was about to marry another guy. And her fiancé was straight out of central casting for a jilted-heart romantic comedy. Strikingly handsome, a bona fide Olympic athlete, he was a fundamentally good man adored by everyone who knew him. In the words of one of my best friends, who was with him at UCLA, "He's a lot like you, dude, just a little better in every way." At the time of this writing, he is still the devoted husband and father she always wanted—and truly deserved. I then limped into the next relationship a wounded fool too heartsick to enforce any healthy boundaries with a woman of a very different character. And that one had just ended in comedic disaster outside of the men's room of a boutique hotel in Napa, California.

I had been to a ton of other weddings, of course, and none of them were mine. Gay weddings, straight weddings, Greek Orthodox, Indian, Catholic, Jewish, you name it. I had stood there as a best man, a groomsman, and even once as a bridesmaid. I watched friend after friend proclaim their love and pledge themselves completely to the person standing next to them. One by one, they were all in and fully committed to the new adventure of marriage, and I was genuinely happy for them. But it meant my circle of close friends was shrinking, vow by vow. We would keep in touch, of course, and talk on the phone sometimes. I would see them at fantasy football draft night, or for the odd round of golf, but their priorities naturally shifted to their homelife, and then eventually in most cases to paint colors and baby names. Perhaps the most important responsibility for a best man or a groomsman, once the ceremony is over, is to get out of the way. I wanted my friends to find fulfillment in their new lives as spouses and parents, but I would be lying if I denied also feeling a growing sense of loneliness along with a slight pang of envy. This is where I had envisioned my own life at age thirty-five. I felt like I would have been a good husband, and a good dad, but there was no denying that at that point I was very much the odd man out. As I sat there watching the sun set over Eastern Indonesia, it struck me that in the grand game of marital musical chairs, the music had stopped and everyone else seemed to have a seat. Suddenly I was all alone.

Clearly, I sucked at relationships.

And that's when it hit me.

Maybe that idyllic homelife of my friends was simply not meant for me. Maybe I suffered the spectrum of romantic failure because I wasn't supposed to experience that kind of happiness. Maybe I could stop beating myself up, and just accept that it wasn't in my future. Maybe the focus of my passion, my energy, and my life force was meant for something else. Maybe I could commit myself fully to something meaningful and, as cliché as it sounds, make an actual difference. Perhaps fate, God, the universe, destiny, or whatever we want to call it had other plans for me. Maybe I was staring right at it.

In the arc of human experience, the death of a loved one is the very worst thing. Death due to murder is the worst of the worst. It means that someone, for terrible reasons, has snuffed out the light of a person we care for deeply. The only thing worse than murder is when the killer gets away with it. It is difficult for most people to put themselves in the headspace of someone thrust into that situation, into the overpowering darkness of that place. Some people even feel entitled to question a parent's fundamental need for justice, but nobody knows how important that is unless and until, God forbid, they are actually there. A parent's grief under those circumstances is a human universal of misery that crosses all economic, cultural, and racial lines.

So maybe a happy family of my own was never meant to be, but as I sat there waiting for one last wave, it struck me that I was in a unique position to help those poor people. Instead of walking a fat dog and watching a movie in a warm living room at the end of a perfectly balanced workday, maybe I could do something meaningful for innocent people who needed a champion. Maybe they deserved someone who was all in.

German philosopher and writer Friedrich Nietzsche famously said, "He who fights with monsters might take care lest he thereby become a monster. And if you gaze for long into an abyss, the abyss gazes also into you." But what if a monster, with nothing to lose, is exactly what is needed? Within the strict bounds of ethics and the law, maybe those poor bereaved families deserved someone fierce. Someone of single-minded intensity and dedication. Someone with scars and teeth and the ability to attack. Someone who would stay up late and lose sleep to achieve justice for their murdered child. Someone who would sit and grind and find solutions to problems that others might give up on. Someone who would guide them through the brutal criminal justice process with as much dignity and empathy as possible. Someone who would care about them, and fight for them, and at the end of the day understand their rage. Maybe for them, with study, and practice, and improvement, I could be their champion. If I truly dedicated myself to those mothers and fathers and families, with nothing to lose in my personal life, maybe I could become their monster.

It was suddenly so clear to me. Forget balance, forget family, forget money, I was going all in. And as far as the abyss, rather than just stare, I resolved to find out what happens when you sprint headlong right into it. It occurred to me that the problem with most destructive addictions is they sneak up on people who are surprised when they get consumed. Work, especially this work, can get addictive—but what if you serve yourself up voluntarily? I decided at that moment to embrace it completely.

A strange sense of relief washed over me as I returned to the boat.

Unburdened from my own heartbreak, the rest of that trip was a joy. On surf charters in Indonesia, you basically spend the entire day surfing in eighty-degree water before everyone gathers on the boat for dinner. You laugh, discuss the next day's projected weather, and eventually end up "talking story" with the other guys. A lot of your energy on those trips is focused on things like swell direction, wind conditions, and phases of the moon, and it is remarkable how much you can soothe a troubled mind by reconnecting with the natural world. After the beers start flowing at those dinners, the conversation inevitably tends to get a little looser. On that trip, the boat captain was a man named Gary Burns, and one night under the stars he let slip just a little more about his past life than he might have other-wise. Gary lived on the fifty-foot sailboat with his wife and young daughter, spending half the year in Australia before returning each spring to Indonesia for the surf season. Gary had lived on boats for his entire adult life, and there was very little he did not know about the ocean, or the people who live on it. One night, he told me about some colorful encounters he had with smugglers, fugitives, and drug dealers inside the boating world. He was amused to have a prosecutor on board to chat with. I had gained a new friend, one I would soon depend on in ways that had nothing to do with surfing.

CHAPTER 4

"NO BODIES, NO MURDER"

I RETURNED FROM Indonesia with a new sense of purpose and dedication. I had recharged my batteries, I was totally single, and I hit the ground running. I prosecuted some short jury trials in rapid succession. A murder in a bar, a love triangle between homeless parolees and the mentally ill woman they were fighting over, a child abuse homicide, and even a serial rapist they passed along to me from the Sexual Assault Unit. All wins. I was honing my skills and moving through my caseload at speed. But it wouldn't be long before I embarked on one of the most downright diabolical cases of my entire career.

I was pulling into the parking lot of the DA's Office a few short months after Napa when I got a call from Detective Dave Byington. "Hello, counselor, we have a weird one...." Dave explained that a couple had gone missing while attempting to sell their yacht in Newport Beach. "Hoping you can swing by with your investigator today and we can break it down for you."

Looking back through the lens of everything we uncovered regarding the disappearance of Tom and Jackie Hawks, it's easy to forget that the case began as a pure mystery—and the more we learned about who Tom and Jackie Hawks were, the worse it all looked. There was no way to rationalize what happened to them, the way that we try sometimes to convince ourselves that we could never be the victim of a gang murder. Tom and Jackie were good people, living a good life, who fastidiously made good decisions.

Tom Hawks was a fifty-seven-year-old former probation officer who had been financially responsible to the point of being frugal. He had saved enough to retire early and live his dream, buying a fifty-five-foot yacht with his wife, forty-seven-year-old Jackie, and outfitting the boat to serve as an incredible home on the water. Their dream, quite literally, was to sail off into the sunset. They cruised around the Sea of Cortez and in and out of Newport Beach Harbor in Southern California for more than two years.

Tom had two children from his first marriage; Jackie, a widow whose first husband had died in a motorcycle accident that left Jackie injured and unable to have children of her own, had raised them with Tom. Tom, Jackie, and the kids, Ryan and Matt—then young adults—were a close-knit family, and Matt, living in Arizona, had just become a father for the first time. Tom and Jackie fell in love instantly with their new role as grandparents and, led by Jackie's enthusiasm, decided that two years of living on the water were enough. They had a new plan: Sell the yacht, use the proceeds to buy a smaller boat, and move back to Arizona to help raise their baby grandson, Jace. Jackie was over the moon.

Tom—still careful with money—didn't want to pay the typical

15 percent commission if you use a broker to sell a yacht, and so he took out an ad in *Yachting World* magazine to see if he could find a buyer himself, at a listed price of nearly $500,000. Soon a young man reached out to him—Skylar Deleon, twenty-five years old. It seemed too easy. Tom and Jackie told friends that Skylar was a former child actor with plenty of money who didn't even want to haggle about the price. Like test-driving a used car, the plan was for Tom and Jackie to take Skylar on a sea trial, then close the deal. Jackie called a friend from the boat in the late afternoon on November 15, 2004—they had plans to meet up that night—and told him they were still on the water, and she'd give him a call when they got back to shore.

That was the last time anyone heard from Tom or Jackie Hawks.

By the next day, their family was already concerned. Jackie never turned off her cell phone, and yet their calls were going straight to voicemail. It wasn't like them to be out of touch for even a day. Had they closed the deal and spontaneously decided to take a road trip with the proceeds? It seemed unlikely. Tom's brother, Jim Hawks, was a retired police officer. In fact, he had been the chief of police in Carlsbad, California, about an hour south of Newport. As soon as Ryan and Matt reached out to tell him they were worried, Jim drove up to the boat dock. There, he found the dinghy Tom and Jackie used to get out to the yacht, which was moored in its usual spot—but something didn't feel right. And the dinghy didn't look right either. Tom was meticulous about his boat and its upkeep, and Jim saw that the motor was still in the water and the boat was tied up improperly. When he made it out to the yacht, things looked just as sloppy. There were tarps on the deck and a towel hanging out of one of the portholes. Jim knew his brother would have never left the boats that way. Jim Hawks left his business card on the yacht with his phone number and a note saying he was trying to find his brother.

Soon after, he got a call back from a woman who identified herself as Jennifer Deleon, Skylar's wife. With both concern and annoyance, she told Jim that she and her husband couldn't track down Tom and Jackie either. She said that they had bought the boat, in cash, and that Tom and Jackie were supposed to show them how to operate it and come get their stuff. Jim called Tom and Jackie's friend down in Arizona who took care of their finances when they were on the water, figuring that if they'd gotten the money, she'd know—or at least the bank would know. But there was no activity on the account.

The family filed a missing persons report with the Newport Beach Police Department. Dave Byington and his team searched the boat, but it was clean. Too clean, in fact. They requested a second CSI team, this time from the sheriff's department, to come process the boat, too. Again, they found nothing. When my investigator Larry Montgomery and I arrived at the Newport Police Department, Byington explained: "We have a missing couple, we have no evidence of a struggle, but we can't find their car, nobody has heard from them, the family says they were looking at property in Mexico, but the whole thing is super weird."

The one thing they did find on the boat was a receipt from Target—for trash bags, Clorox wipes, and a bottle of Tums. They were able to get surveillance video from the store, but it wasn't Skylar or Jennifer who'd made the purchase. Turned out, it was Jennifer's father, Steve Henderson. Most people don't know that Target keeps a video record of every transaction at their stores, which is frankly pretty awesome. We were able to track down Steve, and he brought us to Skylar and Jennifer—who were volunteering at their church, their toddler daughter, Hailie, in tow, and Jennifer very pregnant with a second child.

The church, the pregnancy, and the fact that they were cooperative in every way made Skylar and Jennifer seem like an innocent young couple caught in a mess. They presented as the perfect all-American family. Police separated Skylar and Jennifer and interviewed them. Each told essentially the same story that Jennifer had told to Jim Hawks. The boat had been purchased, with cash, and Tom and Jackie had promised to instruct Skylar on how to properly operate everything. Skylar and Jennifer had answers for every question, expressed concern for the Hawks, and even added a kicker that made them sound completely legit, if a little mercenary: "Once you find these people, can you please tell them they need to make good on their promise to show Skylar how to properly operate the boat? We would hate to have to sue them."

When police huddled up after the two interviews, they matched perfectly. Not to mention, the young couple offered a persuasive bonus to the story: Jennifer provided police with original bill of sale documents, which also contained the stamp of a percipient witness and notary public named Kathleen Harris. The documents appeared to have the Hawks' signatures, and even their fingerprints. They looked convincingly official. The documents were taken by detectives, photographed, and immediately sent to the FBI for analysis.

////l\\\\

Here's where our suspicions and beliefs quickly diverged from what we could prove. With every minute that ticked by, and the more we learned about Tom and Jackie, we *believed* that something terrible had happened to them. It was pretty clear it had something to do with that sea trial. But the only evidence we had at that point was that the Deleons had bought some cleaning supplies and had done such a good job cleaning the boat that there were no fingerprints to be found, no DNA, no signs of a struggle, nothing.

So what do you do?

Things got more complicated the more we investigated. The produced and notarized documentation from the sale was for a sum $200,000 less than what Tom had been asking for. Even stranger,

Jennifer also produced a signed and notarized power of attorney form giving Skylar the right to access Tom and Jackie's bank accounts. And that was striking. Why would Tom and Jackie have given this power to a near-stranger? And where did Skylar and his wife get that kind of cash? More alarming, Skylar was on probation and had recently spent time in jail for armed burglary. Yes, he'd been a child actor, like he'd told the Hawks—sort of. A few commercials, and a nonspeaking role as an extra in two episodes of *Mighty Morphin Power Rangers*. The rich kid Tom and Jackie had told their friends about wasn't real.

But Skylar was incredibly smooth. In his initial interview with detectives, he had an explanation for everything. First, the bill of sale was lower because Tom wanted to avoid taxes. Second, the cash was money he was trying to illegally launder—related to drug trafficking in Mexico, linked back to his father, who had a police record going all the way back to the 1980s when he did federal prison time for drug smuggling. Skylar even brought up his burglary, which was super strange in its own right, explaining that it was part of the cartel business involving his father. Third, the power of attorney—Skylar said that Tom and Jackie wanted to buy property in Mexico, and that Skylar had offered to help them open a bank account down there, using his Mexican citizenship and connections.

All of that checked out . . . to a degree. It was true that Tom and Jackie had talked to their family about buying some property in Mexico with the leftover proceeds from the sale. And it seemed entirely bizarre (and thus perhaps believable) that someone would admit to money laundering and drug trafficking in their police interview—when Skylar could have just as easily said that the cash came from gambling winnings or the repayment of some kind of a debt. The fact that his explanation was so thorough—and that on top of that, we had a licensed notary saying she'd witnessed the whole transaction—seemed strangely convincing. And we interviewed notary Kathleen Harris no fewer than five times, and her story was nearly perfect—*nearly*. (We'll get there soon.) By admitting to laundering money while he was on probation, Skylar could have been sent to prison for eight years. Why would he do that if he wasn't being honest?

The genius of the story—and what made it so easy to buy—is that Skylar put himself in legal jeopardy. No one does that. It is very common that when you finally get a coconspirator to crack and tell you the "truth" about what happened, that truth somehow magically puts the blame on everyone but the guy who is talking. The potential witness, in a sea of bad behavior, would come off utterly without fault. "I didn't know it was going to be a burglary." "I didn't know my friend had a gun." "I have no idea where the bullets came from." These people end up useless as witnesses because it's obvious to the jury that they're not telling the whole truth. The people who acknowledge their own culpability are rare—and therefore we tend to believe them.

The hours turned into days, and the days turned into weeks, and we essentially still had nothing. We had no witnesses, no physical evidence, and no sign of a struggle on the boat. We had a bizarre story from Skylar Deleon, but we also had cell tower pings from Tom's and Jackie's phones near the Mexican border on the night they went missing. We had boat sale documents, which the FBI was now telling us contained Tom's and Jackie's actual signatures (almost—more soon) and fingerprints, and Hawks family members even corroborated parts of the house-buying plan in Mexico. We still had not found their car. We also had Skylar's wife Jennifer, Skylar's buddy Alonso Machain (a former jail guard Skylar had come to know when he was serving time for the burglary who Skylar said had joined them on the test run), and notary Kathleen Harris (who had never been in trouble a day in her life) all backing Skylar's account.

We asked to see Kathleen's notary book, and she said it was full and that she had sent it to the state office in Sacramento. The state had no record of receiving it, but she produced the receipt from the post office to prove it had been mailed. We couldn't poke any holes in her story, except one—she described Jackie as having long brown hair, but Jackie's hair was spiky, short, and dyed blond. Did Kathleen simply not remember? Did she confuse Jackie with Jennifer? We weren't sure, and, more importantly, we still couldn't prove a crime had taken place.

Again, there are things you suspect, and there are things you can prove.

I could hear the defense attorney's closing argument in my mind: "Who is to say that couriers from a Mexican drug cartel didn't deliver the money and then decide to take things into their own hands when Tom and Jackie drove out of the parking lot? Their cell phones were pinging just north of the Mexican border right after the transaction, and people have been murdered for a lot less than $500,000 in cash."

We were stuck. The Hawks family was worried sick, we had dead ends everywhere, and we were left with next to nothing. So now what? With still no word from Tom and Jackie, it was hard to think there would be a happy ending here, but we needed something irrefutable that I could point to. We knew it must be out there. We just didn't know what it was.

Forensic scientists are excellent at what they do. Similarly, the detectives assigned to that case were among the finest I have ever worked with. But none of them had received any specialized training on what to look for when examining a boat, and neither had I. Ultimately, the final decision about who to charge, and for what crimes, fell to me. I know some rich people with boats, but none of them have a clue about crime. We needed a break. If only there was someone we could call . . . not a yacht club type, but somebody who had seen the grittier side of the boating world. Someone who might have met a genuine scallywag or two. Someone who had seen the darker side and would feel comfortable enough to talk to us.

Thank God for cheating girlfriends.

I called Charter Captain Gary Burns in Australia. He had just wrapped up the surf season in Indonesia. I told him the facts and asked him: "If there was a murder on a boat—no blood, no DNA, nothing—what would you look for?" He didn't skip a beat before giving me the answer.

"If they were selling their boat, there would be a manifest of everything on board. And if you're trying to figure out if there was a murder on a boat," Gary said, "you look for missing anchors."

"Gradually, then suddenly," as Hemingway wrote. It's how so many of these cases go. We checked the boat, and, sure enough, one of the anchors was missing. It had been staring us in the face the whole time. There should have been two anchors on the bow, and now there was only one. We even had photos of the other anchor from Tom and Jackie's adventures in the Sea of Cortez. Gary to the rescue.

At that moment, we knew—or at least I felt very confident that we knew—what had happened to Tom and Jackie Hawks. The implications were chilling. Wherever that anchor had gone, we believed Tom and Jackie had gone with it. It wasn't the whole story, but it was something simple, understandable, and undeniable. At that point, I believed I could prove that these two innocent people had been murdered, but exactly what had been done to them, and by whom, was still an open question.

I could have charged Skylar at that point, maybe with second-degree murder, but the real question was how to establish the fullest extent of accountability for everyone involved. That's another thing that you don't realize until you're invested with the decision-making authority of a prosecutor: It should never be enough to simply get *a* conviction. To do these families justice, you have to hold every guilty party responsible for the full scope of their actions. I didn't just want to get Skylar on second-degree murder. He would already have been long out of prison by the time you read this. If he had planned this—and if others had helped him—I wanted to make sure they were all accountable to the maximum extent possible, for everything they did.

We brought Skylar back in with this new evidence. He brought his toddler, Hailie, perhaps hoping we wouldn't arrest him with a baby in his arms. As soon as he realized how much we knew, he got nervous, and I think the kid could tell. Hailie suddenly vomited right on Skylar's lap. We let Skylar go, and the next day, we arrested him on charges of his admitted money laundering and probation violation, buying us time to keep building the murder case.

Next, I approached Jennifer's lawyer with a deal. For the first time in my career, I offered what is known as full *transactional immunity*—not realizing how deep her involvement really was. Transactional immunity, as opposed to what is known as *use immunity*, is what most people think of when they hear the term. It means *immunity* immunity. It means confess everything you have ever done wrong in your entire life and receive complete absolution. It's not just a get-out-of-jail-free card; it means the recipient never goes to jail in the first place. All she had to do was tell us what happened and she would never have to serve a single day in custody.

Astonishingly, she turned it down, letting young love win out over reason, sound legal advice, and any notion of doing the right thing. I was enjoying a rare round of golf on a Sunday morning when her lawyer, Mike Molfetta, gave me the news. Mike is one of the best lawyers I know, and his client control is unmatched. "She's got nothing more to say," he told me. I couldn't believe it. She was going all in.

Jennifer would visit Skylar regularly at first. They would speak on phone lines through glass, just like you see in the movies. And—not suspicious at all—they would often whisper. The lines were recorded, of course, and we would enhance all the tapes to the limits of available audio technology. Much of what they said remained unintelligible, but we did get one true nugget. As Skylar was reassuring Jennifer that he would be home soon, he whispered, "Remember . . . no bodies, no murder." Boom.

With Skylar in jail receiving regular visits from his wife, we turned to the media. That's when the dominoes really began to fall—almost a full month after Tom and Jackie had disappeared. We put Ryan Hawks—grieving, telegenic, compelling—on *Good Morning America*, *Larry King Live*, and anywhere else we could in order to try and find out if anyone out there knew anything, if anyone had seen Tom and Jackie, or perhaps seen their Honda SUV, which had been missing all along. Incredibly, the day after the media blitz, detectives got a call from a woman in a trailer park in Mexico who said she had seen Ryan on television, and she was looking at the car right now, Arizona plates, outside her window. She sent a photo, and it matched. If there was any last bit of hope we would find Tom and Jackie, here it was—maybe, just maybe, they had gone to Mexico and somehow couldn't reach their families, maybe something had happened to their phones, maybe they'd been kidnapped but were still alive.

Dave Byington went down to San Miguel, Mexico, with a group of his detectives. Dave is of Mexican ancestry, and I actually had a connection with the chief of Homicide in Ensenada. The Mexican police rolled out the red carpet for us, and the Homicide chief himself arrived at the San Miguel trailer park with three or four of his police officers to assist Dave and his team. Sure enough, there was the car. Dave knocked on the door of the house, and there was a local family inside.

"Hello, can you please tell us where you got the car?"

"Our friend gave it to us."

"Who's your friend?"

"Skylar Deleon."

Home run—or so we thought, until a brand-new twist suddenly emerged. The friendly police chief stepped up. "Did you say Skylar Deleon?" he asked the family in Spanish. He then stepped inside the house and closed the door, leaving Byington outside staring at his shoes. The chief emerged about twenty minutes later. In a cloud of dust, he pulled his men, got in his vehicle, and left with no explanation other than declaring "You cannot have the car." What in God's name just happened?

As we would soon find out, Skylar Deleon was a known entity to Ensenada's chief of Homicide—they'd investigated him in connection with an entirely different murder, ten months earlier, involving a man named Jon Peter Jarvi, who had been found with his throat slit on the side of a Mexican road between Ensenada and Tecate. That investigation culminated in a personal meeting between Skylar and our suddenly-not-so-friendly chief of police. At that point, we had no idea any of that had happened, and we still have no idea what they discussed, but charges were never filed against Skylar and the investigation suddenly came to a halt. At least until we got a hold of it. *El jefe de homicidios* did exactly nothing from that point forward. Suddenly, the red carpet was yanked out from under us, and we were being blocked from continuing our investigation.

It was a moment for heroes.

Dave Byington, unarmed, in a foreign country—and in a move for which I will love him forever—looked at his guys and quietly announced, "Fuck that shit."

He watched the Mexican police cars leave the trailer park, one by one, then removed a spare set of car keys given to him by Jim Hawks, put on a pair of latex gloves, and straight up repossessed the Hawks' car—it was our evidence, after all. He drove it out of Ensenada, through the city of Tijuana, and right across the border into the US. Now we had a missing anchor, Skylar's jailhouse tapes, and the car—and pretty soon, we would have bank security footage from Arizona, where Skylar and Jennifer had tried to use their power of attorney to gain access to Tom and Jackie's accounts days after the disappearance. Fortunately, the bank manager knew the Hawks personally and could not believe they had given a POA to these strangers who were showing up to claim their money.

Legally, they presented a notarized power of attorney that had been properly filed and recorded by the County Clerk of Prescott, Arizona. According to the law, that is all they needed to do. But the law of common sense and human loyalty denied them their goal. "I'm not giving you access to their accounts until I hear from Tom and Jackie themselves," the bank manager told them, and so Skylar and Jennifer—caught on camera with grins on their faces as they thought they were about to solve their money problems forever—went home empty-handed.

We then searched the home of a dive shop employee who connected Skylar and Jennifer with the notary, Kathleen Harris. The search yielded exactly one clue, but it was a big one. A crumpled color photocopy of Tom's and Jackie's drivers' licenses was found wedged between a wall and the wastepaper basket it was supposed to have been tossed into. Oops. Jackie's driver's license photo revealed that she had long brown, curly hair before she had moved onto the boat and chopped and colored it. That's why Harris had described Jackie with long brown hair. She was basing her description off a photo. That meant I could prove she had never met her. So now we had the notary, too.

With all of this, we got a search warrant on Skylar and Jennifer's garage apartment—and there we found Tom's and Jackie's laptops, their video camera, and more, along with the business card of an Interpol detective who'd been investigating Skylar in connection with the Jon Jarvi case. And that's when we started to connect the dots

THE BOOK OF MURDER

with what had happened with Dave Byington's red carpet rejection down in Mexico.

After the searches, our notary, Kathleen, was the next one to fall. After multiple dishonest interviews, she came back with a lawyer, looking to talk. No, she'd never seen Tom and Jackie—her descriptions were, in fact, based on the photos on their drivers' licenses, and she'd been paid $2,000 in cash to fake the paperwork, having no idea there was a murder involved. We ended up giving her immunity in order to secure her testimony.

Instead of going back to Jennifer—who had previously told us she wouldn't cooperate—I reached out to the lawyer for Alonso Machain, who had fled to Mexico. I told him we would find Alonso and extradite him from Mexico; Mexico would only require us to take death off the table before they turned him over. Alonso drove back to the US and turned himself in. We offered what is known as a *proffer*—an agreement between a prosecutor and a witness where they agree to talk and we agree not to use what they say against them—and he told us everything: every conversation, every meeting, and every single detail of what happened on that boat. The truth was more horrific than we had ever imagined.

In an interview that lasted several hours, Alonso explained that Skylar had told him he was an international bounty hunter, paid to make bad people disappear. A lie, but Alonso was an unsophisticated and unworldly twenty-year-old who still lived with his parents in Pico Rivera. In truth, Skylar and Jennifer wanted the boat and whatever money was in Tom and Jackie's bank accounts—and were willing to do literally anything they needed to get it. Skylar promised Alonso one million dollars to help get rid of—murder—the Hawks (he would never have seen it, of course), and Jennifer was a full participant right from the start. Seeing the ad in the boating magazine sparked a plan, weeks in the making. Skylar recruited Alonso to help, and then, upon meeting Tom for the first time and seeing that he was a big, fit body-builder, Skylar called around for more muscle, finding a former gang member from the Long Beach Insane Crips, improbably named John Fitzgerald Kennedy, to pose as his accountant and join them on the test run.

Indeed, when Tom—savvy from his days as a probation officer—seemed skeptical of Skylar's intentions, Skylar had called Jennifer to come down to the harbor, bringing Hailie with her, to reassure him and Jackie that they were a kind, loving family. These people literally used their toddler as a prop to gain Tom and Jackie's trust, then murdered them in the coldest blood imaginable.

They bought stun guns and architected a plan. On the afternoon of November 15, 2004, Skylar, Kennedy, and Alonso drove to Newport Beach for the sea trial. Skylar introduced Kennedy as his accountant as they boarded the boat and the trip was soon underway. Tom steered the yacht out of Newport Harbor and into the open ocean. Once they were far enough from shore, Skylar and Kennedy overpowered Tom, and when Jackie heard the commotion, Alonso hit her with a Taser and subdued her as well. Jackie pleaded, "How can you do this, Skylar? You brought your wife and baby on board! We trusted you!"

Tom and Jackie were handcuffed and forced to sit on the couch in the main salon of the boat. They were then presented with bill of sale documents and a power of attorney form that Skylar had prepared. He told the Hawks that if either of them refused to sign, he would hurt the other one. Tom repeatedly assured him that they would cooperate as long as Jackie remained unharmed. Jackie, sending future investigators a signal, in fact signed her name incorrectly—"Hawk," without the letter s—with enough presence of mind to hope the error would indicate to someone out there that something was wrong. After signing the documents, Tom and Jackie were taken downstairs to the main bedroom and placed on the bed they had shared for the past two years. Skylar then set a course for the deepest part of the ocean.

And Tom, handcuffed back-to-back with Jackie, stroked her hand and tried to calm her. She had been begging for her life, telling Skylar she just needed to see her grandson one more time. "It's okay, sweetheart," Tom told her. "Where we're going, we're gonna be together." Alonso described how they brought the anchor from the bow and attached it to Tom and Jackie, who were blindfolded, duct-taped, and now face-to-face on the fantail of their beloved yacht. Alonso said that when Tom heard Skylar behind him, he kicked and almost knocked Skylar off the stern of the boat. Almost. Kennedy then came running up and punched Tom in the side of the head, apparently knocking him out, or at least stunning him enough to end the fight. Jackie was screaming as Skylar threw the anchor overboard, the line going taut, yanking Tom and Jackie violently into the cold November ocean.

We have all had that one conversation as kids. The one where we contemplate the most horrible way to die. "Would you rather burn to death, or freeze to death?" "Fire ants, or get eaten by a lion?" The question I couldn't stop thinking about was, How do you cry and try to hold your breath at the same time? Truly awful stuff.

On the ride back to shore, Skylar threw the Hawks' family photos and possessions into the ocean like they were Frisbees. John Kennedy grabbed a beer from the fridge, found a fishing pole, and tossed in a line off the side of the boat. These were cold-blooded killers, utterly lacking in any sort of human remorse. It is perhaps the cruelest case I have ever encountered, and Skylar is perhaps the scariest sociopath I have ever met. We put the pieces together for Jon Jarvi's murder as well—Skylar was in a work release program in jail at the time and convinced Jarvi, a pilot who got into painkillers and associated legal trouble, that he had a big score for the two of them down in Mexico. He convinced Jarvi to give him $50,000 in cash and then drove him across the border, slit his throat, and left him to die on the side of the road. Skylar was late getting back to jail that night, but it was okay, because his friend Alonso Machain was in charge and fudged the attendance sheet.

Watching the Hawks' home videos was an experience. I decided to view them sequentially, and started with the first tape as I was working alone in my office late one evening. Tom and Jackie had carefully documented their lives on board the yacht—which they'd named the *Well Deserved*—for the better part of two years. We found those tapes in Skylar and Jennifer's crappy converted garage, as if they had also stolen their warmest memories. As the prosecutor of their murderers, I had a unique opportunity to really get to know my victims by watching those tapes. It was hours and hours of touching, raw video: Tom swimming with a whale shark in the Sea of Cortez, Jackie giving the viewer a tour of the interior of their lovely home on the water. You can see their wonderful sense of humor and how much they loved each other. So many amazing adventures.

There was a bodysurfing video from when Ryan and his dad were back in Newport Beach. I don't know why, with all the horror in this case, but for some reason, watching that particular clip, showing them laughing together as Tom got knocked down by a wave, it all suddenly got to me. Not the anchor, not the begging for life, not the sheer brutality, but that poignant moment between a father and son. The tears started and I broke down crying. It gets me every time I think about it, and it's making me choke up again even as I write this. That, of all things, is what finally broke my heart for these people and that family. I have never shared that before. It's funny how the little things can catch your emotions so completely off guard.

The trials in this case were so involved, and so detailed, that I would almost need another book to walk you through it all. Each was very different. The first to go was Jennifer, and she was represented by the formidable Mike Molfetta. He had very correctly advised her to cooperate and take my offer of immunity. She hadn't, which left him to have to formulate a defense where, in essence, she blamed Skylar for everything. She was not on the boat at the time of the murders; Skylar was, in fact, a genuine psychopath; Jennifer had a family to worry about. Molfetta argued, quite persuasively, that had Jennifer not met Skylar, she would likely never have committed a crime in her life.

Among the problems with her defense, however, was that Jennifer Deleon knew all about the murder of Jon Jarvi ten months earlier. In fact, Jarvi parked his car in front of Jennifer's parents' house, and it sat there for days before Skylar finally got rid of it. When police came looking for him, Jennifer was the person who answered the door. The officers informed her that the owner of the car had been missing and had been found dead in Mexico. On the same day that the car turned up, Skylar had come home with $50,000 of Jarvi's cash. This money was immediately used to get them out of debt, buy a new Toyota Highlander for Jennifer to drive, and . . . believe it or not . . . purchase a $900 sex toy that Skylar found online, on his desktop computer, before returning to Seal Beach City Jail and checking in with Alonso.

Fair to say, Jennifer knew everything. So, when Skylar asked her to "come down to the boat and bring Hailie in order to put these people at ease," Jennifer knew exactly what she was doing. This was a woman who used her child to lure an innocent couple into a false sense of security so that her deranged husband could murder them and steal their boat. Phone records from the night of the killings were also very telling. When Skylar arrived in Newport, he called Jennifer. When the Hawks were tased and subdued, he called Jennifer. When they were taken out to sea and dumped overboard like trash, he called Jennifer. There were more than a dozen calls between them. She was not only operating with full knowledge, but was a critical component in the entire plan.

Molfetta argued that her knowing involvement only took place after the fact, and only because she was terrified of her psychopath husband. She only went along to protect her family. . . . "Where is the smoking gun?!" he demanded during his closing argument.

"You want to see a smoking gun?" I asked in rebuttal. I zoomed in on Jennifer's face in the enhanced video grab from the bank. The Cheshire grin on her face was clear as could be. "A picture says a thousand words, ladies and gentlemen. Does that look like the face of a woman who is terrified of the man next to her, or someone who is about to solve all of her financial problems? You make the call."

Jennifer's parents were deluded until the very end. We knew from listening to the jail tapes that they had said to her lawyer, "I know Jesus will be in the courtroom with us."

"If Jesus shows up," Molfetta responded, "you can rest assured he'll be sitting with the Hawks family."

After an offer of no prison time in exchange for the truth, Jennifer cast her lot with Skylar and is now serving two life sentences without the possibility of parole. One day the state of California will probably release that woman . . . but they shouldn't.

Skylar was next. And while you might think we could bring in Jennifer's guilty verdict here, in a severed trial like this we actually couldn't. Given the horrific nature of pretty much everything in the case, we sought the death penalty. This meant his trial was bifurcated into a *guilt phase* followed by the *penalty phase*. In such cases, first the jury must decide whether or not he did it, and then they must decide the appropriate penalty: life without the possibility of parole, or death. We knew Skylar was likely to never get executed, at least not in California, but when the case truly merited it—less than 4 percent of the time, as it happened—we felt it was appropriate to seek death even though it took perhaps five times the effort as compared to a regular murder case.

One of the unfortunate aspects of prosecuting death cases is that not everyone involved in the process approaches their task with the same dedication to fairness and the law. Former California Supreme Court Chief Justice Rose Bird, for example, is reputed to have taken great pride in the fact that she reversed every single death penalty case that came before her, sending them back to be retried in lower Courts. This was perhaps a wonderful flex for her when surrounded by her ideological supporters, but it was catastrophic for the victims' families, who had to relive the trial all over again. The position of Justice Bird, and others, is difficult for me to intellectually distinguish from that of a "pro-death" justice affirming a case with clear error because they ideologically believe *in* the death penalty. Both approaches are equally wrong.

Skylar's trial began with a dramatic moment that I will never forget. Gary Pohlson, one of the finest attorneys I have ever encountered, didn't want to blow his credibility in the guilt phase of a bifurcated capital trial. In his opening statement, he announced that Skylar was guilty of all three murders, but that mitigating evidence would convince the jury that he should not receive the death penalty. This is a move that most lawyers simply don't have the guts to make. He knew it would win him points in the penalty phase because the jury would remember his honesty, and that even while he couldn't get his client cleared of the murders, he would have a fighting chance to spare his life. Credibility is everything in front of a jury. You see defense lawyers guided by zealotry more than strategy get up and argue fantastical nonsense on behalf of their client during the guilt phase, and then once there is a conviction, they have to go in front of that same jury and somehow argue to spare their client's life. If the jury knows you tried to fool them in the guilt phase, you run a substantial risk of losing credibility when it really counts.

The penalty phase brought out excuse after excuse for why Skylar didn't deserve the death penalty. One of the defense witnesses was

Skylar's mother, who told the story of his abusive drug dealer father, and how there was once a big party at their house and little Skylar fell in the swimming pool, and no one noticed. Someone had to jump in and save him, and he was spitting out water, gasping for air. She didn't see the irony. As a general rule, I almost never cross a defendant's mother. It is very risky to go too hard on them, but with her I couldn't resist.

"That must have been terrible," I said.

"Was he blue?" I asked.

"Did he seem terrified?"

"Was he tied to an anchor?"

Sorry if two decades of this work means that I have little sympathy for cold-blooded murderers, or those who testify on their behalf. Skylar was convicted, sentenced to death, and now is (symbolically, at least) a "condemned prisoner."

Skylar's story took a somewhat unexpected turn after the murders. Skylar has claimed to be transgender, and while in county jail sought to move to the cushier women's facility, even making an attempt—a feigned one, I'm confident—to cut off his penis. Why am I so convinced that this is a manipulation, and a sick attempt to take advantage of the sympathies of the transgender community? To begin with, Skylar is a pathological liar. His entire life, Skylar has been manipulating people along these lines. For years, Skylar told people he was a hermaphrodite. There was no truth to it. Since his conviction, he has insisted that he needed the Hawks' money for gender reassignment surgery—but this is also nonsense. After the murder of Jon Jarvi less than a year earlier, Skylar drove home with $50,000 in cash. Instead of getting the surgery when he had the money (a procedure that would have cost him $17,000 out of pocket), he blew it on a car, credit card bills, and his robotic sex toy. (When we carried the sex machine out of their apartment, past all the neighbors watching outside, Jennifer's deeply religious mother shouted into the street, "That's not mine!")

In San Quentin, he has changed his name to Skylar Preciosa Deleon and grown out his hair. I worked for years with a transgender colleague and saw the struggles she went through. She was one of the best people I've ever worked with and a truly wonderful human being. To see a manipulative sociopath attempt to take advantage of the feelings of people simply trying to pursue their own happiness in life should be revolting to everyone, in my opinion. Anyone who has spent any time at all trying to understand Skylar Deleon learns two things: Skylar will say and do absolutely anything, and Skylar can never, ever be trusted. I'm sorry, but it is all a con. At least those who believe Skylar this time won't die as a result.

Finally, there was John Fitzgerald Kennedy—the muscle. Signed on at the last minute to fill in for a guy way too smart to show up for Skylar, Kennedy had actually been training to be a pastor when he agreed to go on this mission. Right before the anchor went overboard, Kennedy threw perhaps the most cowardly punch in the history of all sucker punches when he hit Tom Hawks as he was blindfolded and tied up but still fighting for the life of his beloved wife. There was one memorable wrinkle in his trial: Alonso Machain (who testified as our witness against all three defendants) had a hard time remembering whether Kennedy had facial hair or not. Given the enormity of the events, and the relatively short time he interacted with him, Alonso just couldn't remember. We know Kennedy certainly had a goatee the night of the murder, but how important is facial hair, really, in our ability to remember a face?

I borrowed an argument from my colleague Larry Yellin that I saw him use back when we were working Misdemeanors together. I had the benefit of PowerPoint, so I put up a silhouette of Michael Jordan in his famous Air Jordan ad. Not only is Jordan arguably the greatest basketball player to ever live, he is also perhaps the most successful pitchman, selling everything from shoes to cologne. For whatever reason, companies love to put his silhouette in their ads. The man is so recognizable, we literally only have to see his shape to know who we are looking at. We have all seen him, at least virtually, hundreds if not thousands of times.

So . . . ask yourself . . . does Michael Jordan have facial hair? If you don't immediately know the answer, does that mean you have never seen an image of Michael Jordan? Does that mean you couldn't identify him in a courtroom? Take a few seconds and think about it. The answer is that he has had a mustache ever since his college career at North Carolina. You have seen Michael Jordan, and Alonso saw Kennedy. The jury agreed.

In all three trials, the courageous act of Jackie Hawks signing her name without the "s" had a tremendous impact. In order to understand this, we have to consider exactly what she was thinking at the time. There she was, on the boat, knowing she was about to die, deliberately leaving a tiny clue so that her murderers wouldn't get away with it. In her final moments, she wanted justice. I asked the jury: Who was she actually communicating with? "The police can gather evidence," I told them, "the prosecutor can present it, and the judge can preside over it, but the only people who can actually hold these terrible individuals accountable are the ones on the jury. Ladies and gentlemen, I respectfully submit, Jackie Hawks was talking to *you*."

The whole series of trials haunts me to this day. The Hawks could have been any of us. Good people, living their lives. It's a reminder to take nothing for granted. Gary Burns and I are still buddies, and I try to get back to Indonesia every year. It's amazing to think about how that ridiculous moment of drunken betrayal, in that little Napa hotel, could result in friendship and then justice. And every time I set foot on a boat now, the first thing I look for are the anchors.

CHAPTER 5

WEALTHY MEN ONLY

WHEN YOU ARE a Homicide prosecutor, most cases come to you. The murder is committed, police reach out, and you respond. You go to the scene, review the reports, file charges when appropriate, and present the case. There is profound satisfaction that comes with catching killers and charging them quickly. You get to help victimized families in the lowest moment of their shock and grief, the murderer is in custody, and you generally feel very good about where you are devoting your professional energy.

The typical cold case—an older crime that hasn't yet been solved—may not have a fresh scene to visit, but it often comes to you as well, landing on your desk after there has been a DNA hit. Often rape-murders, these cases can linger for years or even decades as pure mysteries—classic whodunits—for which there are no remaining leads. Imagine a woman found beaten, raped, and strangled with no viable evidence other than the forensic swabs that haven't yet caught up to the killer.

What happens is that the perpetrator's DNA—or the DNA from a close family member—winds up in CODIS, the Combined DNA Index System, often from some new crime scene or an old item of evidence recently reprocessed, and the police department gets notified of the hit. I haven't yet talked much about the science behind DNA, but, in a nutshell, the forensic application of DNA is simpler than some may realize. Although it seems a little intimidating at first (or at least it did for me as a young Deputy DA), understanding its evidentiary significance is not hard at all. In fact, DNA evidence is a little bit like a cat video sent to you on Instagram. The math and science underpinning how that image appears on your screen may be vastly complex, but understanding what you are looking at is easy—it's a video of a cat. Similarly, the biochemical components of DNA (deoxyribonucleic acid) might take years of formal study to truly understand, but when the genetic profile from a sperm stain found at a murder scene matches your suspect's, you don't need a degree in biochemistry to understand what it means. A jury doesn't need expertise in the actual science of DNA to properly consider it during deliberations. Neither do you.

The British evolutionary biologist and Oxford professor Richard Dawkins once said, "DNA neither cares nor knows. DNA just is. And we dance to its music." I have always liked that quote. It reflects the utter lack of bias inherent in DNA evidence. It may not know or care, but when it comes to solving murder cases, it sure can tell us a lot.

An easy way to understand DNA is to think of the famous image of the double helix, which looks a bit like a twisted ladder. The rungs of the ladder can be thought of as a long street with houses on both sides.

Each house has a unique address, but most of the houses are rather dull. They have exactly two rooms and two occupants. The two occupants are our genes, and they determine if we are going to be plants or animals, how many legs we will have, whether we will breathe air or water, and more. This genetic material comes from exactly two sources: our mother and our father. The vast majority of DNA on the human genome is exactly the same from one individual to the next. In fact, almost 99 percent of our DNA is indistinguishable from a chimpanzee's.

But there are a few places where science has found significant variation. As we drive down the chromosomal street, like a home development where almost every house is the same, suddenly a mansion will appear. A bigger house, with many rooms, any of which can be taken by the two occupant genes who live there. An individual address is called a "locus," and these have been given scientific names like D3S1358 or Tho1. Forensically speaking, these are the fun spots. If there are thirty potential "rooms" at that location (known as an "allelic ladder"), scientists simply assign a number to each one. An occupying gene in that particular room (known as an allele) will get numbered based on the room it is in. For example, mom's gene may be a 3, and dad's may be a 25. Their offspring will then be a (3, 25) for that locus. Whether the gene is for red hair, big feet, or any other inherited trait doesn't matter. It's the numbers that count. A person's DNA will never change, and in every single nuclear cell in their body, for their entire life, they will have a 3 and a 25 in that location.

There are currently twenty-one different locations on the human chromosome where scientists check for variation. When you examine each of those twenty-one locations, you end up with a near-infinite number of possible combinations. Figuring out the chances that two people would happen to have parents who provide them with the same genetic combinations at all twenty-one loci produces odds like one in seventeen quadrillion. In other words, if the DNA recovered from the murder scene happens to match yours in all twenty-one spots, there is a one in seventeen quadrillion chance that the DNA at the murder scene actually belongs to someone else.

Considering that there are "only" about eight billion people in the world, and there are a million billion in a quadrillion, you can feel plenty confident that a "hit" means that the suspect was at the scene. While false positives are not mathematically impossible, the chances are so fantastically remote that it would be like a criminal defendant hitting the worst lottery in scientific imagination. There may be perfectly innocent reasons why a person's DNA is found at a crime scene, but in the real world, it is absolutely their DNA. By the end of a well-presented case, it is all very easy to understand. DNA doesn't care, it just is.

So, when there's a DNA hit, the investigations usually don't require much involvement from the prosecutor, and they tend to be pretty easy to prove. All you need are enough people still around from the original investigation to lay a legal foundation for the evidence and you're in business. As I just detailed, sperm fraction DNA from a rapist-murderer is hard to explain away when it matches up perfectly to the DNA taken from the dead victim. These hits are huge for the families who have been denied justice for too long, and it is rewarding to help put the bad guy away. But it is just another reactive role for the Deputy DA, waiting for the case to show up. And for a strong case, it proceeds through the system in essentially the same manner whether it lands on your desk or on a colleague's who is assigned to the next city over.

There is another kind of cold case.

Certain cases become cold not because the police don't have a viable suspect, but because the reviewing prosecutor doesn't feel like there was enough evidence. From the perspective of the surviving family, this can be devastating. Imagine the situation where you know who killed your loved one, and the police agree with you, but the DA feels like they can't prove it. Unless something changes . . . that's it. The murderer, or murderers, get away with it. Unless and until someone steps up and intervenes, justice will never be achieved.

The decision to refuse a case is very subjective, and there is no statute of limitations on murder in the state of California. As a prosecutor with access to unsolved cold cases, you can be the person who prevents a killer from getting away with it.

It is tempting, for sure, to shy away from cases that have been refused before. Another experienced prosecutor has taken a look and taken a pass—and usually for good reason. This type of cold case is always going to be difficult to prove, and whatever the issue was years earlier typically hasn't improved with the passage of time and the fading of memories. On the other hand, if you're really all in, screw difficult. If you are in the position to stop someone from getting away with murder, why wouldn't you?

To do it right, these cases need to be reworked from the ground up. This means you actually go to the police department and dust off the old files. It means you gather your team, roll up your sleeves, and get to work. Opening the old bankers' boxes feels a little like Indiana Jones cracking the seal on some ancient tomb. Instead of treasure, inside you find bloody death, and hopefully some piece of evidence that was missed back in the day.

The idea is to pore over the old files, not really sure what you're looking for until you find it. Sometimes you can identify an item to forensically test, but most of the time you can't. My team and I found some amazing things in those old boxes. Once we found a ligature—an object used for strangulation that had been removed from the neck of the victim—and it had the killer's DNA all over it. If the case is old enough, investigators had no clue about the future of genetic testing. If you can let modern forensic science do the heavy lifting, great. Most of the time, however, there is no smoking gun to test. Instead, what a case might need is simply a new set of eyes. These are the cases where the individual prosecutor and the assigned detectives can make a huge difference. This is where you as a prosecutor must affirmatively go out there and pick the fight.

There is a different—and perhaps even more profound—reward that comes from reaching back into the past and finally delivering justice to a family that has been denied it for so very long. But there is a problem that comes with the consuming and intense nature of these cases. On my trip to Indonesia, I had made the decision to dedicate myself completely to the job and see what happened. By giving up on the idea of family, I sought a purity and purpose in my work, from which I derived a great sense of meaning.

Father Allender, one of my Jesuit teachers in high school, used to quote Gandhi: "The best way to find yourself is to lose yourself in service of others." I am beyond flawed, and far from pious, but the hug from a bereaved mother at the end of a hard-fought trial is an intensely satisfying experience. In fact, it is downright intoxicating. With alcoholic parents of my own, and with the "curse of the Irish" pretty rampant in my family, I resolved at a very young age that I was never going to let that happen to me. Through high school, college (including a four-year stint living in a fraternity house), and all of law school, I never touched a drop of alcohol. To this day, I have never really been drunk. I never wanted the monkey of addiction on my back.

The odd thing, and what they don't tell you in Al-Anon meetings, is that addiction can come in many forms. After I had spent about ten years in Homicide, my old mentor Rick King, current California Superior Court Judge and former head of the Unit, used to joke, "You got the needle in your arm, buddy, I can see it. . . ." And he was right. The problem is that to get the same feeling, you have to go out and pick tougher and tougher fights on tougher and tougher cases.

I had heard about the murder of Bill McLaughlin on my first day in Homicide. My predecessor, Debbie Lloyd, told me that I should take a look at it at some point—she believed that one day it could be solved. "And the family is so nice," she told me. She was correct on both counts. As soon as I had the opportunity, I dove in.

Jenny and Kim McLaughlin loved their father immensely, and that love didn't stop when he was gunned down in the kitchen of their childhood home while making himself a sandwich on the evening of December 15, 1994. They had their assumptions about who was responsible, as did the police, but it would take a full fifteen years before murder charges were filed. Rather than yell, or publicly criticize the investigation, these women sent cookies to the Newport Beach Police Department each year on the anniversary of the slaying. It was the gentlest of reminders not to forget about their dad. These were wonderful human beings showing grace under the worst circumstances imaginable. Meeting them for the first time broke my heart, and the more I learned, the more motivated I became.

The case was beyond compelling. In fact, it reminded me of the plot to the old movie *Body Heat* starring William Hurt and Kathleen Turner. There was money, betrayal, sex, and murder. Bill McLaughlin was fifty-five years old at the time of his death, and had been a brilliant businessman. Born without much in the way of economic security on the South Side of Chicago, Bill was the first in his family to go to college, and had big ambitions. After a stint in the Marine Corps, he joined the biotech industry and became a hugely effective salesman. After working in sales and marketing for a number of companies, he went off on his own and founded a company that developed a new dialysis catheter, ultimately selling it to a medical device manufacturer. Then he teamed up with a scientist to think even bigger, and together they built a business around an improved method for separating plasma from blood.

The technology they produced represented a breakthrough in the field. Their machine essentially allowed blood to be extracted from a donor, the plasma removed, and then the blood returned right back, without the need to send it out to a lab. Bill and his partner sold the company for tens of millions of dollars, and the technology is still widely used today, for both serious medical purposes as well as cosmetic skin and scalp rejuvenation procedures. Bill's work made genuine contributions to modern medical science, and saved lives.

It also made him incredibly rich, with a net worth of more than $50 million in 1994 dollars. He owned a private plane, two homes in Las Vegas, a boat, two Mercedes-Benz cars, and an avocado ranch. He traveled the world, and his home base was a magnificent water-side property in Balboa Coves, a luxury community in Newport Beach where the houses now sell for an average of more than $6 million. He also owned a nearby beach house on Fifty-Fourth Street in Newport, where his youngest child, his handsome son Kevin, used to surf.

It sounds incredible, but life was far from perfect for Bill. Four years earlier, his twenty-four-year marriage came to an end when his wife filed for divorce—a divorce Bill did not want. He was also involved in hugely contentious litigation with his former business partner over the patents and royalties for their breakthrough medical technology. In addition, Kevin still lived with his dad because three years earlier, at age twenty-one, he was hit by a drunk driver while skateboarding home and suffered massive cranial trauma. Kevin was in the hospital for months, and was still coping with the disabling aftereffects of the traumatic brain injury. Even after three years, Kevin could barely speak. He would likely need some form of care for the rest of his life, and Bill was providing that.

Bill's daughters had moved out to live their adult lives, and, post-divorce, he was lonely. He made the decision to put himself back out there and start dating again. I'd be lying if I claimed I didn't identify with Bill just a little bit, given my own history of romantic fiascos. Certainly, it is easy to imagine that Bill's divorce messed with his self-esteem as well as his selector switch when it came to potential romantic partners. We will never know how Bill met Nanette Johnston (there have been a number of stories over the years), but we do know that she took out a personal ad in a local magazine, brazenly searching for a sugar daddy. "Wealthy men only," her ad said. "You take care of me, and I'll take care of you."

It turned out that Nanette was probably the single worst woman in all of Orange County whom Bill could have met. More than twenty-five years his junior, already divorced with two kids, she longed to live the high life, and Bill's generosity—fancy trips, plastic surgery, gifts for her kids, access to a joint bank account—was helping her do just that. Nanette and her kids moved in to the Balboa Coves home after the couple had been dating for a year. Nanette pressed Bill for marriage, and convinced him to take out a $1 million life insurance policy with her as the beneficiary. She even managed to get written into his will with a $150,000 bequest. "She's using you for your money," Bill's daughters would tell him, and he'd say that he knew and sort of laugh it off. He stayed with her anyway.

And then, on the evening of December 15, 1994, just after he'd returned from a trip to Las Vegas, Bill was confronted by a gunman in his kitchen. It all happened in an instant. He was shot six times, including multiple fatal shots through his chest, and ended up flat on his back on the kitchen floor, dying in a pool of blood. Detectives could immediately tell that Bill had seen his killer—he'd put a hand up to block a shot, the bullet ripping through one of his fingers.

Kevin was upstairs, there were no surveillance cameras, no

eyewitnesses—and no fingerprints left at the scene, no footprints, no DNA, no sign of a physical struggle, no murder weapon. By the time Kevin hobbled his way down the stairs, having heard the gunshots, the killer was gone. Kevin's 911 call is heartbreaking to listen to, as he tried to articulate—his speech practically unintelligible from his brain injury, compounded by grief as he watched his father fading fast on their kitchen floor—that he desperately needed help.

Finally, he was able to get the operator to understand that she needed to dispatch police. "Is it your father or your dog?" the operator can be heard asking on the tape. "Your father or your dog?"

Police arrived within minutes, and Bill was pronounced dead at the scene.

There were exactly eight critical clues left at the house. A brand-new, freshly copied Ace Hardware key was stuck in the front door lock, a pedestrian access key to the gated community had been dropped on the mat just below, and six expended shell casings from a 9mm semiautomatic handgun were scattered around the kitchen. But as detectives surveyed the rest of the pristine home, there wasn't much else. They were left to ask: How do you find the killer, and—the question that kept the case unsolved for fifteen years—how do you prove it?

The case was submitted to the District Attorney in early 1995 and was refused. It was submitted again later that year and once again refused. But Debbie had encouraged me to take a look, and so I did. The files at the Newport Beach Police Department brought me right back to 1994. We knew the killer had a key to the McLaughlin home, as well as an original pedestrian gate key distributed by the Balboa Coves HOA. The number of people who had keys to the house was small—six, as far as the detectives knew, aside from Bill himself. There was the elderly neighbor, Mr. Kennedy, who liked Bill and had nothing to gain. There was Mary, his housekeeper for decades, who had only kind feelings toward Bill and plenty to lose. Bill's daughter Jenny lived an hour down the California coast. His other daughter, Kim, was an English teacher in Japan. Both loved their father to death. Kevin wouldn't have needed a key; he was already in the house. Police at the scene tested him for gunshot residue and found none, but no less important, he seemed so genuinely bereaved that it wasn't difficult to rule him out as the shooter.

The only other person with a key, as far as detectives knew at the time, was Nanette. And, it just so happened, she was missing her pedestrian gate key.

But Nanette had an alibi. She was at her son's soccer game earlier that evening and had a receipt from a Crate & Barrel store, where she had bought a vase shortly after the murder. A Post-it note was found on a lamp at the murder scene, written by Nanette: "Bill + Kev—we won our game, so we play again tonight—see you later. Nanette." Indeed, witnesses saw her at the game, and though she left in time to make it back home before the murder, the store receipt proved she was not there. Nanette finally returned to Balboa Coves about an hour after Bill was killed, the house swarming with police. Things got more interesting from there. She asked few questions. She didn't ask to see Bill's body. She didn't cry. Strangely, although sitting outside in her car for over an hour, with a phone right in front of her, she called absolutely no one. This behavior was all suspicious as hell from the detective's point of view, but people deal with grief differently, and certainly it wasn't enough to charge her with anything.

Kim and Jenny were always very nice to Nanette, although they were uncomfortable with the relationship. They felt she was after Bill's money, and didn't see a lot of redeeming qualities to balance that out. Above all, they just wanted their dad to be happy. Even with knowledge of the million-dollar insurance policy and the $150,000 bequest in the will, it was not clear—to the family, or to the detectives—that

Nanette would have sufficient motive to kill. After all, Bill had a lot more than $1 million, and he had been freely sharing it with Nanette and her children. But Nanette's behavior seemed coldhearted and bizarre, even for her. Suspicion continued to mount.

It is worth noting that Kevin wasn't supposed to be home that night—he was typically out of the house on Thursday nights, at an Alcoholics Anonymous meeting. For some reason, he skipped that night. But the fact that the murder happened at a time when Kevin was supposed to be gone made it appear that perhaps the killer had been aware of both Bill's and Kevin's schedules. An interesting idea, but not enough to charge anyone. Still, the fact that the killer just happened to pick a short window when Bill was supposed to be alone in the house wasn't something that escaped the minds of the detectives.

Perhaps the most obvious suspect at the beginning, at least the person with the greatest potential motive, was Bill's former business partner. The man had recently suffered a substantial setback in the litigation against Bill, and it looked like McLaughlin was going to win the lawsuit. Detectives immediately looked into him, and just as quickly determined he had nothing to do with the killing. He was in Santa Barbara at the time, 150 miles away—and had no access to Bill's house keys, had never owned a firearm, and had never threatened Bill or made any statements indicating that he wanted him dead. The ex-partner cooperated fully with the investigators, and, while there was clearly animosity between the two men, given that Bill's estate and legal rights survived his death, the former partner had nothing to gain financially from Bill's murder.

Let's put ourselves in the detectives' shoes: What do you do when there's scant physical evidence, no witnesses, no weapon, and no real leads? Was there anyone else in the business world who wanted Bill dead? He had quite ominously told his brother just the night before that he felt like someone wanted to kill him. But who? The plot quickly thickened when Jenny and Kim gained access to Bill's bank records and immediately made a shocking discovery. There was no money. How could that be? Jenny and Kim pushed the investigators to look more closely at Nanette.

A surveillance team was assigned, and the true shadiness of Nanette's world started to take shape. Not long after the killing, undercover narcotics officers assigned to watch the beach house observed an unknown male walk into the waterfront home like he owned it. Muscular, tall, and with a bag of Christmas presents slung over his shoulder, he looked like some sort of young Santa with an attitude. Who the hell was this guy? Almost immediately after seeing this new player enter the scene, detectives got a call from Nanette's ex-husband, Kevin Johnston, and the story got even more questionable. Mr. Johnston told police that Nanette had indeed been at the soccer game, just like she said. But unlike the way she described it to police, she wasn't alone. In fact, she had recently called him and said, "Bill was murdered, but I have an alibi, and don't tell the police I was with Eric at the game."

Eric? Who was Eric?

Between the tip from Nanette's ex and the plate on the Nissan Pathfinder parked in front of the beach house, police were able to identify Nanette's gift-laden visitor as Eric Andrew Naposki. Naposki, police would learn, was a former NFL linebacker and a bit of an athletic freak of nature. An imposing six foot two, with 240 pounds of lean muscle, Eric had successfully walked onto the New England Patriots football team, where he played outside linebacker. Walking onto a team in the NFL is virtually impossible, but Naposki did it. After a handful of games for New England, he suffered a serious groin injury and was done for the year. He was cut from the roster and bounced around the NFL for a few more seasons as a practice squad player before washing out of the league and landing in Tustin, California, essentially broke. He finalized a divorce from his wife and got a string of jobs as a personal trainer, security guard, and bouncer.

Nanette, not so big on fidelity to Bill, met Eric in late 1992 at an expensive gym called Sporting Club Irvine where Eric worked as a personal trainer. Within about a year, they were sleeping together. Eric would later claim that as far as he knew, Nanette and Bill McLaughlin were business partners—and she was living in his house purely platonically as they worked on medical innovations that Nanette was happy to claim credit for. Nanette told Eric that she had a business degree, and that Bill was riding her coattails.

As her relationship with Naposki developed through 1994, Nanette became increasingly bold. They started going on trips together (financed unwittingly by Bill), including to New York City and Jamaica. Nanette brought Eric as her date to her sister's wedding. She helped with his bills. She paid his rent at least once. She bought him nice clothes. She paid for an expensive gym membership, and she took him to Chicago to meet her grandmother. In fact, Eric later said he was planning to propose on New Year's Eve, just two weeks after the murder. It would have been news to Bill, who detectives believed had no clue Nanette had been sleeping around on him. But the closer the young couple got to the fateful evening of December 15, the bolder Nanette became with her side relationship, even bringing Eric to her son's soccer game in Bill's town of Newport Beach.

Eric Naposki was definitely someone the police wanted to speak to, and, in a way, he made that very easy. When they ran his license plate, they learned he had an outstanding arrest warrant for a traffic violation. Eight days after the murder, police arrested Eric and impounded his car. The short list of evidence was about to get a little longer. Police began questioning him, and he was more than willing to talk—and talk, and talk. And he spun quite a yarn. First, he said Nanette was just a friend . . . and only after repeated questioning did he admit they were sexually involved. He said he didn't own a gun ... then later admitted he'd bought one in Dallas, but said he had given it to his father after he got mugged back home in New York. Around forty-five minutes into the interview, Naposki was asked again about firearms. "So just to be clear, you only owned that one gun?" Naposki paused. "Oh yeah ... well, I did have a second handgun, a Beretta 9mm. . . ." This one, Eric explained, had been lost. He said that he gave it to his friend Joe David Jimenez, and the gun was later stolen from Mr. Jimenez's car.

Naposki went on to describe the night of the murder. He said the evening started with him and Nanette watching her son's soccer game in the city of Walnut, about thirty minutes from Newport. The game went into triple overtime, which wasn't expected. They left in a hurry so he wouldn't be late for work. Eric explained that he was the head of security at the Thunderbird nightclub, which was interesting news to detectives. As Humphrey Bogart famously said in the movie *Casablanca*, "Of all the gin joints . . ." The Thunderbird was well-known to detectives. Not only because it was the source of most bar fights in the city, but also because it was a mere 137 yards from the front door of Bill McLaughlin's home. And Eric began working there on December 1, just two weeks prior to Bill's murder. Eric went on to say that Nanette had dropped him off at his apartment in Tustin around the time of the shooting—9:10 p.m.—and that he rushed to get dressed and head to work for his 10:00 p.m. shift.

In a later interview, Naposki told police that he thought his timing gave him an alibi for the killing. When detectives explained that he did not have an alibi—that the timing made the crime entirely possible based on everything Naposki had told them—Naposki's story suddenly changed again. He added a convenient detail he had left out before: that his boss had paged him while he was on his way to work, and that he had returned the call from a pay phone at a nearby

Denny's. So he went from trying to get to work in a hurry to adding a page from the Thunderbird and a stop at Denny's.

When the bar manager was contacted, he steadfastly denied ever paging Eric, explaining that he would have had no reason to do so. During the course of our investigation, I made our poor detectives drive and redrive Eric's stated route from Walnut, to his apartment, to Denny's, and then to the murder scene. They did it on the calendar anniversary of the murder, the first day of the Newport Beach Boat Parade, the night before the boat parade, and every other conceivable variation of Naposki's story that I could think up. Each and every time, they made it, on video, with plenty of time to commit the murder. We even contacted a traffic engineer for Newport Beach to find out the pattern of the local stoplights back in 1994, to see how that might have affected the timing. No matter how many times we did it, the result was always the same: Eric Naposki did not have an alibi.

The circumstantial evidence kept piling up. The keys at the scene were made at an Ace Hardware store; the clerk at the Ace Hardware store near Eric Naposki's apartment recognized Naposki as someone he'd made keys for, twice. "We're one of the very few Ace stores to give away those rings," the clerk said. "There is a high probability that key was made in my shop." He also said that when Naposki visited the shop, he asked about making a "prop" silencer for a 9mm pistol. Not suspicious at all.

Even more: There was a notebook recovered from Naposki's car when police impounded it. Among the to-do lists and "errunds," there was a series of numbers and letters written on one of the pages that looked like it might be a license plate. When police looked it up in the DMV database, it came back as the Mercedes-Benz located in Bill McLaughlin's garage. Naposki would later claim that he wrote that down after the murder, wanting to do some checking to see if Bill had been bad news, or if Nanette was in trouble. The problem is those databases are only available to law enforcement, and having a license plate number wouldn't actually help Naposki at all.

According to Nanette, she got a call from Bill after he landed his plane, and she and Eric left the soccer game quickly afterward, before trophies were handed out to the kids. Nanette asked her ex-husband to take the kids for the night, telling him that Eric had an appointment. There was plenty of time to get from the soccer field to Bill's house before the shooting at approximately 9:10 p.m. In fact, there was more than enough time to drop Eric off next to Bill's house and then backtrack to Crate & Barrel, where Nanette could make her purchase and get her alibi receipt. At 9:11 p.m., Kevin called 911. By 9:12 p.m., the police were on their way. At 9:52 p.m., Nanette got a two-minute call on her car phone from an unknown number, a call she failed to mention to police. At 10:00 p.m., she arrived at the scene. After being escorted to the beach house, once the police left, she returned to the car and checked her messages, then paged Eric Naposki at 1:36 in the morning and received a four-minute incoming call just afterward.

Nanette didn't call any family members the morning after the murder, but she did call Eric again. After getting a distraught phone call from Kevin, Bill's daughter Jenny called Nanette to find out if her dad had actually been killed. Nanette responded curtly: "Yeah, it sucks."

Beyond that, life continued in a shockingly normal way for Nanette and Eric. They went Christmas shopping at the mall. They went shopping for motorcycles about two hours after Bill's funeral, which is the same day that Eric moved out of his studio apartment and into the beach house with Nanette (Bill's will had given Nanette the right to use the beach house for a year after he died). The following day, with less than $1,000 in his bank account, Eric bought Nanette a $600 Movado watch.

As the investigation intensified, police learned that Nanette and Eric had met with a real estate agent in the months before the murder and were looking at houses in the exclusive Turtle Rock section of Irvine. These were million-dollar homes. (Remember the million-dollar life insurance policy with Nanette as the beneficiary.) Nanette told the agent they planned on moving in together with their kids, but not until after the first of the year. These were two people with no assets outside of Bill's money. Eric had bad credit, debt, child support payments for the two kids he had with his ex-wife, and was driving a beat-up Nissan Pathfinder registered to his father. Nanette, despite what she may have told Eric, had no assets, no degree, no job, no profession, no income, and no job skills. In fact, she owed Bill $35,000.

Detectives continued to try to put the pieces together, and to find a smoking gun. Or, even better, the actual gun used to kill McLaughlin. In January 1995, police served a search warrant on Naposki's apartment. Nanette was there when they arrived. Police did not find any guns, ammunition, ammunition magazines, gun cleaning equipment, owner's manuals, holsters, gun storage boxes, or anything else relating to firearm ownership. Naposki had already admitted to owning two guns—a .380 and a 9mm handgun—so police questioned him again. This time he was downright hostile. In fact, as I listened to the old cassette tapes, I accidentally started the interview in the un-rewound middle and heard someone yelling words to the effect of "You expect me to believe that? You keep lying to me!" and thought it was one of my old detectives going hard on Naposki—until it became clear it was actually Naposki yelling at the police.

One problem for Eric is that police followed up with Joe David Jimenez, the friend to whom Naposki said he'd given his 9mm handgun, which had then been stolen. Jimenez was pleasant, cooperative, and more than happy to help. And he had a bombshell. He explained that Naposki had hired him to do a security job. He said it was true that Naposki lent him a gun, and also true that he told Eric it had been stolen from his car. But Jimenez went on to explain that Eric had stiffed him for the work, so he actually sold the gun to help cover his losses—it wasn't stolen. And he said the gun wasn't the 9mm Beretta as Naposki claimed to the police, but instead the .380 that Eric claimed he had given to his father. Jimenez said he could get the .380 back from the buyer.

Sure enough, police recovered the .380, and it was, in fact, the gun Naposki had purchased in Dallas. And the .380 had been loaded with Federal Hydra-Shok ammunition, the same brand used by the killer and scattered all over Bill McLaughlin's kitchen the night of the murder. So where was the 9mm, and why would Naposki have lied about which gun he loaned to Jimenez? The police had never publicly revealed that the murder weapon was a 9mm. Had Eric not known that the murder weapon matched one of his guns, why would he try to conceal the truth from the investigators?

"That's my statement," Naposki said to police, and refused to answer any more questions about the gun. "You know we play[ed] the old mind fuck game between each other that night, okay," he said. "I mind fucked you with the gun, and you mind fucked me with what happened to me that night."

So Nanette lied about Eric, and Eric lied about the gun.

All of this added up to what felt to detectives like a convincing picture in many respects. Eric had probably made the keys, he probably had the right gun, and he certainly had enough time to commit the murder. But this was what the defense would call circumstantial evidence, and the answer to one big question was missing: Why? Why would Eric Naposki want to kill the man he thought was his girlfriend's business partner?

Bill's daughters continued to push for answers in the months following their father's murder. Nanette's behavior continued to create red flags. All mail to the Balboa Coves home was mysteriously stopped (she forged a forwarding address form). Nanette refused to return Bill's Cadillac (she forged the title documents). She refused to leave the beach house. She cleaned out Bill's office. She wouldn't return phone calls. Meanwhile, Jenny and Kim kept digging through Bill's banking records looking for the missing money.

Jenny and Kim decided to repossess Bill's Cadillac in April of 1995 and found a treasure trove of additional financial documents in the trunk. After they took the car back, Jenny received an angry phone call from Eric, which she recorded. Eric had moved into the beach house by that point and alluded to legal action against Jenny and Kim for taking the car back. A car Eric had been seen driving around Newport. Just imagine this from the family's perspective, being threatened by the boyfriend of the woman you think murdered your father. The more I learned about Eric Naposki and Nanette Johnston, the more grotesque they became.

As Jenny and Kim combed through the financial records they found in the trunk, they realized that Nanette hadn't just been their father's gold-digging girlfriend, but she had, in fact, been forging his signature on checks to herself for almost a year. It had started small—a few thousand dollars here and there—but the problem had grown larger: $15K, then $25K, then $75K. The day before Bill's murder, she had written a check to herself, from Bill's account, for $250,000. It's hard to imagine that Bill wasn't going to find out. The closer they looked, the more fraudulent checks they found. It turned out that Nanette started bleeding Bill dry a full year before he was actually shot.

Nanette had an explanation for everything, of course, and denied all wrongdoing to Bill's daughters. But theft, even if they could prove it, still wasn't murder. Nanette's motive to kill Bill was clearly money—the life insurance, the will. But she still had her alibi, and the

DA at the time felt the evidence wasn't there. Nanette was arrested and charged for the forgery and grand theft. She was convicted, and sentenced to a year in jail. Her answer was to file a palimony suit demanding half of Bill's estate, which would have included half of the money that had been set aside to take care of Kevin. The unbridled arrogance of that woman was astounding. And to make it go away, the daughters actually settled the case. In the end, Nanette made a substantial amount of money. She had taken a small hit, did less than six months of jail time, and was released. By the time we looked at the case, she had been free for a decade and a half and was on her third marriage. She was enjoying the quintessential lifestyle of a wealthy Orange County housewife.

Eric's motive in 1994 was a little harder to tease out, and despite the mountain of circumstantial evidence, the District Attorney in 1995 was still unconvinced. As mentioned, the case was submitted to the DA twice in the immediate aftermath of the murder, and both times it was refused. That could have been the end of it.

But fourteen years later, Larry Montgomery and I huddled up with Newport detectives Joe Cartwright and Tom Voth, and we went to work. I have to give so much credit to Larry, the investigator who never gave up, as he kept combing through the files to figure out if something had been missed.

One of the first things we did was submit the expended shell casings for DNA testing. The lab laughed at us and said that DNA will always burn off a casing in the process of a bullet being fired. This was a fact I did not know. The keys were similarly devoid of any DNA. But the shell casings themselves revealed an important clue. Back in 1995, the crime lab was able to narrow the murder weapon down to seventeen possible firearms. Forensic technology had advanced to such a point that when we resubmitted the shell casings fourteen years later, the lab came back with a single gun. A Beretta 92F. Not only the exact kind of gun purchased by Naposki in the months before the murder, but the one that he lied about, and couldn't account for. This was huge.

Then came another epiphany moment. About six months into our review, Larry came into my office and sat down. "We've got her," he said with a smile. He pulled out a one-page police report from the initial surveillance, conducted a mere four days after the murder. It was from the night before Bill's funeral, and written by none other than a youthful Detective Dave Byington in December of 1994. He was working as an undercover narcotics officer at the time, and was put on "Nanette duty." He was on the sand outside of the beach house when he observed Nanette decorating a Christmas tree inside with her two children.

I had seen the report before, and, on the surface, it didn't seem to mean anything. "Think about it," Larry said. "If Nanette is innocent, then there is a killer on the loose. A killer who she's been told had the keys to Bill's house. With her sketchy history of stealing from men, why wouldn't she suspect the killer was actually looking for her and not Bill? If she is innocent, why wouldn't she wonder if the killer might also have a key to the beach house as well? By all accounts, she loves her kids, so of all the places they could spend the night before the funeral, with a killer on the loose, who might be after her . . . she decided to bring them to the beach house?"

Dave Byington was an undercover narc staking out the house. No uniform, no grooming standards, and formally trained in how to kill. "The killer could have been Dave, right outside on the sand," Larry explained, "and yet Nanette didn't even bother to draw the curtains. She knows those kids aren't in any danger from some mystery killer, because there is no mystery. Nanette knows exactly who the killer is because she put him up to it. The locks to the beach house weren't changed for twenty-nine more days. Like I said . . . we've got her."

Larry also pored through the old tapes from an ancient hotline that had been set up after the murder. There were two taped calls of great importance. Both had been missed in the original investigation. The first came from a woman who said her fiancé had information that might help. She said he had met Nanette at the Sporting Club Irvine, and she wanted to invest in his company. In the background, a male voice can be heard asking if she was talking to the police. She said, "Yes, Bob, they want to talk to you," at which point the male voice asked her to hang up.

This isn't much . . . unless you're investigator Larry Montgomery. Larry dove into the records from the gym back in 1995 and looked for every "Bob" and "Robert" on the membership list who might have owned a company. Incredibly, he located a man named Robert Cottril who had a computer startup back in 1994. Sure enough, he was the "Bob" from the phone call. Larry and I drove to North County San Diego to see what he remembered. He said that he had met Nanette and told her about his startup without realizing she had any access to funding. It was more of a friendly conversation about a project he was excited about. He distinctly remembered that in the weeks before the murder, she said she expected to come into some money and that she wanted to invest upward of $100,000 in his company. As with the real estate agent, where did she think that money was coming from? This was new information, and Bob was willing to testify.

The second call was from 1998—after detectives had already shelved the case—from a woman who had been afraid to come forward before, and in fact still feared for her life at the time she made the call, worried that Eric would go after her. Her name was Suzanne, and she told the detective that she had been Eric Naposki's neighbor in 1994. She said Eric had talked to her about Nanette and Bill, before the murder, saying that Bill had tried to force himself on Nanette, and that he was going to blow up Bill's plane. And then they had a second conversation, after the murder, during which he asked her not to talk to the police, and made a chilling statement with a knowing grin: "Did you hear about Bill McLaughlin? Maybe I did, maybe I didn't." He also told her that he once owned the same kind of gun that the killer used. Again, this was before any details about the gun were revealed to the public. Suzanne had not been willing to come forward when detectives spoke to her in 1998, but when Newport Beach Police Sergeant Pat O'Sullivan reached back out in 2009, she was relieved that the case hadn't been forgotten and now, this many years later, felt safe enough to testify.

Larry Montgomery met with her, and I tagged along. I had no doubt about Eric Naposki's guilt even before we talked to Suzanne, but this was the testimony that made it a case I felt very comfortable we could win. Larry told her he didn't want to scare her, but her testimony was key. She agreed to help us move forward.

With Suzanne's memories of her conversations with Eric, the motive became very clear. It is entirely possible that Eric genuinely had no idea that Nanette and Bill were romantically involved. He may have had no clue Nanette was living a double life. Nanette likely told Eric a story that they had separate bedrooms in the house, and, in order to convince him to murder Bill, Nanette claimed that Bill had forced himself on her. In police interviews, again and again, Eric insisted that he would have broken up with Nanette if he knew she was sleeping with another man. She wanted it all—Bill's money, the easy life, a hunky boyfriend—and masterminded this plot. Naposki might have been manipulated, or maybe not, but when you take someone's word, and then choose to enter the home of a man you don't know for the purpose of killing him, you're responsible for the full weight of that decision. No matter what Nanette told him, Eric knew Nanette would benefit financially from the murder. Even if that was only a small fraction of his thinking, under California law, it is enough, and Eric would still be on the hook for a first-degree murder with the special circumstance of murder for financial gain.

When putting together a list of suspects, you start with the population of the earth and whittle it down from there. In this case, putting all of the evidence together, we knew that the killer was in Newport on December 15, and needed a reason to want to kill Bill McLaughlin. We knew Naposki was in Newport on December 15. We knew from Suzanne that Naposki thought Bill had tried to force himself on Nanette. The killer knew that Bill would be home. Nanette knew Bill would be home. The killer used an original pedestrian gate key. Nanette was missing her original pedestrian gate key. The killer had access to the house key. Eric had access to the house key. The key was made at an Ace Hardware store. Eric had keys made at an Ace Hardware store. The killer planned the murder. Naposki inquired about a silencer for his gun. The killer used a Beretta F-series 9mm. Eric owned a Beretta F-series 9mm. The killer used Federal Hydra-Shok ammunition. Naposki used Federal Hydra-Shok ammunition. When the killer traveled toward the murder scene, Eric was traveling toward the murder scene at the same time . . . according to him. To get to work, he had to pass within one hundred feet of Bill's front door. Nanette tried to hide Eric's identity from the police. Eric was not buying cars and Bill was not selling cars, but Eric had Bill's license plate in his notebook. Eric lied about his relationship with Nanette, he lied about where he was, and he lied about which gun he had loaned when no one but the police and the killer knew what gun was used in the murder.

It is hard to build an effective case when there are no witnesses and no physical evidence, no murder weapon, no fingerprints, no DNA. But circumstantial evidence this overwhelming is impossible to ignore.

By 2009, Eric and Nanette were living entirely separate lives, and in the fifteen years since the murder, they each had to have delighted in the idea that they had gotten away with it. Nanette was married again and probably never even gave Bill another thought. Eric had attempted to return to football, but the murder investigation wasn't something the NFL was eager to look past. His lawyer even sent a letter to the DA's Office trying to get them to clear Naposki's name.

Eric went to Barcelona to play football in 1996—he'd played over there before the murder, too—and helped the Barcelona Dragons win the 1997 World Bowl. His coach recalled in *Sports Illustrated* that he even asked Eric about the case: "'I said, 'Eric, what's that all about?' ... And he said, 'Coach, it's something that happened over there, but believe me, I wasn't part of it.' And I didn't pursue it. I just said, Okay." He ended up returning to the US, moving to Connecticut, getting remarried, having two more kids, taking college classes, and opening a gym.

We had worked the case for over a year, and it was decision time. How did they know Nanette would be coming into money after the first of the year to buy a house or invest in a business? She had nothing, Eric had less, and neither of them had a crystal ball that could have predicted Bill's murder. Many cold cases get solved because of forensics, and others get solved by old-fashioned common sense and gumshoe police work. These people weren't just killers, they were arrogant killers. I made the decision.

The first person I called to share the news with was Kim McLaughlin.

"Hi, Kim, I just wanted to give you a heads-up that we filed charges today."

There was a long pause: "Against who ...?" she inquired with a sheepish tone.

"Well, Nanette and Eric," I replied.

There was another long pause.

"For what . . .?" she asked.

"Well . . . for the murder of your dad, of course."

Upon hearing that, Kim broke down in tears and cried and cried. Her father had been murdered by his girlfriend for money, and her brother Kevin, tragically, had drowned while swimming in Hawaii in 1999, five years later. He had moved there so his mom could care for him after his father was killed. It's not hard to wonder if he would still be alive if Bill had never gotten mixed up with Nanette Johnston.

The people who did it—the mean-spirited, greedy people who did it—had made out just fine and had been left free to live their lives. To Kim, that phone call represented the day that justice finally arrived. Most people have no idea what a family goes through under those circumstances, and hopefully they never will. These are the monsters you find in Friedrich Nietzsche's abyss. Despite sacrificing most of a personal life to do the job as well as I possibly could, moments like that make it hard to have any regrets.

We still had arrests to make. And I still had cases to try. We set up two teams, one in Connecticut and one in Orange County. The idea was that we would give Eric one last chance to do the right thing. We would give him the opportunity to call Nanette on a recorded line and get her to make admissions.

On May 20, 2009, with the assistance of Greenwich Police, we arrested Eric Andrew Naposki on his way to work. Larry Montgomery and Newport Detective (now Chief) Joe Cartwright accompanied Eric to an interview room. He yelled at the two detectives as Larry tried to conduct another interview. He interrupted over and over, saying, "You know I didn't do this" and demanding to know what new evidence existed. Larry finally finished the interview. "I know you did," he said, causing Naposki to fly into a rage. When asked if he would be willing to put a call in to Nanette and assist in the investigation, he said words to the effect of: "Fuck you, see you in Court." A little like my Russian mobster Ramadan Dokovic in that convertible Mercedes: long on bravado, short on brains.

At that point, still early on the West Coast, I gave the green light for the Orange County team to arrest Nanette. The detective sergeant in charge was none other than Dave Byington, who had been the young undercover narcotics officer on the sand outside the beach house the night before the funeral. Byington walked up to the door with a search warrant and an arrest warrant. He knocked politely.

"Hello, Nanette, remember me?"

"No."

"Well, I remember you, and I am here to arrest you for murder."

"Which murder?" she said as she tried to close the door in his face.

"I don't know how many you have committed, but this one is for the murder of Bill McLaughlin."

This was early in the morning, and it didn't break our hearts that with a woman that vain, her booking photo—the one that would be distributed widely in the media—would reflect her at her unmade-up early morning worst. Seemed strangely fitting.

I had launched the proverbial missile, but now I had to actually prove the case. Somehow, Naposki managed to put together an amazing legal team. A former friend of his had become a well-respected defense lawyer in New York City. He included two fine former prosecutors named Rich Portale and Angelo MacDonald. Local counsel was Gary Pohlson, recently retired from the Orange County Superior Court and the defense lawyer on the Skylar Deleon case. These were very good lawyers.

Nanette was appointed a public defender named Mick Hill, who is also a tremendous trial attorney in his own right. Originally from Ireland, Mick has an acerbic wit that juries tend to love. I had my work cut out for me and I knew it.

Nanette's arraignment was a circus. Unbeknownst to her attorney, someone had encouraged members of her church to show up and ask for her release. That's right . . . her church. There must have been fifty well-meaning people there asking to address the Court, and each one of them had been duped. The judge asked for my input, and I explained that we had been working on the case for well over a year and we knew Nanette Johnston far better than they did. I predicted that while they certainly meant well, once they had the opportunity to research the McLaughlin case and her alleged involvement, none of them would come to the next hearing. Sure enough, her support evaporated quickly and only her adult daughter and husband attended the continued arraignment a couple of weeks later. Nanette was not released.

Duped just like Bill, Nanette's then-husband was also an innocent caught up in her world of lies. He had no clue what he was getting himself into when he hooked up with that woman. Among the items recovered during the search of their home were unpaid credit card bills for which he was financially responsible in the amount of almost $200,000. He had no idea the cards even existed. As he listened to the evidence pile up during the preliminary hearing, he reached out to investigators and provided us with a series of photographs he'd later found in Nanette's belongings. They depicted Nanette and Eric in the weeks leading up to and immediately after Bill's murder. The ones right after the murder showed them living a happy life with smiles all around.

Eric's defense, not surprisingly, was to blame Nanette. His team also went all in on the purported phone call from Denny's. According to Naposki, he had a phone bill from a calling card back in 1994 that showed he returned the page from the bar manager at 8:52 p.m. from Tustin. But the bill had been lost. There are two fundamental problems with that defense. First, an alibi, in the immortal words of my colleague Larry Yellin, is when you're in Vegas at the time of a murder, on casino video, sipping a piña colada next to an Elvis impersonator at the bar. Not ten minutes away and heading directly to the murder scene. A call at 8:52, even if it was true, still would have given him plenty of time to get to Newport, and into Bill's kitchen, by 9:10 p.m.

The second problem requires a little more thought. Naposki knew he was a suspect within days of the murder. We had all the angry interviews with police to prove it. If you knew you were a suspect in a murder that you did not commit and had a phone bill that you believed cleared you of that murder . . . how does that get lost? If you were truly innocent, how many rooms would you wallpaper with copies of that bill? We accumulate birth certificates, social security cards, and other important documents over the course of our lives and usually find a way to hang on to them. In the life of a murder suspect, nothing would be more important than a document that you think proves your innocence, and yet the only person who had a clear recollection of ever seeing it was Naposki himself. Ignoring the fact that the phone bill, even if it existed, would not have provided a legitimate alibi for Eric, for him to claim that he lost the one piece of evidence he believed might save his life is a hard story to swallow. The jury rejected Eric's defense.

Nanette's trial was pretty much the mirror image of Eric's. She claimed that Eric was jealous of Bill and killed him to get him out of the way. The fact that she stole so much money, and had so much to gain financially, was simply coincidence. To an objective jury, the accumulation of evidence against both of them was just too much. Nanette was cheating on Bill in an increasingly brazen way, *and* stealing from him more and more, the closer they got to December 15. Which was Bill going to find out about first? Either way, she would be out on her butt with nothing. From Nanette's point of view, Bill had to die. And, besides, when I stood in front of the jury and explained the Christmas tree decorations with wide-open shades at the beach house the night before the funeral, I think I had all twelve deliberating jurors nodding along. A jury needs to be convinced of the legal case, absolutely—but life experience plays into it, for sure. You need the evidence to make sense on a human level. And here, it was hard to conclude anything except the fact that Nanette knew who the killer was.

Eric Naposki and Nanette Johnston were each sentenced to life in prison without the possibility of parole. Eric has never stopped talking and trying to argue for his innocence. After his conviction, he asked to speak to us one last time. We went to the jail, and his latest story was a doozy: He said that Nanette had asked him to kill Bill and he refused, but that he connected her with a hit man who could do it—but only if he could use Eric's gun, which he says he'd given to Nanette as a gift. This comes after years of insisting he had nothing to do with it, and then turning around and saying Nanette did it.

The problem with this latest story, apart from it being entirely false, is that not too many hit men are likely to ask if they can borrow your gun. The beauty is it also makes him a full coconspirator in a murder committed for financial gain—which is exactly what he was convicted of. C'mon dude. Naposki yelled at me as he was being led out of Court after his sentencing: "Ya fuckin' blew it, Murphy. . . . Ya fuckin' blew it."

Naposki was trying to tell me I'd put the wrong guy in jail. Fortunately, the Court of Appeal disagreed with him.

There was a photo taken that shows Kim McLaughlin the moment the guilty verdict was read in Court. It shows a woman at the end of a long road, bursting into tears, because the people responsible for murdering her father were finally going to face justice. Sometimes, when I'm feeling down, I will google that image, just to remind myself that every once in a while the good guys can still win.

CHAPTER
6

SADISM, SERIAL KILLERS, AND BACHELOR NUMBER ONE

I'VE ALREADY MENTIONED my good friend Dennis Conway, one of the colleagues I was so privileged to work with over the years. Dennis and I used to spend hours strategizing before trials, especially when it came to our cross-examination of defense experts. Dennis was promoted from the Gang Unit, where he had worked for years with Howard Gundy and Mike Murray—the former Marine and the West Point graduate, respectively—and the three of them were thick as thieves.

Dennis, the youngest of eleven children in a blue-collar Irish Catholic family, grew up in a small town outside of Boston. He had a difficult homelife as a kid, and hitchhiked to California not long after his seventeenth birthday. He worked as a bartender for several years in Newport Beach before his girlfriend became pregnant, and he found himself a single dad without a college degree.

Dennis wanted something better for his son, so he took advantage of a little-known provision of the California Professional Code that allows a person to practice law without an undergraduate education, as long as they graduate from a California-accredited law school and somehow manage to pass the bar exam. Nobody does it this way, because it is nearly impossible, but Dennis scraped and saved and studied, going to school at night for five years before finally graduating and passing the test. Stubborn and determined, Dennis pulled it off—all in the service of creating a better life for his boy.

Years later, when we rotated into Homicide together, his office was flanked on one side by Carolyn Carlisle-Raines, a graduate of Yale Law, and on the other by Mary Ann McCauley, a smart and effective advocate and genuine debutante from the American South. The women were refined, genteel, and rich in impressive educational pedigrees—and sandwiched right between them was Dennis. Unpolished, strong-willed, and an enormously talented trial lawyer, Dennis, like Howard and Mike, was very much a part of Lew's mutant warrior rebuilding plan for the Homicide Unit. His law degree might not have impressed anyone, but the way he got it sure did. His grit was admired by the people who ran the office back then, just as it should have been. In trial—as in life—Dennis was an absolute scrapper.

As we were walking through the parking lot one day on our way to the gym, we ran into Mike and Howard, who were entering the building from the opposite direction. They were bickering like an old married couple. "It's the same argument they have been having for a week," Dennis said with a laugh. "It's about Doppler radar. Neither knows jack shit about it, but they won't give an inch. If they ever tried a case against each other, it would literally never end."

I had known them both for years, and considered them friends, but I didn't know them anywhere near as well as Dennis did. "Those guys have been fighting somebody their whole lives," he said. "Tell them they can't and they'll die trying to prove you wrong."

That quote has stuck with me ever since. Dennis had an unconventional education, but he is as smart as anyone I have ever known, and a keen student of human nature. "Haven't you ever noticed," he asked with a grin, "that everyone in the Unit who has ever done anything worthwhile comes from a fucked-up home? Including you, Murph."

I had never thought about it before. Lew had been terribly poor as a kid before joining the Marine Corps. Rick King had been one of those lost young men who got into trouble in the late '60s and received a stern "suggestion" from a judge that he consider the military instead of going to jail. The military in those days meant Vietnam, and Rick enlisted anyway. He did two combat tours as a Navy Seabee and came home a decorated war hero.

Like Dennis, Mike and Howard each had rough childhoods, which drove Mike to West Point and Howard, like Lew, into the Marines. These guys were fearless, lived for the fight, and were positively dominant in trial. They also seemed to take personal offense whenever a defense expert was trotted into Court to testify about some killer's supposedly hard childhood.

In comparison, I was very fortunate as a kid. I grew up in a nice area, my parents had money, and I can't for a moment compare my circumstances to what some of my colleagues experienced. My father was a good person, and I was proud of him, but it is fair to say that our relationship was more than a little strained. A brilliant man—a genuine prodigy—and a renowned physician, he graduated from Northwestern Medical School with a full-ride academic scholarship.

The "curse of the Irish" runs very deep in my family, as I've mentioned, and a raging case of functional alcoholism eventually led to his sobriety when I was seven and my parents' divorce when I was ten. He just wasn't around much when we were little, which was fine, but my mother, Canadian with Scottish roots, had alcohol issues of her own. Although she initiated the divorce, when my dad moved out, she went well off the rails and into several years of very heavy drinking. She loved us to death, and had no malice, but it was a particularly rough situation for my younger sister and brother. I reached a point at age fourteen when I could no longer handle the chaos, or the deteriorating conditions of my mom's house, so I moved in with my dad a couple of miles away. It was a dramatic decision and it broke her heart, but I had to do it. In her boundless empathy, particularly for animals, we had a home full of dogs and cats, half housebroken at best, that she had rescued at one point or another and couldn't place. We had a parrot, a guinea pig, and, for a time, even a chicken. Every animal in that house, and therefore every person who lived there, had fleas.

As she drank more and more, it felt like the place was descending into madness, and I had to get out. Though she was a sweet soul, and as well-intentioned as they come, her drinking and emotional lability when doing so made it difficult for her to properly protect herself or her kids. She never abused us in any way, but might have been a little blind to some who would. Still, I loved my mom, she loved us back, and real love from a flawed parent is really the best any of us can hope for anyway. Despite her drinking, I loved her dearly for the rest of her life.

My father's home was the opposite. Clean, quiet, and perfectly organized, it had been my sanctuary, and I jumped at the chance to move in. Although sober and well-meaning, my father possessed a raging temper that swung from person to person like a cannon turret. After I had lived in his house for a year, the cannon swung toward me and he kicked me out at fifteen. I couldn't move back to my mom's, so I slept on the floor of my best friend's bedroom for a week until my dad calmed down and let me come back.

From that moment on, I was on notice. True stability, at least at home, just wasn't going to be a part of my world. A year later, as I was preparing for the SAT exam, he did it again. This time it was when he was away at an AA retreat and I threw a small party for a few friends (okay, perhaps twenty-five). I thought I had plenty of time to clean up, but he came home two days early—in an age without cell phones to give me some warning.

It was a good example of the "what can possibly go wrong?" logic of a sixteen-year-old kid, and I deserved to get in trouble. My dad walked in like Dean Wormer from the movie *Animal House*, and exploded like the cartoon character Yosemite Sam. So out I went . . . again, this time for the better part of two months. I must have crashed on the couch of every friend I had, before the kindly parents of one of them learned of my circumstances and let me "move" in with them. They were incredibly nice people to whom I am grateful to this day. But it took a heavy toll on the relationship with my father, and after one more good rage when I was in law school, we didn't talk for almost twenty years. He did send me to a Jesuit high school—the very best—as well as help me pay for college, and he allowed me far more opportunity than some of my buddies in the Unit got from their parents. I carry no bitterness toward my father, and really never have. In fact, I see myself as very lucky.

Alcoholism is a monster, though, and from the perspective of a kid growing up in that environment, I suppose I had been fighting something my whole life as well. When Dennis and I got back from the gym that afternoon, it occurred to me that perhaps I had a lot more in common with my impressive colleagues than I might have felt when I first arrived in the Unit. I began to relate to them in ways I had not before. I started feeling like we belonged together, at that time, in that place, doing that job. In the years to come, my colleagues became my bickering, wonderful, brilliant brothers and sisters, and the Homicide

Unit was as much a home as I have ever known. They all had demons of their own, and I loved them all the more for it.

But demons in the form of addiction, anger, or loneliness are all metaphorical. Lew was about to come into my office and introduce me to a real one.

//////\\\\\

The summer of 1979 was an interesting time everywhere, but particularly in Southern California. Trying to get out of my mother's house as much as possible back then, I got my very first surfboard in June and spent every minute I could with my friends at the beach. While the rest of the country was listening to Michael Jackson and buying the first generation of Sony Walkmans, a group of surfers from Santa Monica had taken advantage of the newly invented urethane skateboarding wheel and were in the process of revolutionizing the sport.

Skateboards had gone from being children's toys with clay wheels to the apex of cool for the kids growing up in the coastal communities of Los Angeles, San Diego, and everywhere in between. Young skaters like Tony Alva and Stacy Peralta began landing the first legitimate aerials in drained backyard pools across the affluent areas of Venice and Santa Monica. Pretty soon, every kid in a beach community wanted a pair of Vans skateboarding shoes, and the trend was to personalize them by writing on the white rubber outsole. While the rest of the country was still grooving to Donna Summer and the Bee Gees, disco had become decidedly unhip in surf culture at the time. For teenagers living in that world, the summer of 1979 was all about Pink Floyd, Lightning Bolt shirts, skateboarding, and those crazy Vans shoes.

On June 20, 1979, twelve-year-old Robin Samsoe went to the beach in Huntington with her best friend, Bridget Wilvert. They were sitting on towels near the water when they were approached by a man with long hair and a camera who asked to take their pictures. He was in a photography contest, he explained, and could win a prize if they would pose for him. Robin was willing; Bridget was cautious. And when Bridget saw the man reach over to touch Robin's leg, Bridget pulled her friend back and reminded her that she needed to leave soon to get to the ballet studio where she was answering phones in order to pay for her dance classes.

A nearby mother of one of their friends didn't like what she saw either and chased the man away. Shortly afterward, Bridget lent Robin her bike to get to the dance studio . . . and Robin was never seen again.

"I said, 'Don't stop,'" Bridget told ABC News, but when Robin did not arrive at the ballet studio, and then never came home, it became increasingly clear that something terrible had happened to her. As hours turned into days, Robin's mother was beside herself with worry, and the Huntington Beach Police Department went to work. Among the officers assigned to the case was a brand-new twenty-seven-year-old detective named Craig Robison. Craig was young, hungry, and dedicated. He immediately wondered if the "photographer" at the beach was responsible for Robin's disappearance. He arranged for Bridget to sit down with a forensic police artist named Marilyn Droz, and they created a composite sketch of the man who had approached them on the beach. The resulting image was released to the media along with a photo of the young, innocent, twelve-year-old Robin Samsoe.

Not long after the sketch hit the television news, Detective Robison received a call from a parole officer. "I just saw the sketch you guys released. You need to take a look at one of the parolees on my caseload. His name is Rodney James Alcala."

It was the end of the day, and investigators had been up for almost twenty-four hours at that point. Work breaks are critical for detectives in cases like this because fatigue often causes mistakes. Detective Art

Droz, Marilyn's husband, left the police department soon after they were contacted by the parole officer. He planned to go home, grab some food, catch a little sleep, and return to the station a few hours later. He collapsed into his couch and mindlessly turned on the TV.

In case you aren't old enough to remember *The Dating Game* television show from the 1960s through the '80s, here's how it went: Three bachelors were introduced, on one side of a partition, and then a pretty, young bachelorette came out on the other side, unable to see the men but able to hear their voices. She would ask a series of questions to the three contenders, usually loaded with silly double entendres, and ultimately choose her favorite to go on a date with. It was G-rated, harmless, and from a more innocent time in pop culture when the airwaves weren't inundated with cringey reality television. As Jim Lange, the show's host, cheerfully introduced the contestants, Droz nearly fell off the couch. "Bachelor Number One is Rodney Alcala!" Literally as Detective Robison was in the process of learning as much as he could about Alcala, and generating a search warrant for Alcala's mother's home, there was the potential suspect—on TV, laughing, joking, and smiling. Droz couldn't believe what he was looking at. Years later, it is striking to watch the video (and it's available online, if you're curious) knowing who he was and what he'd been doing both before and after the episode aired.

On the evening of June 26, 1979, Detective Droz watched in amazement as Alcala, in front of a studio audience, presented as handsome, charming, and quick with a joke. Introduced as a "successful photographer" who might be found skydiving or motorcycling during his off-hours, the truth was that he had taken pictures of hundreds of young women, young girls, and young boys, luring them in front of his camera with compliments and attention, and often getting them to take off their clothes. Alcala was, in fact, a trained photographer. He had graduated from UCLA's fine arts program, and detectives later learned that he had even sold some of his photos to pornographic magazines.

"The best time is at night.... Nighttime is when it really gets good," he told bachelorette Cheryl Bradshaw. She asked the three bachelors what kind of food they would be if served for dinner. "I'm called the banana, and I look really good," Alcala said. "Peel me."

Cheryl Bradshaw chose Alcala over the other two *Dating Game* contenders, drawn in by the same charm that likely lured his victims. But once she was able to spend some time with him backstage, she wasn't so sure. The executive producer of the show at the time, Mike Metzger, had also found Alcala a little creepy—a "strange personality," he told ABC—and didn't want to cast him, but his wife, Ellen, the show's contestant coordinator, thought he was handsome and overruled her husband. Bachelor Number Two, actor Jed Mills, agreed that something seemed off about Alcala, and remembered later that backstage Alcala told him, ominously, "I always get my girl." But, somehow, he had an appeal to women, and the ability to read them, sense who was vulnerable, and know just what to say to get their guard down.

Before their scheduled date, Cheryl Bradshaw called the show's producers and said she was feeling uncomfortable. She decided to cancel. For her, the decision may well have saved her life.

////|\\\\

It may sound strange coming from a career prosecutor, but serial killers are mesmerizing. They occupy a unique space in our collective imagination that seems to tap into some deep and genuine primal fear. It makes sense that humans, like every other animal, would evolve with an innate understanding that we, too, can become prey. In the modern world, lions may not pose the same danger they once did, but there are still plenty of predators lurking in the dark—smarter, much harder to catch, and far less understood. Both terrible and compelling, serial killers are the quintessential "boogey-men," the stuff of legend, the sources of myth, and the targets of cutting-edge forensic science. Serial killers have been the subject of countless books, movies, and even musicals. *The Threepenny Opera* and *Sweeney Todd* are examples of serial murder literally put to song.

The term *serial killer* is really more of an academic concept than a legal one. There are no statutory criteria for what constitutes a serial killer, and when prosecuting one of these cases, the category they fall under is the far more mundane *multiple murderer*. But in the academic world (as well as in the FBI) there have long been attempts to study, define, and understand the minds of those who commit these horrific crimes.

Entire seminars and symposia have been dedicated to crafting a definition of what it means to be a serial killer, with most ultimately landing on a statement so anodyne as to be meaningless. "The unlawful killing of two or more victims by the same offender(s), in separate events," offered one FBI study. But under that definition, any active gangster with good aim and a little luck would be included, along with plenty of drug dealers, mafia hit men, and even some medical personnel in states that prohibit assisted suicide.

These are not the same as the sadistic, sexual predators like Ted Bundy, John Wayne Gacy, or Jeffrey Dahmer, who would fit any definition we might want to apply. I prosecuted thirteen defendants during my time in Homicide who met the most basic requirements, but only six were true serial killers, and between them they likely accounted for well over a hundred murders, and certainly over a hundred separate sexual assaults. They were clever, prolific, and incredibly cruel.

One of the most common questions people ask about serial killers is: What on earth would make someone do that? We yearn to make sense of otherwise senseless killings. Blaming childhood abuse seems like an easy explanation—reassuring, understandable, and safe. Like a zombie bite, a person only turns into a monster if they have first been bitten by one. Avoid a bite, and avoid those who have themselves been bitten, and all is well. No monsters in, no monsters out. The problem is that in reality, the idea that abuse is to blame for serial killing is almost as fictional as zombies themselves.

I shared that common misconception when I first arrived in Homicide. I thought serial killers would be like the character Buffalo Bill from the movie *The Silence of the Lambs*, who kidnapped women in order to kill them and wear their skin. I imagined grotesque loners who were the twisted products of terrible childhood trauma, social outcasts who had been driven into mad, misogynistic bloodlust from prolonged ill treatment and the omnipresent pressures of modern American life.

I looked for years, but I couldn't find Buffalo Bill. Instead, I kept encountering defendants who were pretty much exactly the same as the serial rapists I had been prosecuting in Sexual Assault for the previous four years. Instead of sad, lonely outcasts, serial rapists tend to be arrogant, narcissistic, cruel, and entitled. They typically have jobs, steady relationships with consenting sexual partners, no shortage of academic ability, and social success. In my experience, most of them have no misconceptions regarding their moral compass. They know their actions are wrong—they just don't care.

Soon after my arrival in Homicide, the District Attorney asked me to try the case of a particularly vicious serial sex offender named Douglas Hopper. Hopper was a multiconvicted rapist who had been to prison several times. During his most recent prison term, after manipulating an unforgivably gullible prison psychologist, he had been deemed to have a low risk of recidivism and was released. He immediately set about raping more women. His final spree involved the rape of at least two real estate agents in the Brea Canyon area of Orange

County, the final one culminating in a high-speed and extremely dangerous chase with police.

Hopper, married and gainfully employed, would peruse local real estate listings and select targets based on the headshots of female agents he found attractive. He would make an appointment to view one of their listings, break into the house before the agent arrived, hide in a bathroom or closet, and then ambush and brutally rape them. His personality and methods were virtually indistinguishable from the bona fide serial killers I would prosecute later in my career. The only difference was that he didn't kill his victims.

Not long after the Douglas Hopper case, I was assigned another prolific and brutal serial rapist named Victor Miranda-Guerrero. Miranda-Guerrero terrorized downtown Huntington Beach in the spring and summer of 2000. He was employed as a dishwasher at a local restaurant and would attack women as they left the busy bar scene late at night. His methods were not as refined as Hopper's. He would simply follow the women, repeatedly bash their heads until they lost consciousness, and then rape them where they lay. Not unpredictably, this eventually led to the death of one of his victims, a young woman named Bridgette Ballas.

When police served a warrant on the place where Miranda-Guerrero was living, they found a collection of trophies from his victims. Not unlike antlers on a wall or a fish over a fireplace, little keepsakes, or mementos of their victims, are saved by many of these predators to remind them of their successful hunts—a classic sign in cases like these. We found a ring belonging to Ballas, an undeveloped roll of film taken from the glove box of another victim (a woman who actually jumped out of her moving car to get away from Miranda-Guerrero) and several other items of women's jewelry we couldn't at the time link to any known victims. Serial sex offenders are remarkably consistent in this behavior.

Miranda-Guerrero was eventually convicted and sentenced to death, but I still had so many questions about this type of killer. Lew, also an alumnus of the Sexual Assault Unit, called Miranda-Guerrero a "textbook example of what these guys are all about." But I wondered: Where was the textbook? Where was the definitive academic authority that had figured out these monsters? I wanted to learn more.

A judge friend recommended the book *Mindhunter* by FBI profiler John Douglas. Douglas had made a strong effort to answer many of the same questions I had. The book led me to an excellent paper presented by the Behavioral Science Unit of the FBI in September of 2005, which further led me to a textbook called *Psychopathia Sexualis*—sexual psychopathy—published in 1886 by the German psychiatrist Dr. Richard von Krafft-Ebing. This is perhaps the earliest known attempt to gain a psychiatric understanding of what we would now call serial killers. To say the book was captivating would be an understatement.

Dr. von Krafft-Ebing's goal in his research was to understand human sexuality in general, and paraphilias—sexual deviancy—in particular. "Sadistic lust murders," as Dr. von Krafft-Ebing called them, comprised a relatively small portion of the book, but an important one. Contrary to my own misconceptions, it turns out that serial killers have been around for as long as there have been people—neither the modern world nor America is to blame. After discussing the well-known case of Jack the Ripper, Dr. von Krafft-Ebing discusses the far lesser known Vacher the Ripper, who stalked the French countryside in the late 1800s, murdering perhaps two dozen people. He would rape, strangle, and mutilate his victims, who included girls, women, and boys. It was said that he was born "of honourable parents and belonged to a mentally sound family. He never had a severe illness, [and] was from his earliest infancy vicious, lazy and shy of work."

In the end, the final judgment read as follows: "'His crimes are those of an antisocial, sadistic, bloodthirsty being, who considers himself privileged to commit these atrocities because he was once upon a time treated in an asylum for insanity, and thereby escaped well merited punishment. He is a common criminal and there are no ameliorating circumstances to be found in his favour'— V. was sentenced to death."

Like many of the individuals I would prosecute in the years to come, there was not a single hint of childhood abuse.

It seems that Dr. von Krafft-Ebing might have been onto something from the very beginning. He attempted to understand "sadistic lust murders" by placing them on a relational spectrum with other paraphilias and associated acts of sexual deviancy. In other words, he considered lust murders to be sex crimes—brutal, sadistic, and terrible, but motivated and intertwined with twisted sexual desire. Rape and rape-murder are certainly crimes of power, but I think we are deluding ourselves if we ignore, as current definitions of serial killer seem to do, the sexual motivations of this type of murderer.

There is another definition you repeatedly encounter in this area of study that always struck me as a little odd. The "psychopath" in virtually every academic definition, from the *DSM-5,* to the Hare Psychopathy Checklist, to just about every article ever published on the topic, is characterized as having (among other traits) "a lack of empathy." It seems strange that we would try to define something that almost all of these offenders actually have (a nameless, violent, perverted drive to prey upon others) through the lack of something else (empathy). It seems that the lack of a thing would just take them to neutral. Some psychologists, especially when testifying as defense witnesses, even go so far as to say that the psychopath is *incapable* of perceiving the fears or feelings of others.

In my humble opinion, based on an admittedly anecdotal sampling of a mere half dozen or so of these individuals, this truly misses the mark. In my experience, these guys are not only perfectly capable of perceiving the emotions of other people, they are highly attuned to them. They lustfully enjoy the imposition of fear, pain, and cruelty on innocent others. Not only do they perceive this suffering, they derive immense sexual gratification by inflicting it.

This driving desire is not the absence of a thing, but a thing in itself. It is a burning, lustful, joyous desire to prey upon, dominate, and then inflict as much fear and pain as possible. We just don't seem to have a word for it. *Cruelty* partially fits, *sadism* comes close, the German word *schadenfreude* (taking delight in the suffering of others) is in the ballpark, but there isn't a term I am aware of that accurately describes what compels these people to do what they do. I believe in science, but the farther you go back in the historical record, the more you encounter a simple word, religious in origin, that may most accurately summarize the mindset of true serial killers. It seems to fit better than anything else: *evil.*

At the same time, the uncomfortable truth is that the person standing in front of us at Starbucks could be a serial killer and we would never know. The reason why "Jack the Ripper" was never caught, I believe, is precisely because he was able to walk away from those horrific crime scenes and instantly blend in with everyone else in 1880s London. "Jack the Ripper" was successful precisely because he *wasn't* Buffalo Bill.

But I will go a step further. Not only are many true serial killers perfectly capable of functioning in society, and not only are their actions usually *not* the product of childhood abuse, in my experience many of them grew up in circumstances that were the exact opposite. Many of them, to put it lightly, were spoiled rotten as kids. They had every advantage and opportunity in life and came from a psychological position far closer to extreme entitlement than victimhood. They kill because they want to. They kill because they sexually get off on it. They kill because, to them, killing is fun.

To that end, Rodney Alcala was afforded every opportunity to live a great life. Although his father passed away when he was young, Alcala grew up in a clean, stable, and loving home. He was raised by his mother as well as an affectionate aunt, who were both very present in his life. He had siblings who went on to become successful adults; his brother, like my friend Mike Murray, even graduated from West Point and distinguished himself during the Vietnam War.

In addition, Alcala was born with exceptional intelligence and had a documented Mensa-level IQ of 135. This placed him in the ninety-ninth percentile of measured human intelligence—and it showed. Alcala attended Cantwell High, a well-regarded private college prep school in East Los Angeles, where he worked on the year-book committee and earned a varsity letter on the cross-country team. Interestingly, Rodney transferred to Montebello High School for the final semester of his senior year, declaring to his mother that he had enough of religious education. At both schools, Alcala achieved what psychologists would call great "social success." He had friends, he had girlfriends, and in decades of subsequent investigations, there was no record or reference to him ever being bullied or abused by anyone.

One of the first things Detective Droz noticed, watching on television, was how much Bachelor Number One resembled the composite sketch developed from the memory of twelve-year-old Bridget Wilvert. Alcala's hair was a little shorter, and his chin perhaps a little squarer, but the similarity was striking.

On July 3, 1979, as detectives continued to compile background information about Alcala, they received word that the "scavenged" remains of a young girl had been found in the foothills above Altadena, California. *Scavenged* is a common term you hear working homicide cases in Southern California, which essentially sits on the edge of the Mojave Desert.

Commonly, when a body has been dumped into the chaparral near some hiking trail or unpaved fire road, the animals will get to it long before police do, and they will often eat ("scavenge") much of what remains of forensic value. In this case, a fire abatement crew stumbled across a few bones near the skull of a young female. The front teeth, noticeably missing, had almost certainly been knocked out before her death. Not far away in the scrub was a shock of blond hair and a single personalized Vans skateboarding shoe—which was immediately recognizable as belonging to Robin Samsoe. Dental records would soon confirm the worst. She had also been wearing a small pair of gold ball earrings, but they were nowhere to be found. Perhaps they were eaten, or scattered somewhere on the vast hillside. Robin's mother was positively devastated by the confirmation her daughter had died.

On July 14, detectives served a warrant at Rodney Alcala's residence—his mother's house. The first thing they encountered was Rodney's Datsun B210 station wagon parked in the driveway. Detectives impounded the car and later searched it. While they did not find the smoking-gun evidence they were hoping for at the time, the search did reveal several important clues, one of which would only become apparent decades later.

The car by itself told quite a story. First, the windows were heavily tinted, long before it became fashionable to do so. Whatever Alcala had going on in there, he clearly did not want people to be able to see inside. There were binoculars, and there were street maps, meticulously organized inside the car. The carpeting had recently been replaced in the cargo area in the back. The car appeared to have been modified to aid in kidnapping most effectively. It had almost certainly been recently cleaned.

The inside of the house was also meticulous. Three weeks had gone by since the media began airing stories about the missing girl from Huntington Beach, and there was little found of dramatic evidentiary value—at least at first. The search warrant was limited to weapons, Robin's belongings, and the instrumentality of a crime, none of which were found. Police weren't allowed to seize anything else or look beyond what was in plain sight, but as they searched the home, effectively finding nothing, there was one moment of truly brilliant police work. One of the officers assigned to the search happened to notice a printed receipt for a rented storage locker in Seattle. Thinking quickly, and knowing they couldn't physically take the document, he simply wrote down the details. Not only would that one decision turn out to be hugely impactful in their investigation, it certainly saved many lives.

Alcala was arrested and taken to the police department for questioning. He denied all wrongdoing, of course, and seemed to have an answer for everything. After the interview, but while he was still in custody in Huntington Beach, Alcala received a visit from his sister. Police provided a room, where the two of them proceeded to have a conversation in Spanish. Unbeknownst to Rodney, the phone sitting on the desk between them was wired for sound, and when officers reviewed the tape, they heard him asking his sister to clear out a storage locker. The request was odd, cryptic, and suspicious as hell. Fortunately, it was also exactly the break Detective Robison was looking for. He immediately went to work writing a warrant for the storage locker in Seattle. It was a race, and the police won.

A few days later, once inside the locker, Detective Robison found a bonanza. There were hundreds of photographs of young women, girls, and boys in various stages of undress and vulnerability. Each person in these images had been persuaded by Rodney Alcala to pose for him, demonstrating just how convincing he was. It is difficult to imagine that the still-unidentified subjects were simply released by the predatory monster Alcala had become.

As police continued to search the storage unit, they also found a small silk pouch filled with women's jewelry—earrings, necklaces, and more. Detective Robison immediately recognized the pouch for exactly what it was: a trophy case. Just like I'd seen with Victor Miranda-Guerrero. Every item of jewelry in that pouch, perhaps thirty in all, likely represented a different victim—a young woman or girl whose light had been extinguished for the sexual pleasure of a man who never should have been released from prison. It disturbs me to this day. Among the earrings, brooches, and necklaces there was also a single pair of gold ball earrings. Robin's crying mother immediately identified them as the pair Robin had been wearing the day she disappeared.

Among the photos, one showed a young woman in a bikini on roller skates. There was a strip mall in the background that Detective Robison recognized as being in Sunset Beach, just north of Huntington. It was approximately three miles from where Robin and Bridget encountered the photographer, and probably only two miles from where Robin was likely abducted. Detectives released the photo to local newspapers, and the young woman was soon identified as Lori Werts, age fifteen, who was fully cooperative. She had been keeping a diary that summer and said the photo had been taken by a man with long hair who said he could win a photography contest if she would let him take some photos of her. She also said he'd tried to convince her and her friend to get in his car. She brought in her calendar and showed police that she met the photographer on the same day Robin went missing. There could be little doubt that Alcala was the photographer who had approached Robin and Bridget at the beach.

But how exactly did *I* end up prosecuting a case that took place when, like Robin Samsoe, I had also just turned twelve years old? The background that I am about to describe might be more than a little upsetting, not just in the brutality of the crimes committed, but for the unforgivable failures of the criminal justice system in the way it handled a prolific sexual predator. The twisted procedural history of Rodney James Alcala fires me up every time I go through it. Forgive me if some of my personal feelings show as I walk you through this.

To understand how Rodney Alcala and I eventually crossed paths requires going all the way back to 1968, and Alcala's first (known) crime, the rape and attempted murder of eight-year-old Tali Shapiro.

Tali was living in Los Angeles at the time, her family temporarily staying at the Chateau Marmont hotel while their home was being restored after a fire. Tali's father was a successful music industry executive, and Tali should have been enjoying a carefree childhood. She was skipping to school on a sunny September day, wearing a dress her nanny had crocheted for her. A man in a beige Plymouth pulled up alongside Tali and told her he had a special picture to show her. Tali told him she didn't talk to strangers, but then the man told her he was a friend of her parents, and so, against her better judgment but having been taught to respect her elders, she got in the car.

The moment she felt that she was in danger was when he wanted to bring her back to his house; she wanted to jump out of the car, but she didn't, and that's the last thing Tali remembers. In the only stroke of luck surrounding this entire situation, there happened to be a Good Samaritan named Donald Hines who had witnessed Tali getting into the car and thought that something didn't seem right. He followed the car until he saw the man exit with Tali, and then he drove to a pay phone and called police. (It's worth noting that eleven years later, when the Robin Samsoe hotline was set up by the Huntington Beach Police Department, Donald Hines read about the missing girl and immediately called in suggesting they look at Rodney Alcala. This was the first time Alcala's name came up in the investigation, and

Mr. Hines made the call before the composite sketch had even been released. Fortunately, police were listening.)

Officer Chris Camacho responded to Hines's call back in 1968. He was a young cop, on his first day back at work after recovering from having been shot in the Watts Riots a few weeks earlier. He knocked on the front door—Camacho recalled years later to the *Santa Cruz Sentinel*—and two other officers went around to the back. The man called out that he was just getting out of the shower. When he opened the door, he was naked—and wasn't wet, and wasn't holding a towel. He asked for a moment to put on his pants. Camacho gave him a few seconds. "Then I heard some moaning," he told the newspaper, and "I kicked in the door."

It was a bloody scene that still brings Camacho to tears. Tali was naked on the kitchen floor, surrounded by a shocking amount of blood. There was a metal bar atop her neck. Camacho assumed she was dead. But then he heard her gagging. The other officers had come around front to help when they heard Camacho kick in the door, and therefore no one was guarding the back exit. Camacho had a choice to make: Does he pursue the man, who was already heading for an escape, or stay behind to try to save the girl? He decided to save her, and Shapiro was rushed to the hospital. Miraculously, after being in a coma for thirty-two days, she did survive, thanks to Camacho's help. She had been raped, struck in the head—and had the metal bar not been removed when it was, she certainly would have died.

In the Hollywood bungalow, police found a UCLA student ID and, just like in the storage locker a decade later, hundreds of photographs of young women, boys, and girls in various stages of nudity and vulnerability. Incredibly, these photos were different from the ones that would end up being found by Detective Robison in Seattle. This was Rodney Alcala's first *known* crime, though certainly not his first actual one.

Looking back, we now know that there were hints of this behavior much earlier. Alcala had joined the Army soon after graduation, and the first records of trouble began to appear. His commanding officer prophetically observed that in addition to being insubordinate, Alcala was often highly manipulative of other soldiers. There were references in his military records to both his high intelligence and an event that took place in New York City, where Alcala was accused of hitting a woman over the head with a bottle. It doesn't appear there was any follow-up investigation, and he was eventually granted a medical discharge after going AWOL in 1964.

After fleeing, Alcala escaped to New York, where he used the alias John Burger to enroll in film school at NYU. In a time before computerized databases, Alcala managed to elude police for more than two years. During that time, he made his way onto the FBI's Ten Most Wanted list until luck, if you can call it that, intervened. He was working at an all-girls' camp in New Hampshire when two campers ducked into a post office to shelter from a rainstorm. There, they happened to notice Alcala's photo on the wall. "That's Mr. Burger," they realized, and they told the head counselor when they returned to camp. He checked it out himself and agreed—and Alcala was arrested and extradited back to Los Angeles to stand trial.

Here we find another lesson in the ramifications of prosecutorial weakness when it comes to predatory defendants. Tali Shapiro's parents had moved the family to Mexico after Tali recovered; California was too difficult for them given the trauma of what had happened. They did not want Tali to have to testify and relive the events of that day. But without her testimony, the squeamish prosecutor felt less confident that he could achieve a guilty verdict. I hate to be too hard on anyone, but frankly, this was shameful and profoundly incorrect from an evidentiary standpoint. The prosecutor abandoned other obvious legal pathways and permitted Alcala to plead guilty to simple child molestation.

Alcala's conviction was still a potential life sentence under the indeterminate sentencing guidelines of the day, but it enabled him to receive a parole hearing years earlier than any competent prosecutor ever would have allowed. As a result, and to the horror of everyone who had worked on the Shapiro case—Camacho, LAPD Homicide Detective Steve Hodel, and others—Alcala was cleared by a prison psychologist who claimed he had received the "help" he needed. The parole board then made perhaps the worst mistake in the history of the California Board of Prison Terms, releasing him after a mere thirty-four months in custody. I still can't wrap my head around that.

Barely two months after Alcala's release, he was back in custody for giving drugs to a thirteen-year-old girl, who he was certainly planning to kill—and was again paroled two years later. He had been declared reformed, *again*, and, incredibly, allowed by a different parole officer to travel across the US, via car, back to New York. At this point, it was the spring of 1977, and Alcala then went on a cross-country spree over the next two and a half years, killing young women in California, New York, Washington State, Wyoming, probably Texas, New Hampshire, and Arizona, and likely even in Europe. Somewhere in there, he also found time to appear on *The Dating Game*.

Following the Robin Samsoe murder, Alcala was convicted and received a death sentence in 1980. Again, that should have been the end of his story. But that conviction was overturned by the California Supreme Court, which determined the jurors should not have been told about his criminal past. He was re-tried and again sentenced to death in 1986, but the United States Court of Appeals for the Ninth Circuit overturned that conviction, saying in part that his lawyers failed to call a witness who could theoretically have supported

Alcala's alibi that he was at Knott's Berry Farm when Robin Samsoe disappeared. Knott's, it should be noted, is a straight shot up Beach Boulevard from the Huntington Beach Pier. Each reversal required the entire case to be re-tried, as opposed to just the penalty phase of the trial.

By the time that second trial was overturned, landing the case back at the DA's Office, returned on *remittitur* (translated from Latin as "it is sent back"), I was in the Homicide Unit and ready for anything. Huntington Beach wasn't one of my cities, but, once again, Lew assigned the case to me in an effort to finally end the torment of the Samsoe family. They had already endured the death of Robin, a trial followed by an appellate reversal, and another trial followed by a second reversal. They had been through the wringer.

I had never heard of Rodney Alcala when Lew handed me the file and began walking me through the history of the case. The most immediate problem was the appellate effect of what is known as *the law of the case.* This means that regardless of the current state of the law, once an Appellate Court finds certain evidence to have been improperly admitted, it remains inadmissible. Despite the Evidence Code in 2003, when we were attempting to rebuild the case for the third time—which would have allowed us to tell jurors about Alcala's criminal past—we would not be allowed to admit that evidence.

Beyond that, both times that the case was overturned, the Appellate Courts knocked out much of the evidence that had been introduced during the first two trials. We couldn't use it this time. In effect, the case had been gutted, twice, and we were left with a very thin list of available evidence. Lew knew it. "What do we typically do with these?" I asked.

Lew's answer was another moment I will never forget. "First, waste no energy lamenting the reasoning of the Court," he said. "You can't do anything about it, so forget about that evidence. In fact, treat it like it never existed." For my own sake, and that of the Samsoe family, Lew encouraged me to resist any temptation to offer a deal or try to resolve the case short of trial. "I would make them try the case, and I would make them beat me before this guy goes free."

Like watching the great baseball manager Tommy Lasorda lead the Dodgers in the 1980s, Lew took the pressure off. All I could do was win.

The language in the opinion of the second reversal did seem a little disturbing, though. The tone felt a lot like the author had bought into the defense's argument that Rodney Alcala had been horribly wronged by the previous prosecutor, Tom Goethals. I knew Goethals reasonably well and always liked him. He was an excellent prosecutor and not prone to mistakes. Ironically, Tom is now an appellate justice sitting on the Fourth District Court of Appeal.

I took Lew's advice, but part of me really wanted to reargue the reasoning of the decision and defend what Goethals had done in the second trial. Besides, when I looked at the photo of fifteen-year-old Lori Werts on her roller skates—the one found in Alcala's locker—I noticed Lori, as well as many of the street signs in the background, cast shadows. A thought occurred to me: Since we knew the date, if we could determine the height of some of those signs, couldn't we figure out exactly what time he took those photos, based on the shadows? If I could put him in Sunset Beach at a precise time, and it was consistent with Robin's encounter on the beach, I could destroy the alibi believed to be so important by the author of the previous reversal. Sure enough, when my investigators put the pieces together, and we had an expert (from the United States Navy, of all places) review the photo, the timing fit like a glove. With the composite sketch and that photo, I suddenly liked my chances at trial. "Lean, mean, and clean," as Lew liked to instruct us.

Not long after we formally submitted our intention to re-try Alcala for Robin's murder, there was a huge development that changed the landscape of the case forever.

When California was about to enter the CODIS system, which requires that all prison inmates submit to DNA testing to be checked against a national database of unsolved violent crimes, the law was challenged—by none other than Rodney James Alcala. Rodney literally led the charge on behalf of all California inmates against the new law because, unsurprisingly, he did not want anyone looking at his DNA. There was, of course, no forensic DNA testing back in the 1970s when Alcala had been raping and murdering his way across the US.

It's shocking, in today's world of background checks and computerized databases, to realize that Alcala had made it onto national television after he had already served two stints in prison, been convicted of child molestation, and (though unknown to police at the time) murdered at least seven women. Looking at the timeline of events, while it's still unknown just how many of the "models" in the trove of photos detectives found were viciously raped and murdered, it was certainly more than he was ultimately held accountable for.

Alcala, as detectives would learn over the years, was among the smartest, most prolific, and most utterly sadistic serial killers in American history. Estimates of Alcala's total number of victims range from the thirteen we know of for sure up to perhaps one hundred, a figure broadly agreed upon by the various detectives who worked his cases. The *Dating Game* appearance was just one bizarre part of the whole drama, reflecting the narcissism, the ego, and the arrogance of a true serial killer. It's hard to believe, after all, that someone in the middle of a string of vicious murders would intentionally decide to go on television and offer their name and face to the world—but there he was. Somehow it all made sense in Rodney Alcala's twisted psyche.

Fortunately, Alcala's legal challenge failed, and the Department of Corrections entered Alcala's DNA into the system . . . which predictably lit up like a Christmas tree. Three unsolved murders from Los Angeles contained previously unknown male DNA matching Alcala's, and he was suspected of a fourth. Each new case seemed more horrific than the last. First, there was the rape, torture, and murder of Jill Barcomb—an eighteen-year-old originally from New York who had moved across the country on her own after high school, and whose body was found on a dirt fire road above the Hollywood Hills. Her left nipple was bitten almost completely off, she had fractures in her skull, face, and teeth, she had been strangled multiple times, in multiple ways, and her body had been posed with her fingers touching her brutalized vagina and lacerated anus.

The next hit came back on the rape, torture, and murder of twenty-seven-year-old pediatric cancer nurse Georgia Wixted. Georgia had been found on the floor of her studio apartment in Malibu with brutal skull fractures, a broken elbow, and severe genital lacerations. It appeared she had been raped with the claw end of a blue wooden hammer that had been found next to her body. There was semen inside her mouth, vagina, and anus, and her bottom lip had almost been torn off her face—a common injury in cases of forced oral copulation, but I had never seen anything that extreme.

There was also the torture and murder of Charlotte Lamb, a kind, thirty-two-year-old legal secretary and aspiring actress from Santa Monica. She had been found lying face up in the laundry room of an El Segundo apartment complex, her body also posed, angled to be seen from the doorway, strangled multiple times with the strap from her sandal.

There was a fourth Los Angeles victim, Jill Parenteau, a twenty-one-year-old computer operator, discovered in her Burbank apartment with large hemorrhages inside of her head, bleeding in her nose, a bite mark to her breast, and bruising and injury inside and around her mouth. Her open jewelry box was on a dresser a few feet away. Jill's case would be the hardest. The investigation had been revived with the DNA hits on the other Los Angeles victims, and investigators were convinced Alcala was responsible for Parenteau as well. After the first trial on Robin Samsoe, once Alcala was convicted and sentenced to death in 1980, somehow the Burbank Police Department managed to lose, or throw away, most of the evidence from the Parenteau scene. The nylon stocking found around her neck, the sheets on her bed, and the swabs taken from her rape kit were all missing. We had one remaining slide that had been prepared for serology, a precursor to DNA, a few photos of the crime scene, and her friends and family available as witnesses. With a lack of physical evidence, the Major Crimes Unit of the Los Angeles DA's Office had already recommended to Los Angeles District Attorney Steve Cooley that the Parenteau case not be filed.

The discovery of three new murders, and possibly a fourth, was obviously a huge development. We had already made the decision to re-try the twice-gutted Robin Samsoe case, but the new murders certainly offered a potential wealth of corroborating new evidence. However, this potential new windfall immediately presented two brand-new problems. The first was that Alcala committed those murders in Los Angeles County, and there would be huge legal challenges involved with Orange County asserting jurisdiction. Not unlike in those old movies in which the bootleggers transporting moonshine "just have to make it to the county line," there had been a jurisdictional defense for murders committed in different counties for decades. Essentially, a criminal defendant would be entitled to a separate jury trial in each county in which a separate offense was committed. Fortunately, the California State Legislature had recently passed a law that permitted multiple counties to combine their cases into one jurisdiction. Unfortunately, nobody had ever used it before, and the law had never been judicially reviewed. We would have to convince the California Supreme Court that Penal Code section 790 passed constitutional muster. This was, believe it or not, the easy part.

The second problem, and really the more daunting, was that I needed to convince the Los Angeles District Attorney's Office to let *me* try *their* murders. In the post–O. J. world of Los Angeles County politics, the conviction of a vicious serial killer with national media attention would be a big political win for the elected District Attorney. The smart political move, arguably, would be to tell me to pound sand and proceed on their three solid DNA cases. I had never met LADA Steve Cooley before, and he didn't know me from Adam. The "right thing," in my view, would be to combine the cases, let me try them in Orange County, and join ranks before the California Supreme Court on the multijurisdictional prosecution issue.

The question: Was Steve Cooley a real prosecutor who was going to make his decision based on what was best for the victims' families, and what was tactically best for the cases, or was he just another politician who would do what was best for his image? I called the assigned LADA Prosecutor Gina Satriano. By the end of the conversation, I had not only made my pitch, but also made a lifelong friend. Gina was, in a word, *wonderful*. She agreed with it all, and we decided to approach Cooley with our plan to try the cases together.

We added ourselves onto the agenda for Cooley's next staff meeting. Cooley had once been a no-nonsense former cop and real-deal prosecutor. But he also had designs on a run for the California Attorney General's Office, where he eventually suffered a razor-thin defeat to future vice president Kamala Harris. He was steely-eyed, obviously smart as hell, and more than a little intimidating. In a room surrounded by perhaps forty of his top lieutenants, I made my presentation. The head of Cooley's Major Crimes Unit replied first, recommending against my request, and again adding in his belief that the

Parenteau case, the one where the evidence had been lost, was untenable and should not be pursued.

This was one of Cooley's main guys, in front of all of Cooley's other top managers and executive staff. The two men had probably known each other for decades and obviously had a great working relationship. This was going downhill fast, but I saw a fleeting opportunity and decided to throw a Hail Mary. Interrupting the trusted division head, I said, "Give me Parenteau and I'll win that case, too."

The room went silent.

Cooley raised his eyebrows and looked at me with an intense expression. I wasn't sure if he thought that was the rudest thing he had ever seen, appreciated the chutzpah, or was about to have me escorted out of his meeting. He cocked his head, locked eyes on mine, and stared. "We'll let you know," he said sternly. "Now ... we have a lot of other business to discuss." That presented a very unambiguous clue that it was time for me to leave.

"Thank you, sir" is what I said out loud as I headed out the door. My internal monologue, however, was a little different. Like many of us, I have a voice in my head far more prosecutorial and biting than anything I have ever seen in a real courtroom. That voice has convicted me a thousand times in the tribunal of internal self-doubt, and always for the same crime: stupidity. My former boss Rick King actually coined a phrase for it in the context of big trials: PAPV Psychosis. This stands for the post-argument/pre-verdict period of time when a jury is deliberating, and you begin beating yourself up for every mistake, and every questionable tactical decision, you might have made throughout an entire trial. This felt very much like that. "Why, Murphy, did you have to interrupt that man?! All this time, and all this energy, with families depending on you, and you turn into a rude jackass in front of a room full of people you don't know. Nice job, you idiot. . . ."

It went on and on until I got a call from Gina about two hours after the meeting. "Okay, partner, we got the green light. And by the way, Steve wanted me to tell you he said you're 'his kind of guy.' You saw a chance and took it. He loved your pitch."

As I mentioned earlier, one of the amazing things about working Homicide is watching the horror of the cases balanced out by the heroes you meet along the way. Steve Cooley, in my eyes and by any conceivable measure, was and will always remain a hero.

It took seven years before we actually got to trial—from 2003 until 2010—with Alcala putting up roadblocks every step of the way. We prevailed in front of the California Supreme Court on the jurisdictional issue, which was another amazing part of the journey Gina and I embarked upon on that afternoon in Cooley's staff meeting. To this day, any time a Deputy District Attorney wants to assert a multijurisdictional prosecution, they cite our decision in *People v. Alcala*. In fact, in the ensuing years, I got to cite my own case as I made the same move on other serial killers I prosecuted. Not to overstate it, but that was *cool as hell*.

After Alcala's assigned attorneys failed to win on his behalf time and time again (for good reason), we experienced another radical twist in an already twisted case. Rodney Alcala, the charming genius psychopath, decided to represent himself. This meant that on a daily basis, for the better part of a year, I had to engage with him not just as a criminal defendant, but as a lawyer.

This, again, was right out of the serial killer handbook. When criminal defendants represent themselves, it is called *pro per* or *pro se* status, which are Latin terms essentially meaning "for yourself." A prosecutor must treat *pro per* defendants like we would any other lawyer. You might not extend all of the same professional courtesies, like exchanging cell phone numbers, but it is still very important that you deal with them fairly. Some of my colleagues hated *pro per* cases, but I never minded. After all, these offenders are virtually guaranteed to make some fundamental mistake you would never see from a professional trial lawyer. And, for me, especially with defendants like Alcala—or rapist Douglas Hopper, who also represented himself—I can't deny that I was also fascinated. Dealing with someone like that on a daily basis during a lengthy trial, you get a solid dose of their ability to manipulate. You come to appreciate how they can lure their victims into positions of vulnerability. I knew everything these people had done (or at least what they had been *caught* doing) and yet, here they were, wrapped in a veneer of normalcy, even charm. In the end, Hopper was convicted of everything and received multiple life sentences. He even sent me Christmas cards for years.

As for Alcala, it was a little more complicated. Gina, quite understandably, recoiled at the idea of having to personally deal with him—who could blame her?—so we decided to use that to our advantage. Perhaps we could tap into his obvious lack of respect for women?

We decided that, in the spirit of moving the case along as efficiently as possible, I would pretend to be Alcala's buddy. Every time we had to deny a request, which was often, I would just blame Gina. "I don't know what her problem is today, Rod. Seemed like a reasonable request to me, but she said no. Sorry, dude." This was how we could move the trial along, leading us to the guilty verdicts I was certain we would get, at least for three of the five cases.

Conventionally, one might think dealing with a monster like Alcala would be a horrific experience. If I'm totally honest, I was every bit as fascinated by the prospect of getting into his head as I was repulsed. To an extent, this was going to be a battle of wits, and I relished the opportunity. Besides, like a tarantula in a jar, he was in a controlled environment and couldn't hurt anyone. All hairy with fangs and beady eyes, he was morbidly intriguing to me.

As a capital case, Alcala's trial would be divided into two parts: the guilt phase—when the jury would decide if he committed the charged murders—and the penalty phase—when they would determine if he would be condemned to die (symbolically at least) or face life in prison without the possibility of parole. Once the trial began in earnest, it was intriguing to watch Alcala's mind work. I've never read this in any academic article, but I've noticed that whatever allows these guys to separate from humanity and commit these crimes in the first place seems to also mean that they have a fundamental problem reading the room. Ted Bundy, interestingly, was exactly the same way.

Like they can't refrain from collecting trophies, psychopaths often can't resist the opportunity to exert power in a courtroom. They love to represent themselves. Alcala had trained himself to do cross-examinations of witnesses that were quite technically sound from a legal perspective. What he seemed utterly oblivious to, however, was that as he pointed out some minor inconsistency in some years-earlier statement made by Robin's mother, all the jury saw was the monster who killed the poor woman's daughter calling her a liar. The jury was horrified at every step as he attacked the families of his victims, forcing them to relive the details of what he had done. It was terrible to watch, but spectacular from the point of view that he was self-destructing in front of the jury, making it more and more certain that they would never be on his side.

There was another surreal moment that happened in the middle of the guilt phase. Rodney Alcala called himself to the stand. For reasons known only to him, he had grown his hair out before the trial in a way that made him look even more like the composite sketch. With a jean jacket and gray curls flowing over his shoulders, he began to ask himself questions in the third person. Again, unable to read the room, defendant Alcala answered questions posed by attorney Alcala, which he read one by one from a yellow legal pad in his lap. He explained all the reasons why he didn't, and couldn't have, murdered

Robin Samsoe. The jury looked like they were magnetically repulsed.

Napoleon Bonaparte once said, "Never interrupt your enemy when he is in the process of making a mistake." I didn't assert a single objection. The spectacle was equal parts bizarre and awesome. It was a living embodiment of an old adage you hear in law school that has been attributed to Benjamin Franklin, Abraham Lincoln, and others who probably never said it. It is true nonetheless: "The man who defends himself in Court has a fool for a lawyer and a jackass for a client." Amen to that.

In dealing with Alcala every day, however, I could also see how so many of these young women would get into his car back in the day. He'd lost some of his charm—and all of his looks—but if I pictured him thirty years younger, a cocky, handsome young man who thought he knew it all, I could imagine exactly how he lured these vulnerable women into helpless positions. It all made sense in his own mind: *The Dating Game* was just one more example of how he craved the attention, the power, the fame, and yet lacked all self-awareness to understand how the world perceived him.

During one conversation I will never forget, he provided a beguiling window into his thought process. The jury had been sent home for the day, and we were waiting for the judge to take the bench. There was no particular hurry, and I had a question for him. We had just sentenced a notoriously violent white supremacist and prison gang leader to death row on an unrelated case. "Hey, Rod," I asked him. "What do you do when guys like that get sent to death row? Are you afraid that he might get to you?" It was a legitimate question. Of all the training you receive as a Deputy District Attorney, they provide exactly none on how death row actually works. I was curious.

"Matt," he responded with surprised disappointment in his voice, "I'm on the Weenie Yard"—a term the inmates gave themselves for those classified as non-dangerous to other inmates and staff. "He'll be on the Heavy Yard, and I'll never see him. You know me. . . . I'm not violent. . . ." He was actually offended. Ponder that for just a moment.

This is a man who had smashed women's faces in with rocks and raped them with hammers. He tortured, sexually brutalized, and murdered his way through the late 1960s and most of the 1970s. In his mind, however, he was not violent. It was an amazing moment, and as much as I wanted to respond with outrage, I couldn't break the character of friendly professionalism. Besides, there was no need. I would get to do that in my closing argument.

I certainly felt for every one of my witnesses, for everyone who had to speak to this man who had tortured and killed their loved one and answer his questions as if he deserved a moment of their time. But I particularly felt for Robin Samsoe's mother as Alcala cross-examined her, calling her a liar, questioning her credibility, insisting she was making up the fact that her daughter was wearing earrings that day, earrings that Alcala had saved in his storage locker stash.

Robin's mother had heard it before. She had been raked over the coals in two trials and extensively during the appellate process. She had been accused by two different defense lawyers and multiple appellate attorneys arguing on Alcala's behalf that she had made up the story of the earrings. Alcala had even written a book called *You, the Jury*, where he goes through each item of evidence introduced against him in the second trial while simultaneously proclaiming his innocence and decrying the horrors of the death penalty. The problem for him is that we had requested the jewelry in the silk pouch be reprocessed. There was no DNA recovered on any of the items . . . except one: a tiny white-gold rose earring with 0.06 nanograms of Charlotte Lamb's DNA. Just like Detective Robison suspected years before, we now had definitive proof the silk pouch was a trophy case. Robin's mother had been right all along.

Jill Parenteau's family attended every day of the trial. There were bits and pieces that matched the details of some of the other crimes. Her screen had been cut on the left side, just like the entry to Georgia Wixted's apartment. (Alcala was left-handed.) She had been strangled, raped, and posed in a very similar manner to Charlotte Lamb. The rare blood type in the serology slide was the same as Alcala's (one out of every ninety-eight people), and of course her jewelry box had been left open on her dresser. The night before she was murdered, Jill Parenteau was at a restaurant in Pasadena called the Handlebar Saloon and had been seen speaking to a man who looked an awful lot like Rodney. So we had some good stuff to work with, and things to argue, but you never know what's going to happen in a jury trial.

At some point, for some reason, Rodney asked me to obtain the owner's manual for his Datsun station wagon, which was still in the possession of the Huntington Beach Police. Detective Pat Ellis, my lead investigator during the trial, went down during the lunch break to see if he could find the manual and returned with a giant smile on his face. "I have good news, and I have great news," he said. "The good news is that I found the stupid owner's manual. The great news is I also found this. . . ." Right next to the manual, in the bag containing the items from Alcala's glove box, was a matchbook from the Handlebar Saloon in Pasadena. Back in the day nobody ever knew to look, because nobody in Orange County knew about Parenteau. "We friggin' got him!" Pat said, clenching his fists. It was an amazing find. "We got him."

The pathologists' testimony was disturbing. They methodically explained how the victims had died: Alcala would strangle these women, but do it slowly, bringing them back, again and again, to the brink of life so that he could violate them in every way possible. There was a copious amount of semen found at every scene. He would keep them alive so that he could recharge and do it again and again before finally deciding to watch the light of life leave their eyes. And then he would pose them and photograph their dead bodies. Rodney Alcala was a *monster*. There is no other word for him.

When it was at last time to give my closing argument, I could finally let loose, and I went pretty hard. I raised my voice, pointed my finger at him, and walked that jury through every single charged, sadistic act committed by the demon in the room with us. I also called him out for his treatment of Robin's mother when she testified. For the first time, he finally realized that I wasn't his buddy.

His response, again, was technically sound enough, but he focused all his energy on the Robin Samsoe case. He kept saying that I had engaged in "magical thinking," a term I'll never quite understand when the facts are perfectly clear. In the end, when you looked at the breadth of everything he had been doing, and compared those photographs of Charlotte Lamb to Jill Parenteau, the bite marks on the breasts of each adult victim, the striking similarity of the composite sketch, along with that matchbook from the Handlebar Saloon, the evidence for all five murders was simply overwhelming. The jury convicted him on all five counts in just a few hours. This was huge for everyone, but I felt particularly relieved for the Parenteau family.

We then moved on to the bifurcated penalty phase. We began with what is known as B-factor evidence, or other crimes of violence. Now we were able to reveal for the first time some of the horrors of Alcala's past. Tali Shapiro, as one of the first witnesses, finally testified against the man who had brutalized her so many years before. It was a brave moment. We had another witness, Monique H., whose rape Alcala had been on bail for when he murdered Robin Samsoe. Imagine that for just a moment. The judge knew about Tali, knew about the parole violations, and had to legally presume he had committed the charged rape. With a duty to weigh and consider public safety, that bench officer still set bail low enough for Alcala to be released.

Monique was fifteen years old when he picked her up in 1979, convincing her to pose for nude photos in a deserted area of the mountains and then turning on her, striking her in the head with a tree branch and knocking her unconscious. She awoke to find that Alcala had gagged her by shoving a T-shirt down her throat and was strangling her with his bare hands. He bit her on the breast until she lost consciousness from the pain and awoke again to find that Alcala had bound her wrists and ankles with a cord. He raped and sodomized her as she pleaded for her life. She promised not to tell anyone. In fact, her exact line was, "We can't tell anyone what we did here today." She convinced him that she cared for him. She was able to get him to drive her back into town. She ran from the car and called the police. He was arrested, bailed out, and then approached Robin and Bridget a week later. So on the day Rodney Alcala encountered Robin Samsoe, he was a registered sex offender on one grant of parole for a child molesta-tion, for which he had received a "life sentence," and simultaneously on a separate grant of bail for the alleged rape and kidnapping of a fifteen-year-old girl. If that makes your head spin, it should.

On cross-examination, Alcala asked Monique if she remembered that he apologized in the car after the attack.

"Just testify that I apologized to you," Alcala said.

It was sickening, but tactically great for us. Monique was facing Alcala again for the first time since that horrible day. No longer a child, she responded by driving nail after nail into his coffin. Between her and Tali, they spoke for every woman and girl who had encoun-tered Alcala but did not survive.

We then got into the A-factor evidence, which includes victim-impact testimony. This means family members get to take the stand and testify about how the murder of their loved one impacted their lives. The entire Alcala penalty phase was striking, but this is where it got profound. These were murders that had been com-mitted more than thirty years before those poor people testified in Court, and I don't think any of them were able to hold back their tears. Robin Samsoe's mother was a shell of her former self, but the emotion was positively raw. In many ways, she had never moved on from the horror of seeing her daughter's battered skull, and it showed. Charlotte Lamb's sister, complete with charming Southern drawl, described how she tried to touch up her beloved sister's makeup for her funeral and was shocked to see that her skin under the foundation had turned a shade of blue-green with the early stages of poorly embalmed decomposition. Jill Barcomb's brother wept uncontrollably. The entire penalty phase was a stark reminder of the human cost and immense multigenerational impact of rape-murders. Losing a loved one under such circumstances truly is the very worst thing.

Alcala, however, had one more trick up his sleeve. For his closing argument in the penalty phase, he played Arlo Guthrie's famous song from the sixties, "Alice's Restaurant." There is a point where Guthrie sings about feigned bloodlust in an attempt to avoid induction into the Army. "Shrink, I want to kill . . . I wanna kill . . . I wanna see . . . veins in my teeth." Alcala, the man who had slaughtered so many for his own perverse sexual pleasure, then told the jury that if they voted to execute him, they would be no better than the man in the song, out for blood for no good reason. In addition to being an entirely ineffective argument, it was positively one of the most bizarre things I have ever witnessed. Again, it is a revealing vignette into the mind of a psychopath. As mentioned before, they just can't read the room.

The jury returned a verdict of death, and Rodney Alcala was sentenced accordingly for a third time. He would never be executed in California, of course, but it represented a huge win for the families who had lost their daughters, sisters, and friends so long ago. The good guys, at long last, had won.

I spent seven years living those murders, alongside the rest of my caseload, and Gina Satriano and I became true friends. As the case was pending, I went through several more relationships, and so did Gina. We'd often find ourselves complaining to each other about the complexities of dating women. Like so many other dedicated Homicide prosecutors, Gina went through a divorce from her wife during our time together on the case. In addition to our work on Alcala, we bonded through our mutual romantic struggles. Gina is another true hero; I love that woman and hope we will remain friends until the day I die.

Rodney Alcala later pleaded guilty to two more murders to avoid a trial in New York. Cornelia Crilley was a TWA flight attendant who was found strangled to death with a stocking in her apartment. A bite mark on her body was consistent with Alcala's dental records. Ellen Hover was found in the woods a year after vanishing; her calendar noted a meeting on the day she went missing with a photographer by the name of John Burger, Alcala's alias. He was also charged with the murder of Christine Thornton, in Wyoming, after her family saw Thornton's photo in an online collection from Alcala's storage locker that was released to the public. (Given the quantity of photos found in the locker, and the fact that no one knew just how many people Alcala had killed, police released the photo collection in the hope that the families of other victims would recognize their missing relatives and come forward.) At that point he was too ill to travel and so authorities simply let the charges sit and did not attempt to extradite him for trial.

Alcala was formally named as a suspect in murders that took place in Washington State, New Hampshire, and Arizona. In 2011, Gina and I assisted investigators in tracking one more murder back to Rodney Alcala, this time in Marin County, California. Photos from the storage locker contained images from Fisherman's Wharf in San Francisco, where in 1977 yet another young woman, nineteen-year-old Pamela Lambson, met a photographer who convinced her to go into a wooded area in Marin County. Like Charlotte Lamb and Jill Parenteau, she was discovered completely naked. Like Jill Barcomb, she was found on a fire road often used as a hiking trail. Like all of them, she was a beautiful young woman, loved by her family, whose earrings were missing when her battered body was found.

Rodney Alcala died in prison in 2021, after fading away slowly with dementia. Before he got sick, however, even when all avenues for possible release had been exhausted and he knew he was never getting out, he still wouldn't agree to work with police to sort out exactly how many people he had killed. Instead, he wasted taxpayer resources on nonsense, suing the California prison system over a bogus slip-and-fall claim, and suing again for failing to receive a low-fat diet, on top of his failed effort to prevent the mandatory collection of DNA samples to check against the nationwide CODIS database of unsolved violent crimes.

I think there is an important lesson here, especially as states like California start to swing back to a policy of therapy and early release. Predators like Rodney Alcala do not reform. There is no "treatment" that can modify the behavior of a genuine sexual psychopath, and attempting to fix these people is nothing short of reckless folly.

When monsters like Alcala are released, they will kill other people. It may not be popular to say this, especially in an era of professed "criminal justice reform," and when we want to believe that *everyone* is redeemable, but Rodney Alcala was living proof that some people are not. Sexual predators do not get better. They may get better at not getting caught, but they do not change. When we release violent sexual predators, it is only a matter of time before more innocent people, and their families, suffer.

Rodney Alcala could have been, and should have been, kept behind bars after his very first arrest. Dozens if not hundreds of lives would have been spared unspeakable pain and grief if someone had just stepped up and put an end to the procedural madness. Instead, Alcala brutalized woman after woman, girl after girl, killing them in increasingly gruesome and sadistic ways. Alcala exists today as a profound cautionary tale, a boogeyman reminder that some people are just plain bad, and those with the power to keep sexual predators in custody have an abiding moral obligation to do so. The innocents who will be preyed upon are depending on them to do their job better than what we witnessed in that case. I can only pray that they heed the lesson. As for the families of Rodney Alcala's victims, they can finally rest. The man who so brutally murdered their loved ones was caught, tried, and condemned, and he died alone in a cold prison cell. He will never hurt anyone ever again.

CHAPTER

7

A CRAZY LITTLE THING CALLED LOVE

ONE OF THE most interesting things about working in the Homicide Unit is the interplay between the job and your personal life. Most of us don't go out and try to score drugs, or run around with gangsters, so a murder committed in those worlds may as well happen on Mars in terms of our ability to genuinely relate to it. But we all seek love in our lives, and most of us know what it's like to be in a bad relationship. Disrespect on a street corner means nothing, but we have all felt the wrenching of a broken heart on a Saturday night.

Sadly, as a Homicide prosecutor, when your phone rings at two in the morning, chances are you are on your way to a private home where a husband or wife has just killed their partner. Always terrible, always heartbreaking, and just like my first murder scene with the scorned financial planner, always a story. Most of us have known at least one emotionally labile drunk, and we have all known someone who has been in a toxic relationship with a controlling partner. According to the National Coalition Against Domestic Violence, one in four women and one in nine men have experienced severe physical violence from an intimate partner, and there are more than ten million domestic violence instances per year in the US. We can all relate to the fundamental awfulness of a case where domestic violence escalates into death—which is far and away the most common type of murder you see in suburban areas.

Long before you try your first domestic violence murder as a prosecutor, you handle trial after trial involving misdemeanor domestic violence. In fact, misdemeanor DVs, as they are known, are perhaps outnumbered only by DUI cases when you first begin working as a Deputy District Attorney. My very first trial assignment as a recently hired twenty-five-year-old rookie was in municipal court at Harbor Justice Center in Newport Beach. "Misdemeanor Land," as Municipal Court assignments were known back then, is where you first begin to learn the craft of trial work.

I was immediately shocked at how many domestic violence cases I saw on my very first day. I began the assignment believing every one of those cases involved a hot-headed thumper of a man beating on a diminutive, submissive woman. While my preconceived idea of domestic violence was certainly true in some instances, the reality you learn very quickly is that most of these cases involve a cycle of give-and-take between people who are both terrible to each other. Many times, the couples involved in these toxic relationships would break up and get back together multiple times before the case even got to trial.

It is very common in DV trials to have the victim, usually a woman but sometimes a man, be entirely hostile to the prosecution of the case. They will yell at you in the hallway, blame the police, and often lie through their teeth on the witness stand. Juries, experts in human behavior, usually have little problem figuring it out.

But keep in mind these are misdemeanors, which usually means there are no serious injuries. You encounter more domestic violence when you get to the Felony Panel, and of course many more in Sexual Assault. You review them, file them, and try them by the dozens over the course of your career.

In Homicide, at any given point, domestic violence–related murders will often compose up to half of your caseload. You see them at the beginning of your career, in the middle, and all the way through to the end. From responding to some of these bloody scenes, I have images in my mind that are even now hard to believe. I saw the body of a woman who had been handcuffed to a bed and tortured with a Taser gun before finally being strangled by her cheating husband. She had found out about the affair and cheated on him in revenge—and he killed her in response.

I went to another scene in Irvine, where a man suspected his wife of cheating. He murdered her *and his mother-in-law*. When we entered the home, we found their naked bodies in a downstairs bathtub. They were iced and wet; when they were removed, with settled rigor mortis and lividity, they reminded me of the dead fish we would remove from the bait tank of the fishing boat I worked on when I was seventeen. The heartbreaking thing about that scene, however, wasn't the bodies of two adult women, but all of the toys spread around the house for the two innocent daughters who lost their mother, grandmother, and father all on the same day. Their lives would never be the same. That one really got to me. I still think about them.

In a different case, I saw the bodies of two men who were murdered in a jealous rage by an ex-boyfriend who had snuck into their home and stabbed them both to death as they slept, focusing the blade savagely (for whatever reason) on their eyes.

There was an ex-husband who waited in ambush during a custody exchange, killing his ex-wife and her father after a bad day in Family Court. He had been insistent in the morning that his wife's attorney be present during the exchange and was no doubt disappointed that he didn't get to kill him, too. In each of these cases, and dozens more like them, you start at the scene, sometimes attend the autopsy, and then always meet with the family. In doing so, you gain a visceral sense of the lasting damage and profound grief these murders cause to the loved ones of your victim.

American 1950s Beat Generation author William S. Burroughs— who, in fact, killed his second wife in a death later ruled to be manslaughter—once famously said, "No one owns life, but anyone who can pick up a frying pan owns death." He wasn't wrong. It is estimated that in 2021, 34 percent of female murder victims were killed by an intimate partner. Given all the cases I saw, I would have guessed the number was much higher.

Over time, you begin to see patterns in domestic violence cases that may be instructive. Very few domestic violence murders happen out of the blue. If I had to pick the four horsemen of an impending DV apocalypse, they would be jealousy, manipulation, anger, and control. They manifest in different ways, but, unfortunately, too often the result is death. In this chapter, I want to explore two different cases of love gone bad, neither one a traditional domestic violence murder, but both fascinating in their own way.

/////\\\\\

The first is the Cathy Torrez case, a murder driven by the toxic trait of jealousy, with an investigation pursued thanks to the obsessive efforts of the detective on the case, Daron Wyatt.

In the world of murder investigations, incessant, unfaltering obsession can be both a blessing and a curse. "Obsession in this business," as my colleague Dennis Conway once put it, "is a gift." In fact, if obsession were a sport, the best investigators and prosecutors would all be world-class Olympians. As we've already seen, some cold cases get solved because of DNA, but some get solved because there is a dogged detective who just can't stop thinking about it. (Of course, obsession in other contexts can be quite toxic. Like some other personal traits, it simply depends on the role. An adult man prone to tantrums would be a nightmare at home, but if you're managing a major league baseball team, angrily kicking dirt on an umpire's shoes can be pure gold, riling up the fans and inspiring your players. Someone who loves to scream orders at people would likely be a tyrant as a parent, but as a college football coach it appears to work pretty well.)

In this case, we can turn the clock back to the winter of 1994, when Cathy Torrez was a student on the dean's list at Cal State Fullerton, just minutes away from her hometown of Placentia, California. Cathy was a high achiever who had set her sights on college from a young age. She dreamed of being a social worker, held down two jobs to earn enough to pay her way, and was absolutely not the kind of young woman who anyone would have expected might get into trouble. On the morning of February 13, Cathy's mother woke up to find that her daughter had never returned from work the night before. She had last been seen leaving the parking lot at eight p.m. and was supposedly heading toward Baskin-Robbins to meet her longtime on-and-off boyfriend, Sam Lopez. She was never seen alive again, and on that morning she and her car were nowhere to be found.

Police began a search, looking at all the places Cathy might typically be and telling the family that sometimes young people her age just drive away to be by themselves for a little while. "That's not Cathy," they said, begging police to continue the search. Her sister,

Tina, and her mother, Mary, were petrified of what might have happened, and insisted that if the police found the car, they would find Cathy.

Sure enough, six days after her disappearance, police woke Cathy's mother up in the middle of the night and asked if she had a spare car key. The officer came to get it and wouldn't look Mary in the eye. In the morning, she was told that the car had been found in the parking lot outside Placentia Hospital, and Cathy was dead in the trunk, having been stabbed more than seventy times.

The scene was intense. There was blood throughout the interior of the car, one of Cathy's shoes was under the floorboard, her sock was covered in dirt, there were defensive wounds on her hands, and there were what may have been finger marks on the inside of the trunk. It appeared that the attack had started inside the car, and somehow Cathy was able to escape—only to be caught again by the killer, stabbed more times, and then placed in the trunk. Her throat had been slashed, and her wrists had been cut. It was as if an initial flurry of random stab wounds had eventually culminated in a very deliberate effort to make sure she was dead. Arterial spurting on the inside of the trunk lid very significantly indicated that she was still alive when she went inside. Alive at least for a little while.

More than a thousand mourners came to Cathy's funeral, eulogizing her as a bright, loving, forgiving person. The investigation proceeded in two directions. First, there was the obvious suspect, Sam Lopez, who Cathy was supposed to be meeting that night. As it turned out, she had been planning to reject his marriage proposal. They had been high school sweethearts who broke up, dated others for a time, but had apparently found their way back to each other. Their families were intertwined; they grew up directly across the street from each other, and Sam's brother Armando was married to Cathy's sister, Tina. Sam had another girlfriend, Perla, but had apparently been seeing Cathy on the side. It became serious enough with Cathy that he proposed they elope. Cathy gave it thought but ultimately decided to turn his offer down.

Why? Among other reasons, she had another boyfriend, Albert Rangel, who had actually attempted suicide just days before Cathy's murder. He was in a coma in the hospital after trying to hang himself, and Cathy was focused on his recovery. She was writing notes to him daily and felt like she was in no state to marry Sam while Albert's fate lay in limbo. Albert, comatose, could not have murdered Cathy. His family insisted they loved her and did not blame her for what had happened. And Sam had an alibi: He said he was with his cousin, Xavier, helping him move. Xavier told an identical story. And Sam's DNA was nowhere to be found at the crime scene—not on the car, not on the body. The investigation quickly went cold.

Daron Wyatt began as an officer at Placentia PD the following year and did not initially intend to work in Homicide. But there was a need, and he soon found himself a detective in that department. By January 1997, the most recent eight murders in Placentia were all unsolved, but the Torrez case was the one that kept Daron up at night. He had recently become a father and couldn't bear the thought of Cathy's mother having to live with uncertainty for the rest of her life, unable to see justice imposed on the person who had killed her daughter.

Daron began to revisit the investigation. In Cathy's car, police had found an unfinished note to Albert, stopped mid-word, shoved into the space between the front seats. It seemed clear that Cathy had been in her car, writing that note, when she was interrupted—by someone she wanted to hide the note from. Who else could that be, Daron thought, but Sam?

By the time Daron was diving back into the case in 1997, Albert, after two years on life support, had died. And Sam was married with a child. Daron put surveillance on Sam and Xavier and noticed that

Xavier often seemed to spend the night at Sam's place. They were cousins, sure, but Daron wondered if something more was bonding them. He realized that the initial investigation had only looked for Sam's presence at the crime scene and had treated Xavier merely as an alibi witness. He decided to test for Xavier's DNA—and hit paydirt.

Xavier's right index fingerprint was on the trunk in an upward orientation, as if he had closed it, and his DNA was mixed with Cathy's, in blood on the left-rear quarter-panel of her red car. Perhaps it was a little tougher to spot a smear of blood on a red car, especially one that had been recently rained on, but there it was. It seemed that the evidence was showing that Xavier might have been there when Cathy was killed. Xavier was brought in for questioning and once again repeated Sam's alibi and denied that either one had anything to do with her murder. He explained there was a time, shortly before the murder, when he had met Sam and Cathy at a record store and might have taken something out of her trunk.

Xavier had no motive as a potential killer: He liked Cathy, and had no reason to want her dead. Xavier also presented as anything but a murderer. Mild-mannered and a little nerdy, he worked as a math tutor and still lived with his parents. And based on the forensics of the day, his story could have explained both the fingerprint and the DNA.

Daron did not believe that Xavier was the primary murderer, but ardently believed he was involved, and certainly had enough evidence to charge him. He believed that if he arrested Xavier and could convince the DA to file charges, Xavier would flip and implicate Sam as the true killer. He arrested Xavier and approached the Orange County DA at the time to file a case. The DA, new to all things Torrez, agreed that Xavier was unlikely to have been the main killer—but without more evidence against Sam, she did not believe the case could effectively be made in front of a jury. She declined to file charges, and Xavier was set free after being in custody for just two days.

This was the era of what is known as *substrate DNA*, when defense lawyers would often successfully argue that a person could touch an object at some unrelated moment only to later have blood from the victim be deposited over that innocent person's DNA. Xavier could have touched the car a couple of days earlier at the record store, and now his DNA could be found mixed with Cathy's blood . . . or so the argument went. Compounding the family's grief, the DA's Office actually declined the case a second time the following year—but Daron was relentless, and I give him a ton of credit for it. It got quite heated between the DA and Daron when it was refused again. The DA told him not to resubmit the case a third time, because it would "never be filed."

It seemed like the end of the line. Daron had nothing to hold over Sam's and Xavier's heads with the DA saying they wouldn't file, and even though he continued to keep the case in mind—and Mary continued to press him to find a way to achieve justice—there was little he could do. Months turned into years.

This is the point in the story when I come in.

I was no longer a naive kid. The decision to dedicate myself to the work had paid off spectacularly well, at least professionally. At this point, I had become one of the senior deputies in the Unit. I had dozens of murder trials under my belt, and had yet to lose one. Due to my assigned cities, my cases had become regular features on national news programs like *20/20*, *Dateline*, *48 Hours*, and more true crime cable programs than I can even remember. My supervisors, the elected DA, and the police departments I worked with all seemed to understand that if they just gave me what I needed, the job would get done and they would look great.

But the problem with any addiction is that you need more and more to achieve the same feeling. In the world of murder, that means you push yourself into harder and harder cases. And if the hard cases don't come to you, then you have to go find them. You have to pick tougher and tougher fights, and I was about to pick a doozy.

I had previously requested and was assigned to one of the two cold case positions in the Unit. I did this to broaden my access to tougher cases, and also because cold cases were just so interesting. This meant I could prosecute homicide cases not only from my current cities, but from any jurisdiction in the county where the assigned Deputy had taken a pass. The person assigned to Placentia in those days was having enough trouble getting the small and poorly funded depart-ment to get their current murders on track, let alone old cases like Torrez. Daron and ace detective Larry Montgomery brought me the Torrez case and I agreed to take a look.

I quickly learned that this case was a notorious mess, complete with bad blood between the police and the well-respected former DA. Daron and I had worked some other cases together over the years and had developed a healthy respect for each other. In truth, he wasn't going to leave me alone until I had looked at it. In fact, I don't think he would have left me alone until I filed it. He is now among my closest and most trusted friends.

By this point Larry Montgomery had been dubbed "The Evidence Whisperer" by *Dateline*'s Josh Mankiewicz. Larry had left me a couple of years earlier to work the Trackers Unit full-time. Trackers was all cold cases, all the time, and they did amazing work. It was great to get back together with Larry and unleash his genius on this one.

Sam Lopez's interviews were a lot like Nanette Johnston's after the McLaughlin murder. On the surface, everything looked normal, but nothing was right. Sam's interview tapes objectively depict a young man denying involvement in a murder and providing an alibi corroborated by others. But the real curiosity was in his reactions, and how he should have responded given what we knew about him.

Unlike his cousin Xavier, we knew Sam to be a hothead with a jealous streak a mile wide. Yet what we saw in the interview was a calm young man respectfully answering questions, and asking precious few of his own. If innocent, he had just learned that his girlfriend—the woman to whom he had just proposed—had been found dead. During the breaks, he examined the soundproofing on the walls of the interview room, sipped a Diet Coke, read the ingredients on the can, and only seemed upset, momentarily, when he discovered a stain on his new hat.

"Aw, man . . ." he said, rubbing dirt off the brim. It was the most emotion he showed. It took him almost an hour before he asked *how* Cathy had died, and then he showed no noticeable response when told she had been murdered. The woman had been stabbed seventy times and placed alive in the trunk of her car. Maybe that was worth some sort of a reaction? It was as if he was trying to play the role of an uninvolved bystander, calmly stating his innocence to detectives in order to check himself off a list of suspects.

The real Sam Lopez—jealous, angry, and theoretically innocent—would have been through the roof when told that Cathy had been killed. He would have been enraged that another person had taken the life of his love, and demanded to know what the police were doing about it. He would have offered to help. In fact, he probably would have demanded it. Either way, he should have shown far more emotion. Even if he wasn't dating her, this was his sister-in-law, and he had known her his entire life. The ho-hum, "darn, my hat" routine made absolutely zero sense.

Putting his behavior in context, this was not a man who was grieving the loss of his girlfriend. He was simply not acting the way an innocent person would, and that is powerful for a jury to see. Juries are made up of human beings, and they are experts at how fellow human beings should behave in different scenarios. When things don't seem right, they know. We may not have had much hard forensic evidence against Sam in the purest sense, but Sam's interviews were pretty damning, or so I thought.

Of course, we also had to answer the jury's questions, biggest among them being: Why? Why wasn't Sam's DNA anywhere at the scene? And the answer comes down to the complexities of science: Some people, known as *shedders*, leave a trail of DNA, and some people simply don't. We knew from his interviews that Sam drove Cathy's car all the time. According to Sam, they were often together, and he always drove. So whether he murdered her or not, if his DNA had been inside the car, it wouldn't have actually helped our case. Sam's DNA *should* have been there, because he drove her car all the time. The fact that it wasn't found meant either nothing, or that he cleaned up, which I doubt. The truth is that some people just seem to leave more DNA around than others. Sam clearly was not a shedder. Xavier, on the other hand, was practically a fountain. Either way, the lack of Sam's DNA wasn't a death blow to the idea that he could still be the murderer.

The other piece of evidence we uncovered was a stash of Sam's letters to Cathy while they were together in high school. The "hothead papers," as they became known to my team, revealed Sam's true personality. In those letters, Sam was constantly apologizing and saying that things wouldn't escalate again. He and Cathy kept getting together and breaking up. It was evidence that he had a propensity to violence and that this had been a stormy relationship. It was really a domestic violence situation, and those, unfortunately, can and do sometimes escalate to murder.

We also had a curious bit of backstory: A week before Cathy's murder, she had come home from a night out with Sam, seeming like she was under the influence of some narcotic. She could barely walk, and she didn't remember what had happened to her that night. Sam claimed he didn't know if someone might have slipped something into her drink, or what had happened, but it seemed like another piece of a story that added up to Sam very much trying to get his way with Cathy—and when she said no to his proposal, and then he walked up and found her writing a heartfelt letter to Albert Rangel in her car, the picture started to take shape.

Placentia police wanted to serve a search warrant on the house where Sam and his now-divorced brother were living. Police had, perhaps overzealously, placed a camera outside the home and also set up a wiretap of the phones. The camera was discovered by Sam. When the warrant was served, the image on Sam's television was actually a direct feed from the camera—he had found a way to hook it up so that he could watch the footage the police were collecting. Naturally, as a result of his awareness of the renewed investigation, there was virtually nothing of value on any of the wiretaps. It seemed like we had all we were going to get. As a prosecutor, what do you do?

I was convinced that Sam Lopez had murdered Cathy Torrez in some sort of jealous fit. But just like in the Eric Naposki case, there was no weapon, no fingerprints, no DNA, and no witness linking Sam to Cathy on the night she was murdered. He had an alibi that brought in a couple of different people, one of them being Xavier, whose DNA and fingerprints were all over the outside of the car.

I was not as impressed by the defense of substrate DNA as the Deputy who had reviewed the case back in 1995. I had dealt with this issue before. But I still had to find a way to prove to a jury that the perpetrator was Sam. I had subjective belief in the viability of the case—but also needed to believe that I could win it. Larry and Daron, two men I respected immensely, were both telling me we could win, and they had each been in the trenches with me for years. Then Daron played his ace: "Just come with me to meet the family," he said. "I've already told them you are not making any promises."

We walked into the modest Placentia home of Cathy's mother,

Mary Bennett, with photos of her beloved daughter everywhere. We were joined by her sister Tina and her brother Marty, who coincidentally worked as a Court Clerk in the Orange County Central Courthouse. I immediately liked them all. This was roughly a decade and a half after Cathy had been murdered, and you could still feel the sadness in that home. Mary was sweet, appropriate, and grateful in all the ways you would expect from a dignified, hardworking matron of a wonderful family. That woman had been wronged, and I knew I was in trouble the second we made eye contact. There was a glimpse of hope, and I recognized it immediately. I explained that I just wanted to introduce myself and that we were working as hard as we could to put the case together. The family expressed their gratitude, and, after a few questions, Larry, Daron, and I left. Daron knew exactly what he was doing.

I would love to be able to say that there is some kind of scientific formula that a prosecutor uses to determine when a case is strong enough to file, some objective schematic that you can plug in with a light that turns green when you reach a certain threshold. The truth is that it really boils down to more of a gut feeling than anything else. The internal process sometimes played out for me like the old plot device where a devil and an angel pop up on your shoulders. But in my head, instead of two figures, it was more like a demon rave with lights and music and many voices all yelling at me at the same time.

The devil, or devils, who were telling me not to file, when I really broke it down, were things like vanity, pride, and ego. I had won sixty-three felony jury trials in a row at that point. You start thinking about your record, and your streak, and end up with a multitude of worries that should have zero bearing on a decision like this. Was I really going to file this case, with plenty of media, and possibly lose a big one on national TV? Wouldn't that be bad for my reputation? How would that look? What would people think? These were the worst possible reasons against pursuing the case.

On the other hand, I had made the decision long ago that I was going all in. I had done the work, honed my abilities, and if anyone could bring it home, why not me? What did my good intentions mean if I wasn't willing to step up on a tough one when I knew the guy did it?

Besides, Sam Lopez had already gotten away with it, and, from that perspective, what did we have to lose? If I was going to die on a hill, or go down in professional flames, I wanted to do it for someone like Cathy's mom. I would love to say that my conversation with Larry and Daron was articulate, legal, and well-considered, but I believe my exact words were "fine, fuck it, let's file."

Thus, in 2007, after building that case for four years, I decided to pull the trigger. We put out arrest warrants for Sam and Xavier. And that's when the fun really started. Once you file a case, seeing the defense lawyer who shows up often feels a little like you're playing a game of roulette. The wheel spins and you have no idea where that little white ball is going to land. Sometimes you get a frumpy guy with thick glasses who smells weird, and sometimes the family raises money and finds a true hitter.

The attorney who showed up for Sam's arraignment was a woman named Jennifer Keller, a terrific lawyer and incredible strategist. Seeing her walk into the courtroom felt more like a game of Russian roulette where I had just pulled the trigger on a loaded chamber. As I stood there, I had lost exactly two jury trials in my career at that point, both very early on: my first misdemeanor DUI, and my first misdemeanor bar fight about two weeks later. Both were among my first five trials, and the second of them was all the way back in 1996. I had gone up against Jennifer in the bar fight case, and she quite simply outlawyered the hell out of me. They say you learn more from the ones you lose than the ones you win, and I learned a lot with that loss. Perhaps my biggest takeaway, however, was just how good she was in a courtroom. She recently represented actor Kevin Spacey in his sexual assault trial in New York. The Manhattan DA learned some of the same lessons I did, no doubt, because Kevin Spacey was acquitted on all counts. She is simply superb. Jennifer Keller, the last lawyer to beat me, wasn't exactly my best draw. In fact, I could only think of one defense attorney who would have been worse. And, spoiler alert, he was about to show up, too, thanks to Jennifer's brilliance.

In the course of our lives, we have all seen those people who seem like they were born to do what they do. There was a surfer in the early 1980s named Mark Occhilupo, who I used to follow as a teenager. He was five foot nine (low center of gravity) with broad shoulders and size 14 feet, and he was born on the Gold Coast of Australia. Looking at him, it appeared as if God sat down one day and decided to create a pure surfer. Or think about Kelly Slater in the surf generation after Occhilupo, with eleven world titles, whose nickname is "the GOAT," for *greatest of all time*. There's Magic Johnson in basketball, Tiger Woods in golf, and Serena Williams in tennis. They are true greats, who make competition look so effortless, and who are so fundamentally superior at what they do that nobody can touch them in their prime—and most can't even touch them outside of their prime.

In the gladiatorial combat of murder trials, the greatest I had ever seen, of course, was my teacher, mentor, and dear friend Lew Rosenblum. He is perhaps the single finest trial lawyer I have ever seen. I used to go and watch him in trial before I ever got to meet him, because I wanted to learn from the best. What I saw was more an avenging force of nature than just a lawyer. He dominated the courtroom in ways nobody had before or since, and he had never lost. He prosecuted sixty-seven murder trials in twelve years and finished 67–0. It was impossible, and yet he did it with ease.

Lew had been retired from the Unit for a few years at this point and was now out on his own. Jennifer Keller knew of our close professional and personal relationship. Incredibly (and no doubt with a substantial financial incentive), she managed to convince Lew to come on board with her and take Sam's case. This was quite a development. I just knew that when the chips were down, Lew was one of those guys who was going to find a way to win.

What made me even more nervous was that Lew was in the Unit back in 1995 when the case originally came through. Which meant that somewhere, at some point, he may have taken a look and hadn't thought he could get a conviction against Sam Lopez either. If he had been spooked, why wasn't I? I never thought I would go up against Lew in a trial, and certainly not in a murder case, especially one he might have declined to prosecute when he was in the Unit. To top it off, neither of us had ever lost a murder trial. Jennifer Keller not only knew how phenomenal Lew was in Court, but she certainly picked him to rattle me. It was a brilliant move, and one that I absolutely respect, even if it terrified me at the time. In fact, I lost sleep for weeks knowing that our combined 107–0 record in homicide cases would inevitably become 108–1. But I had no intention of taking a loss, particularly not in a case where an innocent twenty-year-old college student had been brutally murdered by her boyfriend.

Some might wonder if Lew taking this case represented a conflict of interest—if in fact he had come across the file in our office. At worst, if it was a conflict, it was one that both sides would have gladly waived. Sam would have certainly had no issue with it, and I would have never attempted to deny a defendant the lawyer of their choice. We had done no work on the case while Lew was here, so it was not as if he would have had any advantage when it came to the substance of the trial. Besides, a lawyer of Lew's singular talent doesn't need to cheat to win.

You may also wonder how I felt with Lew having switched sides, and the truth is that Lew had every right to become a defense lawyer, and as a defense lawyer I knew it would be his duty to defend his client with all of his skill and experience, regardless of what I personally thought about Sam's guilt. I might choose not to defend someone like Sam Lopez—but I also believed that the case was so tough, Lew might very well have convinced himself that Sam didn't do it. We've never had that conversation and never will. Lew is one of the finest men I have ever met and he has as much integrity as any person I have ever known. Besides, a professional would never ask, and another professional would never tell. I was ready to do my job, and Lew was ready to do his.

Xavier, meanwhile, was represented by Jack Earley, who was and is an excellent lawyer in his own right, having tried over 125 homicide cases, including the case against Betty Broderick, a woman in San Diego who murdered her ex-husband, claiming she was driven to it by years of spousal abuse—"battered woman syndrome," Earley argued. It was the first case to get gavel-to-gavel coverage on the nascent TV network Court TV back in 1991. Earley eventually lost the retrial after hanging the first jury, but he had a fearsome reputation. I couldn't believe that after all the work we had done, Sam got Lew Rosenblum, and Xavier, idiot that he was, somehow managed to retain Jack Earley. My original plan was to roll Xavier against his cousin and change the dynamic of the case. But Jack wasn't interested. Jack saw all the problems I did, and probably a few I didn't.

It's easy to believe, if you watch enough *Law & Order*, that every murder case proceeds expeditiously to trial. Crime, investigation, and trial in forty-two minutes plus commercials. The truth is, sometimes the best strategy for the defense is to "age a case." With the passage of time, some of our witnesses were getting pretty elderly. While you can in some cases conduct what is known as a conditional exam of a dying witness, and tape it to be later shown to a jury, this requires a terminal illness, not just old age.

There was one witness in particular who I'm sure the defense would have liked to see fade away. She was Cathy's coworker at the Sav-On store where she worked, the last person to see Cathy alive on the night of her death, and the person to whom she casually mentioned that she was going to meet Sam. This is what is known as a 1250 statement under the California Evidence Code, and it was a critical component of my case. That witness was getting up there in years, and the defense knew it. They, very correctly, decided it was in their best interest to take their time and meticulously build their case. I, on the other hand, didn't object too hard to the continuances, because every time they asked to push the trial date, it meant one more day that Sam and Xavier were still in jail. Certainly not prison, but the way I saw it, each day they were in custody represented just a little more justice for that family. Even *if* Lew eventually beat me in trial.

Besides, I wanted more evidence, and those lawyers all knew it. I met with the crime lab and requested they re-process Cathy's jeans. There is a concept in the forensic DNA world known as *masking*, where trace amounts of touch DNA are essentially covered up by the massive amounts of victim DNA when mixed with blood or other fluids rich in nuclear cells. The autosomal DNA of the victim simply overwhelms the small amounts from your suspect, and Cathy's jeans were almost completely covered in her own blood. This is different from the idea of substrate DNA where we worry that two people's DNA might be combined even if they weren't in the same place at the same time. Here, the issue is that one person might not be detected by the lab at all because there is so much more DNA from the other party.

The way to get past this was to pick our samples carefully, hopefully finding locations where Sam or Xavier might have touched Cathy, but also where their trace DNA wouldn't be overwhelmed by her blood. If the two of them had put Cathy in the trunk of the car, for instance, with one carrying her legs and one carrying her upper torso, maybe we would get lucky. We asked the lab to swab the back of her knees, the cuff area of her jeans, and her socks. Sure enough, we got a hit. But once again ... it wasn't Sam. One more time, the DNA came back to Xavier. Still, this development was huge. Now I could argue Sam's alibi, Xavier, who had no motive, held Cathy's legs as Sam had her upper body. With the arterial bleeding on the inside of the trunk lid, Xavier's fingerprint, and Xavier's DNA mixed in the blood smear on the fender, I could show that Cathy was still alive when Xavier helped move her into the trunk. That made him a principal to murder and not merely an accessory after the fact. Even against Lew, I thought I could get Sam, through Xavier.

We had another piece to this case that I haven't yet mentioned: Juan Barroso. Juan was a friend; both Sam and Xavier told police they had gone to Barroso's house that evening. Which, if they did, would almost certainly have been to clean up so they wouldn't go home all bloody. But Barroso backed their story—which, in the view of detectives, meant he should have known far more than he revealed. He told the same story for more than a decade.

Juan was interesting to me because he was an outsider, not part of the Lopez family, and had no reason to take the fall for what happened. Juan was represented by Jake Brower, another great lawyer, and even though he was worried about his own fate, Barroso would not cooperate with us and give up Sam Lopez. The entire Lopez family really circled the wagons around Sam and Xavier. They—maybe twenty people—would show up to every Court appearance at the beginning wearing matching T-shirts with cartoon characters whose hands were up against a wall as if they were getting frisked.

"I've been framed," the shirts said. I felt it was bush league and beyond disrespectful to Cathy's family. Whether or not they subjectively believed that Sam and Xavier were guilty, there was still a family there, grieving the loss of a daughter and a sister. There was one member of the Lopez family—I think they called him "Gorilla"—and he stalked the hallway, listening for information he could feed back to the Lopez clan. Every time I would have a conversation, there he'd be, within earshot. That could be useful, I thought.

They say your best work as a trial lawyer always takes place outside the courtroom. In this case, that was the literal truth. Gorilla didn't pick up on the fact that I had noticed he was always there. I decided to use that to my advantage, suspecting that he might bring back anything he heard. Maybe, I thought, I could shake the tree a little bit and get Xavier to tell us what really happened. I asked Jake Brower if, with his permission, I could introduce myself to his client when we served him with a subpoena for the grand jury. Jake, naturally, didn't mind. Imagining that Gorilla was watching my every move, I had my investigator walk right up to Juan Barroso and hand him a grand jury subpoena. I then shook his hand and said, "I'm so glad we will finally be able to talk and have you share everything you know. I wish we could have met under different circumstances." Legally, I was referring to his obligation to tell us the truth in front of the grand jury.

He likely had no idea what I was talking about, but it didn't matter. I didn't say it for him. I can't say for sure if my gambit worked or not, but the next day (after Xavier had been in custody for almost a decade) I got a call from Xavier's attorney. Xavier—finally!—agreed to talk. Remember, he was facing a first-degree murder charge and life in prison. I offered him a proffer agreement, where he would be afforded a chance to cooperate but we wouldn't be able to use his statements against him. He had been in custody for eight years at that point and might be released if he just told us the truth.

And he took the deal, or, at least, he *sort of* took it. There was strategy on his part, too. He likely believed Barroso was going to tell the truth, and so Xavier decided to tell us a story that would lay out Sam, but not him. I can't imagine he was smart enough to think of this, but his story was so bad that had I called him to the stand, Lew would have destroyed him, categorizing him as the prosecution's star witness, and Sam could have gone free.

Xavier told us that Sam indeed killed Cathy and came to his house after he put her in the trunk. According to Xavier, when he pressed Sam for details, Sam told him he had left the knife in the trunk. Xavier told him he needed to get rid of the knife, so he had Sam drive him back to Cathy's car. He said he opened the trunk (thus the print), rummaged through the trunk to find the knife, accidentally cut himself with the blade, grabbed a rag to stanch the bleeding, noticed the blood on the fender, and, without thinking, tried to wipe it off, thus accidentally depositing his DNA on the outside of the car. His DNA on the back of her jeans must have been from him rummaging around looking for the knife.

Hearing this was like watching a child explain how Santa came down the chimney and stole the missing cookie from the kitchen counter. Feigned intensity at all the wrong times, poor eye contact, fidgeting, and virtually every poker tell that you could ever expect to see in a completely bullshit story. Just like a child . . . only this wasn't cute. My IQ was dropping with every minute he spoke. If I called him to the stand, and he told this ridiculous story, then Lew would shred him to pieces and argue that he had no credibility, because he didn't. The jury wouldn't believe Xavier, and thus they wouldn't believe *me*, and my case would be done. Freedom for both murderers.

I knew exactly what Lew would do because the man literally taught me how to do it. I knew the only way we could win the case was by never letting Xavier and his ridiculous story anywhere near the witness stand. I would go with my original plan and argue the hell out of the interview tapes, explaining how Sam could not possibly be innocent given his behavior. "Lean, mean, and clean," again, just like Lew had taught me.

I ran with the evidence we had, presenting the case piece by piece, and building my argument around the idea that Cathy and Sam had this unstable relationship, along with Xavier's DNA evidence at the scene. I then hit them with Sam's interview tape. Murdered girlfriend, but Sam was upset about the smudge on his hat. I believed I could win with that. It ended up not quite as easy as I hoped.

Looking back, the trial was an absolute war, and far and away the most difficult case I have ever presented. Lew Rosenblum did things on cross-examination that I didn't even think possible. He went after Cathy's mother like a tiger but managed to do so without offending a single juror. At the end of the first day, on a case I had worked on for almost a decade, I realized that I needed to reassess each piece of evidence I planned to use because Lew was going to find every tiny vulnerability and exploit it to death.

In the end, it all did come down to Sam's interview. I closed with perhaps the longest argument I have ever made. I picked the interview apart word by word, line by line, and page by page. Each statement was like a new nail in Sam's coffin, and by the end, I felt like I had all twelve jurors on my side.

The jury deliberated for two days and came back with a guilty verdict against Sam. First-degree murder. At the sentencing, in another move that was pure Lew Rosenblum, Sam made a statement to the Court and to the Torrez family. He admitted everything and said he wouldn't appeal the verdict. I had never seen a defendant do that before, and it was legally pure genius. Sam would be getting a parole hearing someday, and Lew knew the parole board would look kindly on him taking responsibility for what he had done. He could finally get it off his chest, and the Torrez family could finally receive an apology. I don't think it made them feel any better toward Sam, but it was quite a moment, legally brilliant, and a demonstration of pure professional class by Lew Rosenblum.

The truth, as Sam finally explained it: He and Xavier went to meet Cathy. Sam went to her car, and they began arguing. Xavier heard Cathy begin to scream and he went to pull Sam away, assuming he had gotten physical. He didn't realize Sam had a knife and was stabbing her. Xavier accidentally cut his hand trying to pull Sam off her. Cathy got away, but Sam chased after her, and cut her face and her head. Xavier helped Sam put Cathy into the trunk, where Sam cut her wrists and neck, sealing her fate. Just like I had argued. Going back to the example of our two cowboys, the initial flurry of knife wounds could have been a second-degree murder. But the throat slash and cuts on the wrists made it a pure, cold-blooded first-degree offense. They drove to the hospital lot and parked, and left the car.

The Torrez family still calls me on every birthday. I am so relieved that they finally got the answers they had been looking for, even if they were horrifying ones. Daron deserves so much of the credit for bringing Cathy's killers to justice—more than two decades after her brutal murder.

/////\\\\\

The second case I want to explore here is a different kind of love gone bad. When we meet someone in a more traditional way, through mutual friends, perhaps in a workplace or at a wedding, that relationship begins with a point of commonality and some degree of mutually assured reputational destruction. If a person behaves badly, it will eventually get back to someone whose opinion matters. Even if we meet a stranger in a bar, at least we get to see them in 3D, and how they interact in the world. This certainly doesn't always add up to decency, and partners have been doing each other wrong for millennia, but we live in a time when even those safeguards are largely gone.

In fact, an entirely fresh lexicon has popped up to describe dating in the modern world, and none of the terms are particularly positive. Terms like catfishing, breadcrumbing, and ghosting didn't even exist a few years ago, and now we hear them all the time. For the reader who has been married for a while, you may not completely understand. For the reader who is single, you know exactly what I am talking about—the wild, unhinged, broken-glass saloon brawl that is online dating. At first glance, it seems like a playground of abundance. But the sheer number of people out there doesn't necessarily correlate with quality. It takes about fifteen minutes to put together an awesome-looking profile (especially with the use of old photos), and nobody leads with their particular brand of neurosis.

Online dating is an arena where even normally nice people can be tempted to behave terribly. He shows up late? There are a dozen men lined up right behind him ready to show up on time. She let slip a few too many details about her ex over dinner? There are six new messages in your inbox from women who won't.

If you perceive something on a date that isn't exactly what you're looking for, there's no need to waste time talking about it. You can just ghost, block, delete, and repeat. With complete strangers, nobody owes anyone anything, and the resulting behavior sadly shows. There are simply no rules, and I challenge anyone who has online dated for more than a week to say that they have treated everyone with the same dignity and respect they would have if they met, say, at a wedding of mutual friends.

There is virtually no social consequence to mercenary behavior; few can cast stones, and I'm talking about reasonably healthy people. Don't get me wrong, there are certainly wonderful people online, and countless happy relationships begin every single day. For the vast majority of these interactions, the greatest risks are really just bruised egos, broken hearts, and wasted time—but for the predators of the world, this era has enabled an unadulterated gold rush.

I prosecuted several horrific murder cases where my victim met her killer online. Loneliness, and the fundamental human need for interpersonal connection, coaxes some people into letting their guard down in ways that perhaps they shouldn't. We have all been there before, in one way or another, but never within the context of the current format of dating apps and the promises of quick connection, quick sex, and quick love. I could, sadly, fill this book with stories of romantic disaster—but there is one case I want to share where the ending was somewhat less tragic; in fact, it was downright happy.

"Dirty John," the podcast-famous case that I mentioned all the way back in chapter 1, is the true story of online-dating boogeyman John Meehan. Working with the investigators who unraveled his actions, I was reminded of some of the red flags I've seen throughout my career, and they're not necessarily the ones we think of right away.

When dealing with strangers, especially those we meet online, predators often show warning signs that you can spot if you're looking—but that the well-meaning, naive, and forgiving among us might miss. Meehan, a poster boy for what to avoid, spent his life lying, seducing, and terrorizing women, going from one to the next, meeting almost all of his victims online. Of course, he was bad long before the online dating sites even opened for business.

First, there was Tonia Bales, a nurse anesthetist and wonderful woman, who made the mistake of marrying Meehan in 1990. After ten years and two daughters, Tonia discovered that her husband had been living a double life. Not only had he been cheating on her, but he had been hiding an arrest for cocaine trafficking from before they got married.

His real birthday made him six years older than what he claimed, he had just impregnated another woman, and Tonia discovered that he had been stealing pain medication from the patients he was supposed to care for at the hospital where he worked as a nurse. Bales finally reached out to John's mother, a woman he had forbidden her to speak with, only to learn he'd been a pathological liar his entire life.

After John and Tonia's divorce in 2002, Meehan was investigated and charged for the theft of pain medication. After pleading guilty, he ran from police, kicking one officer in the face, before falling into an elevator shaft and knocking himself unconscious. He served seventeen months in prison and was released, a convicted felon, in 2004. He made his way from Michigan to California, where he discovered the nascent world of online dating. John Meehan went to work.

His formula was pretty simple. Find lonely, older women with money, charm them, bed them, promise them the moon, and then take them for everything he could get his hands on. When they figured out what was happening, often too late, he would then threaten them, extort them, and, in one instance in early 2014, stalk them. He had been arrested a year earlier for extorting one woman out of thousands of dollars—which might very well have turned into a $40 million payday had a friend of the woman not looked him up online and found enough information to cause the heartbroken and terrified target to backtrack.

This is a guy who would show up in surgical scrubs for dates. As a former nurse, he also knew how to talk the talk. Meehan extorted a car from another woman, and an RV from a third. He spent a few months in the Orange County Jail for the stalking charge and was released on October 8, 2014. Before he could even get his jail-issued classification bracelet off his wrist, he was already back online looking for his next date.

Which is when he met Debra Newell. Debra was a successful, wealthy interior designer who had already been married four times.

Meehan was charming and handsome, and, just like with the other women, he showered her with time and attention.

"He'd tell me how beautiful I was," she told *People* magazine, "ask me about my day and rub my back. I was infatuated with him." He claimed to be a doctor who had volunteered for Doctors Without Borders in Iraq. In reality, he had only been out of custody *a few days* before their first date. But Debra had no clue about his history and, like the others, was completely smitten.

It can be easy for us to look back with the clarity of hindsight and criticize the decisions of a woman like Debra. How could she not realize that the man in dirty scrubs was telling her things that made no sense? The best answer to really understand this can be seen in a wonderful miniseries starring Connie Britton and Eric Bana that portrays the evolution of their early relationship. Having lived that case, I can happily say that both actors were positively brilliant, and it really is worth a watch. Eric Bana, in particular, nailed it. The charm, the cadence, the manipulation: It is a master class in acting.

Debra's daughters, on the other hand, weren't fooled for a minute. Her oldest daughter, Jacquelyn, hated John and couldn't believe her mom appeared to be choosing this loser over her and her sister, Terra. This was made worse when less than three months after they started dating, John and Debra returned from a trip to Vegas—married.

Unknown to Debra, but certainly unsurprising when later learned by her daughters, John Meehan had been the subject of no fewer than six restraining order applications, filed by six different women. Pretty soon, family members began doing some of the due diligence that Debra never thought necessary. She began learning about Meehan's past and finally started to come to her senses. Debra sought to annul their marriage. Meehan—convincing as ever—somehow persuaded her into reconciling, and they moved into a luxury apartment together in Irvine.

As time went on, Meehan's behavior became more and more controlling. He forbade Debra from speaking to her daughters. When he caught her talking to Jacquelyn, Meehan made a comment about throwing her into the ocean. Eventually, Debra Newell had enough. She told him so, and Meehan's threats and rage then turned on her. Like so many women before, Debra applied for a restraining order. Incredibly, it was denied. She went into hiding. Meehan ended up filing for divorce and demanding half of Debra's money. A lawsuit perhaps not satisfying enough, he then decided to steal her late-model Jaguar and light it on fire. The stalking began in earnest.

On August 20, 2016, Debra's daughter Terra was returning home after walking her Australian shepherd, Cash. Terra couldn't stand Meehan and was relieved her mother had finally seen the light. Still, she had always been very polite to him compared to her sister. Terra, with blond hair and a pleasant Southern California beach vibe, was mellow, nice, loved her family, and really loved her dog.

As Terra made her way through the parking lot of her Newport Beach apartment complex, she was suddenly attacked from behind by a large man with a knife. It was "Dirty John" Meehan, her putative stepfather, and he grabbed her like a grizzly bear. He tried to force her into a nearby car, and the fight was on. Terra, having now been stabbed once, was a foot shorter, and more than one hundred pounds lighter, than the athletic Meehan.

Despite her slight stature and beach-chick vibe, Terra is a genuine badass. She also had Cash, the hero dog, who began biting the living hell out of Terra's attacker. The fight had gone to the ground at this point, and, momentarily distracted by Cash, Meehan took his eyes off Terra. Big mistake. She managed to kick the knife out of his hand.

An avid fan of *The Walking Dead*, Terra knew exactly how to dispatch a monster. She immediately picked up the knife and stabbed him first in the shoulder, then the face, and then directly in his left eye—the knife blade penetrating deeply into Meehan's twisted, maniacal, thieving brain.

With thirteen stab wounds in all, the fight was over. Terra had been stabbed, Meehan lay dying, and Cash was fine.

"I'm sorry, Mom," Terra said when she called Debra, "but I think I killed your husband."

There is a photo of Terra in the hospital that was submitted to me with the rest of the investigation. It showed her in the bed, all hooked up to various machines. On her lap, staring right at the police photographer, was that dog. A little nervous perhaps, maybe even a little suspicious, but more than ready to bite the next fool who tried to hurt his mom. It was an awesome image that I will never forget.

John Meehan died of his wounds four days after the attack, having never regained consciousness. When police got into the car he was trying to drag Terra into, they found a backpack containing a gun, ammunition, tape, zip ties, and cyanide capsules. Not exactly tough to figure out what his plans were for Terra. My friend, investigator Julia Bowman, later described it as a kidnap-and-kill kit. I certainly did not disagree.

Most of the time, your job as a prosecutor is to meticulously assemble a case for criminal prosecution. Sometimes, it is equally important to methodically clear someone from any and all criminal culpability. The more I learned about the case, the more fascinated I became. Not only had Terra done absolutely nothing wrong—but she had, in fact, saved her mother, herself, and likely many others from whatever John Meehan was about to do next. Terra was another genuine hero I was privileged to meet during my time in Homicide.

Too good a story not to share, after Terra had been completely cleared, I called a buddy of mine named Chris Goffard, who works for the *Los Angeles Times*. A fantastic reporter, I thought he might like to share Terra's story with readers of the *Times*; instead, he shared it with the world. He put together the astounding *Dirty John* podcast and a series of articles that are really worth checking out. He dove into Meehan's background and revealed things that even I didn't know. During an associated event put together by the *Times,* I reunited with Terra and finally got to meet Cash. Cash and I hit it off immediately, and Terra and I have become friends. She is every bit as awesome as she sounds.

So, what is the takeaway from this, aside from never underestimating a California beach kid and her dog? The first is not to fall victim to the fallacy that we can do a better job at intuitively spotting psychos than Debra Newell did. When we are lonely, we can be very sympathetic targets to the emotionally unhinged or predatory. Meehan is an extreme example of what can go wrong when meeting and dating strangers online. There are a lot of people out there who may fall far short of attempting to kill a family member, but they can still march you right down the path to relationship misery.

My advice, having prosecuted more online-generated nightmare domestic violence cases than I can count, would be to cut, run, and return to the well if you encounter any of Dirty John's dirty behavioral traits. This list is oriented toward women meeting men, but it can really apply to anyone:

First, any man who asks for money, under any circumstance, needs to be blocked and deleted immediately. I don't care if it happens on your first date or your fifteenth. You should also report him to whatever site you are using.

Second, any man who gets physically aggressive with you, in any way, needs to go. It is beyond unacceptable. Those are the guys who murder their wives.

Third, any sort of criminal conviction, other than one DUI that he takes complete responsibility for, means your man is likely a complete loser who makes terrible decisions. There are exceptions to this, of course, but very few.

Fourth, any man who checks your cell phone is either massively insecure, controlling, or both.

Fifth, any man who seems sketchy about where he is living is either broke, living with his parents, or married.

Sixth, anyone who seems jealous of the time you spend with your own family members will eventually alienate you from anyone who may garner your attention instead of him.

Seventh, and this will be controversial among some men, but any guy who has a major problem with the men you work with, or even ex-boyfriends or ex-husbands with whom you have a positive relationship, is jealous and insecure. They will package their complaint as having a "healthy boundary," but in my view, there is nothing healthy about it. Trust is healthy; telling an adult woman who she can speak to is controlling and often leads to far greater instances of abuse.

Eighth, if a man doesn't have a job, it is only a matter of time before he will be living off your paycheck.

Ninth, any man who lies about his job will be comfortable lying about everything else.

Tenth, any guy who tries to rationalize a previous restraining order, or any prior act of domestic violence, is someone you do not want in your life.

Finally, eleventh, do your due diligence. Get his Instagram, tell your friends about him, and google the guy. If Debra Newell had simply googled John Meehan, her computer probably would have exploded.

When thinking about Dirty John, I can't help but go back to Rodney Alcala and how the *Dating Game* contestant chose him by his words—before she actually spent any time with the three-dimensional version of who he was. She was immediately too creeped out to even go on their date. Monsters can mask their true nature, especially in settings where you get limited exposure to their full selves. The online world can be a predator's playground because these psychopaths have been provided a platform where it is very easy to lie. Once emotions come into play and you've fallen for the predator, defenses are down, friends and family are alienated, and you can be very much alone when you finally realize who and what you are actually dealing with.

CHAPTER

8

NURISTAN PROVINCE

"THERE'S A BODY in my son's apartment . . . a dead body. Jesus, she's cold."

"Is it someone that you know, sir?"

"No, I have no idea who she is. I don't know what's going on."

"Does your son know who it is?"

"He's not here! Jesus, lady!"

"Do you know where your son is?"

"No, I don't. I told you . . ."

"Just keep breathing for me, sir, okay? Where in the apartment is she?"

"She's in the bedroom. She— Looks like there's been some sexual activity. She's dead. There's blood from her head. I touched her on the cheek. She's cold."

"There was blood from her head?"

"Yeah. Honey, I don't know what to tell you."

IIIIΛ\\\

Steve Herr was used to worrying about his son, Sam, twenty-six years old, who had been home a short time since being honorably discharged from the Army in 2009. Sam had served in one of the most dangerous parts of Afghanistan, near the northwestern Pakistani border. For a time, the US military strategy in Afghanistan had been one of interdiction—diverting, disrupting, and trying to destroy the enemy—along the rugged border. Army intelligence had determined that the Taliban had been receiving most of its supplies, as well as many of its fighting young men, from the madrassas—the Islamic religious schools—of this lawless and largely autonomous tribal area across the border in Pakistan, one of the most dangerous and inaccessible places in the world. The idea was to build a series of operating bases to support small combat outposts that could block the critical smuggling routes along the porous border, some of which probably dated back to the time of Alexander the Great. In fact, shortly after his rotation home, Sam's tiny base, Camp Keating, was famously overrun by the Taliban, which was repulsed in one of the most famous battles of the entire war.

The strategy was working, which meant the Taliban reacted as one might expect: They attacked these bases constantly. In one stretch, Sam saw combat eighty-three days in a row. It was far from easy. These outposts, isolated as they were, all ran on electric generators. To call in support, in the form of artillery or air strikes when the bases were under attack, electricity was needed. No generator meant no communication, and no communication meant no protection. But, for safety, the fuel used to run these generators needed to be stored in a different location on the base than the troops or the generators themselves. Under near-constant fire, the last thing they needed was for some lucky shot, or a careless smoker, to ignite the fuel and blow everyone up.

The Taliban knew all of this, so they would engage the base with attacks prolonged enough that the generators would surely run out of fuel and the support would stop—which would leave the soldiers as sitting ducks. When the fuel got low, someone would have to run through the open space, under enemy fire, and bring jerry cans—steel containers first used widely in World War II—of fuel back to the generators. At Camp Keating, in the Nuristan Province of Afghanistan, that poor brave bastard was Samuel Herr.

Sam had grown up in a small town just north of the San Fernando Valley, famous for Frank Zappa's iconic song "Valley Girl," Nicolas Cage's first starring role in a movie of the same name, and *The Karate Kid*. Sam ran into trouble as a teenager, with a major legal scrape when he was in high school. He spent a year in jail awaiting trial on serious charges, but a jury ultimately found him not guilty, and he was released. Much like my old boss Rick King, Sam did not like the direction of his life at that point—so he joined the military, where he learned how to repair those diesel generators he would end up risking his life to refuel.

Although several members of Sam's platoon were killed, and many more wounded, Sam returned home after three years of service without a physical scratch. He had spent a lot of time contemplating his future. He was ambitious, having pursued additional combat training in jump school to become a paratrooper. He wanted to return to the Army as an officer. This is a lot easier with higher education, so, taking advantage of the GI Bill, Sam enrolled at Orange Coast College

(OCC). He got an apartment in a sprawling complex across the street from the school called the Camden Martinique Apartments. It was sort of a Melrose Place, with frequent parties and multiple swimming pools, and was populated largely by other students. Sam made friends and was doing well in school, and his life seemed to be going very well. His parents, Steve and Raquel, were happy Sam was home and, most importantly, safe.

All of which is why Steve was not expecting to arrive at Sam's apartment on the evening of May 22, 2010, to find a dead body in Sam's bedroom—and no sign of his son. Sam was supposed to visit his parents that weekend and hadn't shown up. Calls to his cell phone were going unanswered. So, on Saturday night, Steve drove to Sam's apartment. Sam had given Steve a key, and he used it to open the door . . . and once he got a glimpse of the bedroom, Steve immediately called for help.

In a typical year, there are always a few homicides in Costa Mesa, and many look very similar to this, at least at first. The scene initially appeared to be a domestic violence murder. The victim, whose purse and identification were there in the apartment, was Julie Kibuishi, twenty-three years old, also a student at Orange Coast. She was found bent over the bed, face-down, her jeans around her knees, her head—wearing a tiara—was in a pool of blood on the comforter, and scrawled on the back of her shirt were the words "All Yours Fuck You." There was an open pregnancy test, and a strange pencil sketch of a woman in the middle of a fire labeled "I'm done," oddly left face up in the apartment. Julie's ringtone, Taylor Swift's "Today Was a Fairytale," sounded off constantly from her purse, creating a macabre soundtrack to the whole scene. And Sam was missing, presumed to be on the run.

I was more than two hours away that night, at a birthday dinner for the woman I was dating at the time. She wanted to visit her super-lovely grandparents, who lived in La Quinta, a small desert community near Palm Springs, California. We had just ordered when my phone rang. The relationship wasn't new; we had been seeing each other for over six months at that point, so the fact that my work could call me at any time wasn't exactly a surprise. And she was also a Deputy District Attorney, for Los Angeles County—though, most critically, *not* in Homicide.

There really was a difference, even between Units in the office. When work called in virtually any other assignment, it could absolutely wait until the morning. But when I got a call, it meant a killer was probably on the loose, and my cops needed me. Even if I had the choice to tell them I would deal with it later, I would never have done that. If I stuck around to finish a nice dinner, I would have been doing so at the same time some poor family was enduring the worst thing they could ever experience. Besides, the detectives who called me were more than professional colleagues; they had become my friends, and we'd been through a couple dozen murder cases together by this point in my time in Homicide.

So I didn't even think twice when I got the call—*of course* I was going to jump in the car and be at the scene as quickly as I could—especially with the most obvious suspect in the case assumed to be armed, dangerous, and roaming the streets. As we drove back to Orange County, my girlfriend turned to me. "I have to say, I think this is the worst birthday I've ever had." She repeated the line over and over again as we drove back with take-out boxes at our feet. Unsurprisingly, that relationship didn't last, just like the rest of them. I hate to say it, because of course I cared... but... I kind of didn't really care. Or, put another way, it was regrettable, and yet... I had no regrets. I was, I admit now, a terrible boyfriend.

As detectives began putting the pieces of the investigation together, it appeared pretty obvious that Sam Herr was responsible for this killing. There was no sign a stranger had broken into the apartment, and no clear motive beyond what seemed like anger over perhaps another man in Julie's life. And Sam did have a notable history: In addition to having seen real combat as a trained para-trooper, the legal scrape I mentioned earlier was actually for a murder charge. Eight years earlier, he had been accused of luring a friend to an area where the friend was then beaten to death in a gang-related killing. Sam, who was not in a gang, was also severely beaten. He was charged as an aider and abettor. We didn't know much about the case at that point, except that he had been acquitted, but having been a murder suspect in the past certainly caught our attention. We also wondered if there was a possibility of PTSD, given his service in Afghanistan. This young man had seen actual warfare, he had seen friends killed by the Taliban, and he had likely also killed people on the other side during the horrors of combat. Now there was a dead woman in his apartment, and he appeared to be on the run. Sam could not have been a more obvious suspect.

I attended Julie's autopsy the next morning. The Orange County sheriffs have a viewing room in the coroner's office where you can observe postmortem examinations from behind glass. Julie's was equal parts heartbreaking and thought-provoking. Her fatal injuries were obscured by layers of perfectly cut thick black hair. With the fine group of detectives I had on this case, I felt very confident we would solve every aspect . . . except for one: Where did she go? Where do any of us go?

Autopsies are profound things to observe, and I would often go down the rabbit hole of existential wonder. From a religious per-spective, I know that many would say Julie's soul went on to receive her eternal reward, the meaning of which varies depending on your religious tradition. But what is a soul? Philosopher René Descartes declared, "I think, therefore I am." As sentient beings, each of us knows he was right. When we feel love for the uniquely special traits of someone close to us, we know, intuitively, that there is a soul there.

Of course, cold, hard science might seem to lean the other way, with a rejection of any sort of afterlife. As Stephen Hawking once put it, "There is no heaven or afterlife for broken down computers; that is a fairy story for people afraid of the dark." All the more reason to *really live* now. But I'll see your Hawking and raise you Einstein, who insisted that energy can neither be created nor destroyed, merely changed from one form to another.

Somewhere in the cosmic/religious/ethereal mix, there is also justice. I would challenge philosophical nihilists, who believe that nothing really matters, to sit down with the bereaved mother of a murdered child and hold that view at the end of the conversation. From a moral perspective, what I was staring at on that cold pathology table was an affront to justice in every conceivable way. From the perspective of Julie's family, and the community at large, this was an outrage. Our task, as the law enforcement professionals responsible for this case, was to calmly and methodically untangle this mystery. Then, if successful, and within the strict limits of ethics and the law, we needed to do everything we legally could to set things right.

Police began an intense search for Sam, but Steve Herr was convinced that there was more to this story. He insisted that Sam would never have done this, especially once he realized that the victim was Julie, who was Sam's close, but entirely platonic, friend. Julie had met Sam at Orange Coast—initially tutoring him in an anthropology class, where he ultimately got an A. They had been spending a lot of time together, with Julie even sleeping over some nights in Sam's apartment . . . but always on the couch. To Steve, the fact that Julie had been murdered in Sam's bed made absolutely no sense. From the perspective of the police, this was not the first time they had seen a parent slow to accept that their son or daughter was capable of committing a terrible crime. Still, even in the context of a loving parent, Steve was persuasively insistent.

As the search continued, fruitlessly at first, Steve Herr embarked on his own parallel investigation. He talked to Sam's friends, and one of them, Ruben Salas, reported something surprising: He had called Sam's phone that weekend when Sam hadn't shown up to a party he had promised to attend, and someone had answered—but it wasn't Sam. It was a man whose voice he didn't recognize. "Who is this?" Ruben reportedly asked, and the man said, "I'm busy right now, lots of problems with my family."

"What are you talking about?" asked Ruben, and the man supposedly hung up.

This was more than curious to Steve because Sam was very close to his family—he even had a tattoo on his chest with a heart wrapped by the words "Mom & Dad"—and Steve felt confident he would know if there were any issues. It was also curious to Steve because this was not the only time these so-called family problems had come up in the first few days of the investigation. On Julie's phone, there was a string of text messages from Sam's phone, from the night before Steve found the body. "Can you come over tonight at midnight alone," one text said. "Going out for a bit. Very upset. Need to talk." The text messages painted a superficially convincing picture of a young man in crisis, a combat veteran who had seen terrible things and appeared to be at some emotional breaking point. Perhaps, it seemed, a young man so distraught that he was capable of committing murder.

"Please. No sex. I need to talk to someone," the texts continued. "I'm hurting with some bad fam crap. I can't be alone. No sex. Please, I'm begging as a brother."

Julie had written back, "lol ew Sam we are like bro and sis, no sex."

Again, Steve had no idea what this family drama could have possibly been. There was an earlier text from Sam's phone to Julie: "Not too much. Helping Dan. Then headed to folks for the weekend." So Steve called Dan—Sam's friend and neighbor Daniel Wozniak—to ask about this. Dan mentioned that the last time he saw Sam, he had been talking about having problems with the women in his family. Steve felt like none of this supposed family drama made any sense, and it made him very suspicious that something strange was going on.

Meanwhile, the sexual assault exam on Julie's body was negative, and friends insisted, just like Steve and Raquel Herr had said, that Sam and Julie were not sexually involved. There would have been no need for it to have been a secret affair if something had been going on. They were both single. So the murder scene was looking weirder and weirder, and the texts were seeming stranger, not to mention Ruben's reported phone call.

Another detail that didn't quite fit: Julie's body had marked areas of lividity and blanching on the skin of her buttocks. *Lividity* occurs when the heart stops beating and blood begins to settle in areas affected by gravity. *Blanching* happens when pressure on the skin forces the blood out. The combination results in red and white blotches that begin to set in anywhere from thirty minutes to about four hours after death. So a person who is lying on their back when they die will typically have lividity on their back, their buttocks, and the back of their thighs. Julie had it on her buttocks, in the shape of the back pockets of her jeans. You would expect to see that if she was on her back when she died, but she had been found bent, face forward, over Sam's bed. The crazed sexual assault/murder scenario seemed to be contradicted by the forensic evidence the moment the police got into Sam's bedroom. It suggested very strongly that Julie had been dead for at least thirty minutes, but probably more like several hours, before her jeans were cut off. That indicated a staged scene—but who had staged it, and why?

The questions only got more obvious. Steve had access to Sam's banking passwords and went online to check Sam's account. As it turned out, someone had been withdrawing money—and had even charged a pizza to Sam's debit card. The pizza place was half an hour up the coast, in Long Beach. Police had been tracking this activity as well. They got the video camera footage from the ATM withdrawals—but it wasn't Sam, or anyone known to be associated with him. In fact, it looked like a teenager wearing a hat and glasses to hide his face.

Police wanted to identify this person, so they looked for a connection. Was there someone who knew Sam, who lived in the Camden complex, and who had some connection to Long Beach? Police split up. Some watched a variety of ATM machines, some staked out the pizza place, and some wondered if Daniel Wozniak might be of more help finding Sam, even after Steve's conversation with him. There had been a wedding invitation on Sam's countertop, for the upcoming nuptials of Dan and his fiancée, Rachel Buffett. And Dan had grown up in Long Beach.

They went to one of Dan's listed addresses, and it appeared to be a storefront. When they walked inside, they encountered Dan and Rachel. Dan was cooperative and explained to the police that he had heard about Julie's murder from his friends. He said he had also heard that nobody could find Sam. He said he last saw Sam on Friday, the day before Julie's body was found, and that Sam had given him one hundred dollars to help pay his rent. He said Sam drove him to help take care of some wedding errands, since Dan and Rachel were set to get married that Friday, and that Sam was with another friend, a white guy in his twenties wearing a black baseball hat. Dan said they ate lunch, and then Sam dropped him back at the Camden and drove off with his friend in a black Mazda. Dan said he had not seen Sam since.

But the police were not finished in Long Beach. Later that day, Sam's ATM card was used again, at a Comerica bank, by the same teenager from the previous surveillance cameras—and this time, police had the bank staked out, so they saw the boy interact with someone in a green Smart car and then return to a house on Granada Avenue. The address matched the one detectives had learned was the delivery address from the pizza place. That afternoon, with police watching the pizza place, a second pizza was ordered for delivery to the same address, again using Sam's debit card, and this time they were ready. A police helicopter circled above, just in case, and officers approached the house expecting to find Sam inside, armed and dangerous.

Not quite. Instead, they found sixteen-year-old Wesley Freilich, the kid from the ATM surveillance footage, and his friends, inside Wesley's mother's house—staring wide-eyed at guns coming at them from every direction. Handcuffed and on the ground, Wesley later testified he "crapped his pants"—and as soon as police told him this was about a homicide investigation, Wesley revealed everything he knew. A man had told him he was working for a bail bondsman and needed a third party to help collect money for the city from someone who had skipped bail. He told him it was "kind of legal, not really illegal," and produced a stack of paperwork supposedly proving the legitimacy of the plan. He asked Wesley to take money out of banks using this person's ATM card, and told him he could order some pizzas on the card as a bonus. Wesley—again, just sixteen years old—believed this was legitimate, especially because he knew the man, and trusted him.

Who was the man?

It was Daniel Wozniak.

Suddenly, we were able to start connecting some dots. Wozniak had met Wesley six years earlier, when he was ten years old and involved in a play at a local theater. Wesley's mom was a theater teacher, and Wesley was drawn to acting. Dan was a local performer and had taken

Wesley under his wing. "[He was] a fantastic guy," Wesley later said about Dan. "One of those guys that you actually wanted to be around. Made you laugh. Very sweet person."

Dan may have acted sweet, but at this point, he was also financially desperate. He and Rachel were unemployed local actors, and Dan could barely keep a job. He had worked at Verizon for a short time, then AAA. He trained at another company but never showed up for his first day. He worked at a startup for two months, earning a total of $250. He was being paid nothing for the lead performance in his current play, the Hunger Artists Theatre production of the musical *Nine*.

Just days before Julie's murder, Dan was served an eviction notice. He owed over $3,000 in back rent. His bank accounts were overdrawn. He was trying to borrow money from everyone he knew. The previous summer, he had been arrested on a DUI and failed to appear in Court. The week before Julie's murder, he was stopped for a seat belt violation and arrested because of the outstanding warrant. He scrambled to put together enough money for bail. He was facing pending legal costs, not to mention the unpaid rent and the need for money to cover his and Rachel's everyday expenses. (She was unemployed as well.)

Dan and Wesley hadn't talked in two years when Wozniak called him, out of the blue, on the Tuesday before Julie's body was found. Wesley knew nothing about Julie, and nothing about Sam, except that he had his ATM card and PIN. But Daniel Wozniak clearly knew Sam, and we were starting to wonder if this case was as straightforward as it had seemed.

The investigators knew their next step: They had to talk to Dan again. They believed at this point that Dan had not been truthful earlier, and that he knew much more than he had initially revealed. We thought he was going to be the key to finding Sam, and probably a critical witness in delivering justice to Julie's family. It still appeared that Sam was dangerous and on the run—though others in the investigation were starting to wonder if this was something far more diabolical and complex. Time, as always, was of the essence. Detectives called Dan and asked him to meet for a more formal interview. He said he couldn't talk because he had his bachelor party that night. But when detectives are investigating a murder, you can't just push them off until it's convenient.

Clearly, Wozniak had withheld some information from the police, and at the very least appeared to be an accessory after the fact to murder. That is a felony, so detectives decided to crash his party at Tsunami Sushi in Huntington Beach. They arrested Dan for helping Sam, and transported him to Costa Mesa to conduct a formal interview. Detectives Mike Delgadillo and Mike Cohen, two old-school veteran police officers, began their interview of Dan, and it was like watching an actor who couldn't quite remember his lines. Dan was smooth at first, and quite charming, but his story kept changing in subtle, and then not-so-subtle, ways.

It didn't take long before Dan's tale started to sound bizarre. Wozniak said he was involved in a credit card scam with Sam, helping him cover up Julie's murder. He said that Sam knocked on his door on Saturday morning, told him there was a body in his apartment, and that he needed money. Wozniak said that he decided to involve Wesley, but lied to get Wesley to do it. Wozniak then said that Sam told him the murder was part of a drug-fueled rage when Julie refused to have sex with him. Wozniak said he never saw Julie's body and never saw the gun. He said Sam threatened to kill him and Rachel if he didn't help. He said he drove Sam to the Los Alamitos military base to think, and there they came up with a plan to have Wesley withdraw cash from Sam's bank account and have Sam call in thirty days to get the money. Dan later shifted his story and said he dropped Sam off at a shopping mall in Long Beach and hadn't seen him since.

"I lied and I'm sorry for lying," he told detectives. "I made up the mystery man [in the baseball hat]. I'm an actor, and I lied to Wesley, too."

Wozniak went on to say that Sam was depressed about his family, that he was taking drugs, and that he killed Julie. He told the detectives he had abandoned Sam's car after he dropped him off at the mall. Throughout the interview, Wozniak appeared to be reciting a story he had come up with before. But to the experienced detectives, it was a story that didn't make any sense.

First, why would Sam involve Dan in this at all? Why not just go to the bank and take out all of his money before Julie's body was discovered? And why was Wesley saying that Dan had approached him about the bank card plan days earlier? Why would Dan help Sam instead of calling the police? Why, of all places a person could go to "think," would Sam ever want to go to a military base? Why would Sam want to be dropped off at a shopping mall if he was trying to run away from the scene? Once again, just like with Sam Lopez's initial interview in the Cathy Torrez case, things so often come down to human behavior. Would normal people act like this? If not, what was really going on?

Detectives took a DNA swab from Dan, and it is very clear on the recording that Wozniak thought the interview was finished and he was going to be allowed to leave. He picked up his coffee cup and said, "Hey, that was easy," and started to get up. He clearly believed detectives bought his story, but he also didn't realize that helping a murderer get away is a serious crime in itself. At this point in the investigation, it still appeared that Sam was likely the killer, and Dan had been helping him. I still thought Dan would probably lead us to Sam, he would be arrested, and the case would begin its journey through the system.

Wozniak, however, just kept talking, and his story continued to drift. Dan insisted he didn't know where Sam was, or where the gun was, but he said he really wanted to get to his wedding on Friday, and offered to make a deal. As detectives began pressing him on some of the details of his story, Wozniak said he would tell them where Sam was if they agreed to let him go free. That was . . . not the way these things work. And Wozniak's offer meant that he had been continuing to hold back information.

At this point, detectives decided to employ an investigative technique known as a *ruse*—basically a bluff. DNA results wouldn't be back for days, and more likely even weeks, but it was clear that Dan didn't have a great handle on the mechanics of a criminal investigation. On TV, we often see this kind of thing done aggressively, with angry accusations from the detectives, and voices raised on both sides. Good drama in a movie, but lousy police work in real life. Experienced detectives, the true professionals, often comport themselves with the exact opposite approach. They want the suspect to like them, to trust them, to let down their guard, and, mostly, to keep talking. Like everything in life, it is almost always better to be nice. Here, they politely informed Dan that his DNA was found on Julie's body, just to see where that would take his story. Dramatically, Wozniak raised his voice to a shout and changed the story yet again: "Okay, I saw the goddamned body! Is that what you want to hear?" *The goddamned body?* He then told detectives he had been standing over her, and that must be how his DNA got there. The detectives explained that DNA doesn't just fall off a person and onto a dead body. "I saw two gunshots in her head. And I saw her pants . . . like ripped and cut."

Detective Sergeant Ed Everett had been monitoring the interview closely from another room. We had all either been to the scene, attended the autopsy, or both. For Everett, this was the moment the investigation changed. Unless Dan had been there when the gun was fired, there is no way he could have seen "two gunshots" in her head.

All you could really see was blood and brains. There were no neat holes or clear bullet exits. Just long, stylish black hair, and Julie's tiara. There was just no way. Everett entered the room, and pushed back. Wozniak tried to backtrack. He said Sam told him he shot her twice. Then he said he helped clean up the bullet casings. He was digging himself a deeper and deeper hole, not only putting himself in the position of helping Sam get away, but potentially even being there for the murder. At the very least, he had confessed to cleaning up the scene.

Police brought in Dan's fiancée, Rachel Buffett, to interview her as well. After speaking to her, detectives put her in the room with Dan. Sergeant Everett asked Wozniak to explain to Rachel what he had just confessed to them. When Wozniak started speaking, Rachel's reaction was also notable. She was completely unemotional—clinical, even. It was as if they'd rehearsed their back-and-forth. She was supposedly being told for the first time that their friend Sam had killed their other friend Julie—and that her fiancé had helped him. Detectives were expecting disbelief and horror, but there was no emotion at all. It was as if she knew it all already, which made us think that perhaps she did. Her knowledge wouldn't make her a principal in the murder, but it could mean she was an accessory after the fact, like Dan. At this point, we just didn't know.

Rachel's interview contained some interesting nuggets. At one point, she misunderstood a question and thought detectives were asking about her sex life with Dan. "Well, it's not exactly friggin' awesome," she said, intimating that Wozniak had a small penis. After the police let Rachel go, they sent Dan back to his holding cell. Later, he asked to call Rachel. The jail phone is, of course, a recorded line. It was not monitored in real time, but as detectives listened to the tape afterward, they were stunned by the back-and-forth.

Rachel: *What did you do?*

Dan: *I helped Sam cover some stuff up and helped him get some drugs. That's it. I didn't murder anybody.*

[Later]

Rachel: *My mom's working on canceling all the wedding plans now. And I just talked to Tim and I need to make a phone call to the detective now.*

[Tim is Dan's brother. More about him soon.]

Dan: *Why?*

Rachel: *I need to call the detective first, because I need to call him and let him know before they catch me on this recording device because it looks like I'm not trying to tell 'em right away. Tim says he has evidence with him or he knew where it was or something.*

Dan: *Then I'm doomed.*

Rachel: *Yeah. Do you know that Tim had some evidence?*

Dan: *Yeah. Oh God, oh God, oh God. Okay.*

Rachel: *He was really frantic and he said something and something slipped that he had evidence. So I have to—*

Dan: *No don't, don't, don't, don't, don't. That can't be found.*

Rachel: *You realize they're recording this phone conversation anyways? You're being an absolute ass to try and lie again.*

Rachel had gone to Dan's family's house to let them know Dan had been arrested. His brother Tim told her he had evidence. Once Rachel told Dan that she was going to go to detectives with this information, Dan decided he needed to talk to them himself.

He asked for a meeting. He said he had something he needed to tell detectives. Jose Morales brought him into the interrogation room and was shocked by what he heard. "You said you wanted to talk to me, what's going on?" he asked.

"I'm crazy, and I did it."

"You did what?"

"I killed Julie, and I killed Sam."

We knew Wozniak was in deep, but for my part, I certainly did not expect this. We had no real evidence, until this moment, that Sam wasn't just on the run. Although others suspected Dan was shady, his true involvement was unclear, and I have to credit the detectives who refused to bite on the obvious clues when they first entered Sam's apartment. But this . . . ? Sam was a badass combat veteran, and Wozniak was an out-of-shape, pasty-white, unemployed community theater actor who let his fiancée walk all over him. This was more than a huge twist; this changed everything. Wozniak went on to explain that he had killed Sam first, with Wozniak's father's antique pistol, and that he did it for money—$62,000 that he'd learned Sam had saved in combat pay.

See, as you might imagine, the rugged mountain passes in Afghanistan didn't offer a young soldier much in the way of nightlife, or other opportunities to spend his money, so Sam carefully saved his salary, sending it home for his father, Steve, who helped Sam manage his bank account while he was away. That $62,000 was going to be life-changing for Sam, to help him realize his ambition of going back to the Army as an officer. Instead, it was his downfall.

Dan had lured Sam to the Liberty Theatre on the Los Alamitos military base, saying he needed help to move some stuff. They went up a ladder to an attic above the stage, and Dan asked Sam to bend down to help him lift something. He then drew the pistol and shot him in the back of the head. The first shot didn't kill him. Sam said to Dan, "I need help. Something shocked me." The ancient firearm jammed, and in one of the only competent things Daniel Wozniak ever did in his entire miserable life, he cleared the jam, reracked the next round, and aimed at the side of Sam Herr's skull, shooting him again, this time killing him.

Sadly, Daniel Wozniak was only getting started. This was Friday afternoon. Dan left Sam's body in the attic, took his keys, phone, and wallet—he had to have memorized Sam's PIN at some point, watching over Sam's shoulder at some ATM—and drove directly to involve an innocent sixteen-year-old kid. He picked up Wesley Freilich and drove him to a nearby bank to withdraw the first batch of cash. Wesley had never used an ATM before. Wozniak then began texting Sam's friends, trying to lure one of them into the next phase of his plan. The first potential victim did not respond to the texts from Sam's phone, and her slow response absolutely saved her life.

Tragically, soon after, Julie texted Sam to see how he was doing. This meant she had unwittingly just landed in Wozniak's sticky web. Wozniak knew her, of course. She was often around the Camden apartments, and was frequently visiting Sam with Sam's buddy Lester. She was even Facebook friends with Rachel, Dan's fiancée. Wozniak would have known she was sweet, and fun, and totally innocent. He would have known she was a student at OCC and probably that she dreamed of being a fashion designer. And as someone who would certainly respond to a friend in trouble, she was perfect for what Wozniak wanted to do. What he didn't know, which would later prove to be a critical error, was that her relationship with Sam Herr was purely platonic. Wozniak sent her the first of several text messages. The exchange is a perfect representation of both the cynical manipulation of Daniel Wozniak and the sweet innocence of Julie Kibuishi:

Dan (as Sam): *I really just want to talk. I can't talk about it. I need someone I trust.*

Julie: *You can trust me I promise. Im not going to say anything I promise. Pinky promise.*

[Later]

Dan: *Thank you. Be here at midnight? Ill be back around then.*

Julie: *OK I cant spend the night though*

Dan: *That's cool. Youre saving my life.*

Julie: *Im sorry: (but I promise to be there at midnight*

Dan: *OK. Thank you so much again. I feel I have no one I can share this with. You sure you wont let me down.*

Julie: *I never let my friends down when they need me there no prob:)*

Dan: *Thank you. You are an angel*

So, while Sam's body was beginning to enter the first stages of human decomposition in the attic of a community theater on a military base, the trap for Julie had been set. Dan then proceeded—you are not reading this wrong—to *perform that evening* in his lead role in *Nine*, singing, dancing, and laughing.

For those unfamiliar with the play, it is a musical about a fictional Italian film director named Guido Contini who is reflecting on his fortieth birthday and the mistakes of his life. In one scene, Wozniak was required to croon the song "Getting Tall" to a small boy, representing the director in his youth. It is literally about growing up and taking responsibility for yourself. Wozniak nailed the performance, and utterly failed to contemplate the meaning of the song.

The entire play centered around Dan's character, and he didn't appear to miss a single line. No one suspected a thing. The play ended at around 10:30 p.m. Julie had been at dinner with her brother, Taka, where he asked her to be a bridesmaid in his upcoming wedding. Julie was positively thrilled, and he gave her a tiara to wear on the big day. She was so excited that she put it on immediately. The texts from Dan (as Sam) continued, and Julie told Taka that Sam was having a hard time. Taka, who adored his sister, worried that Julie was going to be out too late. He asked her to text him when she got there.

Dan: *How long you thinkin?*

Julie: *30 minutes*

Dan: *Cool. Just teyt me at fwy. Please don't bring ayone. I really don't want anyone else to know whats going on.*

Julie: *no im by myself*

Julie: *Just exited*

Julie: *hey buddy im here and im walking to your place*

Julie [to Taka]: *I'm at sams*

Julie [to Sam]: *?*

Taka: *Ok! Gnite! We had a lot of fun tonight. Be safe.*

Julie [to Taka]: *ya!!! :) Thank you so much*

Julie [to Sam]: *hey buddy where are you? Im freezing*

Julie [which was certainly Wozniak at this point] [to Taka]: *(Uh oh sam is crying its not good :(*

That was the final text from Julie's phone, and Wozniak confessed that he met Julie outside of Sam's apartment and told her that Sam had asked him to come, too. Dan let them into the apartment, and told Julie she should go see something on Sam's bed. She bent over and he shot her in the head, twice, and then went back to his apartment as if nothing had happened.

He literally killed Julie Kibuishi, an innocent twenty-three-year-old woman, to use her body as a decoy. He wanted to create a false trail of evidence indicating that Sam was on the run and throw police off the scent. As her brother Taka would later testify: "What the hell?"

Two murders already committed, Saturday was a busy day for Daniel Wozniak. First, he returned to Sam's apartment to stage the scene, cutting Julie's jeans (thus the unexpected lividity on Julie's skin), writing the message on her shirt, drawing his weird sketch, and finding and taking Sam's checkbook and passport. He used Wesley to get more cash from Sam's account, then realized he had to deal with Sam's corpse. (Wait, this just keeps getting better.) Realizing he couldn't carry Sam's entire body by himself, he stopped by a friend's house and got some tools. He climbed up the ladder into the theater attic, proceeded to cut off Sam's clothing with scissors, and then hacked off Sam's right forearm with a wood saw and chopped off his left arm below the elbow with a hatchet. Wozniak then *chopped and sawed Sam's head off*. He packed the arms and head in a backpack, then drove to a nearby nature park and threw them into the bushes in a relatively secluded area.

He returned to his apartment, took a relaxing dip in the Jacuzzi, and went back to Hunger Artists Theatre to—of course—perform again that night. He then went to the cast party, where there are pictures of him smiling, laughing, talking, and drinking. Wozniak went back to his apartment afterward, met with his brother Tim, and gave him a backpack filled with things he asked Tim to get rid of. He said there had been some trouble in the Camden apartments. It's not clear if Tim asked any questions, but Tim, loyal to his brother, agreed to get rid of the items.

Tim was a little like the character Jeff Spicoli from *Fast Times at Ridgemont High*, the archetype of a cartoonish, blond-haired Southern California surfer who has smoked way too much pot. Despite his brother's instructions not to open the bag, Tim couldn't resist and found a bloody mess, along with their father's antique pistol. He gave the gun to a friend, and, like a child who thinks something out of sight is "gone," Tim threw the backpack over a fence . . . at Wozniak's parents' house.

When police found the backpack (not hard), it was as if Dan had left us a Christmas present: Sam's clothing, watch, wallet, and phone, and Dan's bloody clothes and gloves. All the evidence anyone might need, just in case, for some reason, they doubted Dan's confession when he told us what he'd done and led us to where he'd dismembered Sam's body, dumped Sam's car, and discarded Sam's forearms and head. (As cadaver dogs searched the nature center, on Sam's birthday, as it happened, Steve Herr later testified he was just "hoping and praying they find my son's head.")

Dan's DNA was found on Sam's bloody clothes. Police eventually recovered the murder weapon, which was forensically determined to have been used in both murders and was also covered in Dan's DNA.

So the physical evidence was very strong. In fact, it was overwhelming.

As the investigation continued, detectives requested forensic analysis of the various phones and computers that had been collected in the case. And it turned out that failed actor Daniel Wozniak, as if he wasn't done providing evidence, had conducted the following Google searches on the desktop computer in his apartment:

"Making sure a body is not found"

"Head gun shot"

"How to hide a body"

"Quick ways to kill people"

Worse, the analysis revealed that after he would do a search related to murder, he would then immediately look at cruise lines to see which one might be best for a honeymoon. He would google the decibel level for a gunshot, then search for awesome vacations for actors in Mexico. You could literally read his mind based on his internet activity in the days leading up to the murders of Sam and Julie. Notably, one search he never conducted was for how to get a legitimate job and pay his rent.

Was this stupidity? Arrogance? Or heaping stacks of both?

Most families who have lost a loved one to murder land somewhere on a spectrum between sadness and anger. June Kibuishi, Julie's mother, was obviously devastated. She loved her daughter, and she was sweet, and kind, and now broken. Steve Herr, on the other hand, was enraged. His son had survived the worst the Taliban could dish out, and he had made it home safely. Now his life had been taken by some loser too lazy and self-important to simply get a job. What do you do with that level of grief in a case like this? We had overwhelming evidence of guilt, and these murders—given the planning, the banality of the goal, and the senselessness of taking a human life so he could stage her like some sort of theater prop—were shocking.

Daniel Wozniak also seemed to have precious little going his way in terms of mitigating circumstances. He was raised in a good home, in a nice neighborhood. His mother and father loved him and provided for him, and he went to a fine high school. He wasn't mentally ill, or a drug addict, and, much like with Rodney Alcala, there was no evidence he was ever bullied or abused by anyone. If he ever was, it certainly wasn't at the hands of Julie Kibuishi or Sam Herr. He was just entitled and in love with his own ability to be clever. With overpowering evidence, a truly horrific crime, and zero meaningful mitigation, the elected District Attorney (my main boss) decided we would seek the death penalty. I certainly did not disagree.

I haven't yet explained what the decision to seek death really means under the law. In California, seeking the death penalty means a careful consideration and weighing of the aggravating and mitigating circumstances in each individual case. Known as the A through K factors, these aggravating and mitigating considerations include the circumstances of the offense, the impact on the surviving family members, other crimes of violence, and whether the defendant was under the influence of alcohol or drugs or under the influence of another person at the time they committed the act.

A juror is tasked with weighing these factors against those in mitigation, which include pretty much anything that lessens or contextualizes the severity of the crime. Was the defendant horribly abused as a child? Was there history between the victim and the defendant that puts the killing into some sort of context? Does the juror have any sense of lingering doubt regarding the guilt of the defendant?

The law allows for very wide latitude in what can properly be considered in mitigation, as it should. In the case of Daniel Wozniak—just like with Skylar Deleon, Rodney Alcala, and others—the District Attorney, Tony Rackauckas in this case, believed the crime was sufficiently shocking to seek death.

The defense team assigned to Daniel Wozniak was composed of two very smart and experienced public defenders. One comported herself as a consummate professional. The other, in my opinion, did not. The problem is that when you inject the emotion of the death penalty, and the near-religious zeal with which some oppose it, a "win at all costs" mentality can creep in. Some defense lawyers will even resort to unfair accusations of misconduct against police officers, prosecutors, judges, and even victims' family members, all in the name of preventing what they believe to be a barbaric result.

The danger of allowing personal ideological beliefs to infect professional decision-making is that you can quickly devolve into holding an "ends justify the means" mentality. If an attorney believes that the death penalty is barbaric, it takes a degree of professional discipline not to take the next step.

It is a very slippery slope, and one that the best defense lawyers manage to avoid. In three thousand years of Western philosophical thought, the ends have never justified the means, and they never will. Lawyers who engage in that form of advocacy—the tactical false accusation—quickly become the purveyors of exactly what they profess to abhor, far too blind by anger and ideology to recognize the hypocrisy of what they are doing. Like former California Supreme Court Chief Justice Rose Bird, they may get cheers from those of a similar ideological mindset, but I believe it is intellectually dishonest and fundamentally unfair to the innocent family members who have to endure years of process that has been designed, after all, to ensure fairness.

I believe the role of the criminal defense lawyer to be sacrosanct in the American system of justice. When a person is accused of a crime, any crime, they are and should be afforded a trained professional who will assert every lawful defense, argue every mitigating factor, and zealously represent the interests of the person who has been accused. What, after all, could be more ruinous to the life of a good person than to be accused of something they did not do?

When an attorney appears to be motivated by ideology as much as by the law, even the fairest judges can reach their limits. After several years of contentious litigation, the assigned judge in this case, the Honorable James Stotler, shocked the Orange County legal community when he announced, in effect, that he was so tired of the defense attorney's antics that he found himself entertaining biased thoughts against the lawyer, which he knew was unfair to the defendant and required his immediate recusal.

Stotler is a good man, a good judge, and it was certainly the right thing to do, but it set us back a year. The various pretrial motions filed by the defense, some certainly legitimate and necessary, ultimately required 192 hearings before the case finally went to trial. The Herr and Kibuishi families attended every single one of them, and it was brutal. Steve Herr developed issues with his heart, and both June and Masa Kibuishi (Julie's parents) developed, and then battled, various forms of cancer while the case was pending. It is difficult to believe all of their health conditions were not made worse by the stress of the criminal proceedings.

We finally got to jury selection five years after the murders took place. Jury selection is critically important in any trial, but especially when you're asking twelve people to vote for death. Still, trial lawyers are some of the most superstitious people I know, and I am no exception. Like the baseball players in the movie *Bull Durham*, everyone has their set of rituals. For me, I have always felt like jury selection is a little like a first date. You want to make your finest impression, and look your best, but you don't want the potential jurors to think you're trying too hard.

I needed a new pair of dress shoes for the trial, and had purchased a brand-new pair of black Allen Edmonds oxfords. I was getting ready for bed the night before jury selection and realized that I had not scuffed the shoes at all. I knew I was inevitably going to cross my legs at some point and the jurors would see the bottoms of my shoes. I didn't want them to look new. (This is the kind of thinking that went through my head before every trial, I promise.)

My most comfortable pajamas were (please don't judge me here) a pair of glow-in-the-dark zombie pajamas that I had been given as a gift. They might have been ridiculous, but they were cozy. I called my lead detective to quadruple-check that all conceivable discovery had been provided to the defense before we started the next day. I also wanted to get his thoughts on a couple of the juror questionnaires. I walked outside to scuff up the bottoms of my new shoes, and was pacing back and forth on the sidewalk outside my house. My neighbor had run his sprinklers, and there was a wet newspaper on my drive-way that I picked up, one of those rolled-up free community papers that I intended to toss when I went back down my driveway.

I was stressed and sad about more than just this case. A stray cat, Carl, I'd adopted the year before had just been run over by a car in front of my house, and it absolutely broke my heart. I was living on a residential street with a twenty-five-miles-per-hour speed limit, and the driver who struck my cat must have been going fifty. The car didn't even stop. I was mad at the street, mad at the drivers, and stressed by the case, and we had national media in the courtroom day after day. I was operating on maybe four hours of sleep a night and reviewing juror questionnaires in my mind. One of the jurors had said they believed the death penalty was the same as murder . . . but that they could be fair. Could they, with a core belief like that? I wasn't sure.

And then I heard the deep, throaty sound of a V8 engine coming down the street. I could tell it was an SUV even though its brights were on. It blew through the stop sign on the corner without even slowing down. A dick move, especially considering how many children live on my street—and this guy was going at least fifty. Carl's murderer, no doubt. I threw the wet newspaper at the side of the car as it sped past, and it turned out to be a good throw. A perfect throw, in fact, landing right in between the "Manhattan Beach" on the top of the front passenger door and "Police Department" underneath. It sounded like I had hit a bass drum with a sledgehammer.

The driver slammed on the brakes, and I was staring at two police officers wondering what had just happened. And they saw some dude in glow-in-the-dark zombie pajamas and shiny new dress shoes with a shocked look on his face. "Hey, Jose," I said to my detective on the phone, "I think you might have to come up here and bail me out of jail, buddy."

There is a great scene in the movie *This Is Spinal Tap* when one of the band leaders explains that the bizarre gardening accident that took the life of their first drummer was a mystery the police said was best left unsolved. I think this was one of those situations.

After a moment, the driver hit the gas and kept on going. I pretended like I didn't throw anything, and they pretended nothing hit their car. Better for everyone.

The absurdity of that moment quickly gave way to serious questions about the trial. When picking a death-qualified jury, you have to be very strategic about the choices you make. Twelve people are randomly selected to be in that box at first, and you get twenty peremptory challenges to start knocking people out who you suspect might not go your way. But the more aggressive you get with your challenges, the more you're inviting your opponent to do the same. It's a very specific skill set, really. How well can you read the mind and read the heart of someone you've never met before—and how much do you want to risk that the next person who fills that seat won't be even worse?

On a previous case, I had learned a valuable lesson regarding death-qualified jurors. The defendant was a man named Jason Balcom, accused of raping, sodomizing, and murdering a newly pregnant twenty-two-year-old newlywed in her apartment in Costa Mesa in broad daylight. It was a cold case from 1988 that we had resurrected with DNA evidence, and I made a big jury selection mistake. There were three social workers from the very same office randomly selected on the jury. All of them, truly, would have been excellent jurors, but I got it in my head that I couldn't allow three people who knew each other from the same office. I kicked one of them, and his seat was filled by a woman who seemed perfect on paper—a rich, well-educated stay-at-home mother from Newport Beach—and I ignored the bad vibe I got from her. I instead relied on her absolutely ideal questionnaire. She ended up hanging the jury 11–1 for death, insisting she would never vote for it. We had to do a whole new penalty phase with a brand-new jury—and he ended up getting the death penalty at the end of that one, but the strategic error stuck with me. I needed, from that point forward, to trust my gut before kicking someone out of that box—and to rely far more on how I felt about them than simply on what they had written in their questionnaire.

Without questionnaires, which are rarely allowed by judges, you generally aren't given any information about potential jurors beyond their names, and you can't go home and research them. So a good lawyer will learn to look at every visible detail when evaluating a potential juror. What are they wearing? How do they carry themselves? What book are they holding as they walk into the courtroom? In the end, jury selection is far more art than science. What is the energy you feel? Are they interacting with other jurors? Paying attention to the judge? Is this a person who will likely listen to you in the end? You must learn to first develop an instinct, and then trust it. Not to sound too Californian here, but it is as much about a person's vibe as anything tangible. As luck would have it, the potential juror who said she believed the death penalty was the same as murder was among the first twelve jurors seated. I had her down as an automatic kick, but I liked everyone else in the box and didn't want to lose them. She was the opposite of my rich lady from Newport. Terrible on paper, but a great vibe. She said while she personally disagreed with the death penalty, she could follow the law. Some of the best judges of potential jurors are the police officers and detectives who have had to read people as if their lives depended on it, because in police work they often do. And Jose was as smart and observant as anyone I had ever worked with. If I kicked her, I would likely lose all the other jurors I really liked. If I kept her, and accepted the first twelve, I would have eleven jurors I really liked and one huge question mark.

Jose said he liked her. "She's with you, buddy," he said. He believed she would be open-minded, and got the same vibe I did, but I didn't know whether to trust it. Here's the thing: We strategized that if we didn't kick her, the defense might believe I had overlooked her questionnaire and also accept the first twelve. If they didn't, then I would excuse her and move on. But I was going to see what happened if I accepted the first twelve, and take the risk that our gut instincts were right. It was a high-stakes game of chicken.

I accepted the panel as constituted, and so did the defense. Wow. We empaneled our jury without exercising a single peremptory challenge. Unusual, but not unheard of. Still, I immediately started second-guessing myself. It was actually a smart move by the defense, and an advanced mental strategy on my part had just become advanced self-doubt. So be it. We had a jury.

The Wozniak trial was a weeks-long slugfest. I have to admit the defense did an excellent job for their client given what they had to work with. In the end, the evidence was simply overwhelming. In order to pay his rent and go on a super-bitchin' honeymoon, Daniel Wozniak elaborately plotted the murder of two innocent and beloved human beings.

Perhaps the most egregious part, when you think about it, is that even if Dan was going to kill Sam for his $62,000, Julie Kibuishi didn't need to die. Once the brutal murder of Sam was complete, all Wozniak had to do was send a text from Sam's cell phone that he was having some issues (about anything at all) and was going to take a few weeks to get his head together. Steve and Raquel would have known that something was dramatically wrong, but an adult male, posing no apparent risk to the community, would have been a very low priority for any police department. People "go missing" all the time who eventually turn up in Vegas on a bender, or in Cabo, or in rehab, and police simply don't have the resources or inclination to hunt everyone down who hasn't talked to their parents in a while.

A disturbed combat veteran on the loose, however, who has seemingly just raped and murdered someone in his apartment, is an all-hands-on-deck, no-resource-spared emergency situation. So not only was Wozniak's plan utterly horrific in every conceivable way; it was stupid.

Killing just Sam would have given him weeks to drain the bank account. Killing Julie guaranteed that every cop in Orange County would be hunting for him. Along the way, Dan literally danced and sang, left a trail of irrefutable evidence, and severed a human head. The jury returned the fastest death verdict in the history of Orange County.

As for Rachel Buffett, we always believed she knew far more than she revealed to police. But she didn't just hold back information—she positively lied. Big lies, little lies; her story never added up. We believed she knew Dan was somehow involved in Julie's murder, but what she knew and when she knew it remains an open question. Without solid evidence that she knew beforehand, or that she deliberately aided in the commission of the acts in some way, we couldn't charge her with either murder. Once again, it doesn't matter how reprehensible someone may be; if you can't prove it, you can't charge it. A prosecutor, above all else, must honor the presumption of innocence. I could prove that Rachel lied after the murders, and that is what we did. She was tried as an accessory after the fact the following year, and was convicted and sentenced to thirty-two months in state prison.

Did Dan really think he was getting away with this? The answer doesn't matter, because he didn't get away with it. He'll never see freedom again.

CHAPTER

9

VEGAS, BABY

LAGUNA BEACH IS a phenomenal place to live—especially if you're a surfer. With Newport Beach and Huntington Beach to the north, and San Clemente to the south, Laguna is an eclectic community nestled on the side of a small coastal mountain range overlooking the rocky coves and kelp beds of southern Orange County. The place has always fostered its own unique brand of surf culture. Timothy Leary—of LSD fame—moved there in the 1960s to "turn on, tune in, drop out," and the Beach Boys sang about it in "Surfin' Safari."

Aside from the surfing, with a thriving and dynamic gay community, expensive homes, fine dining, and fancy galleries, Laguna is also renowned for its many resident artists. Having lived there for my first four years after law school, I may be biased, but I believe it is one of the most picturesque places on the entire West Coast. When most people think about the stereotypical California lifestyle, they forget that much of the state is composed of desert, farmland, and the often-frigid climate of Northern California. But for those fortunate enough to actually live that quintessential surfer lifestyle, places like Laguna Beach are home to some of the happiest people on the planet. One of those lucky few was Chris Smith.

Chris grew up in a small town near Santa Cruz, California, in a house on a lake, where he and his younger brother, Paul, fell in love with all things water. From a very early age, Chris was obsessed with surfing, and for a time even hoped to become a professional wakeboarder. An injury to his Achilles tendon redirected him into the business world, and he moved to the Southern California community of Temecula (not quite on the water, but not too bad of a drive), where he took a job in the advertising business.

Like pretty much every young surfer at one point or another, Chris spoke openly of his dream of one day sailing off into the sunset, with a surfboard under one arm and a good-looking woman under the other. But he had a career to build first—and money to earn. After a couple of years, Chris met another young man in the advertising world, Ed Shin. Ed worked for a different company, and the two often crossed paths. They instantly liked each other.

Chris and Ed were both young, handsome, and ambitious. But there were differences between them. Chris was very smart, but more of an artist at heart than a businessman like Ed. An adrenaline junkie who loved fast boats, faster cars, and big waves, Chris was always looking for adventure and the promise of a life of freedom on the water. Like me, he took regular surf trips to Costa Rica, Mexico, and Indonesia, and while he loved his family—he was very close to Paul, Paul's wife, Leah, and his two young nieces—he enjoyed the single life.

Ed seemed the model of stability in comparison. He had a business degree from UC San Diego, a devoted wife, and three young children. Shin was active in his church and participated in biweekly Bible study classes. He loved taking his kids to Disneyland. He had even found his job through a businessman he met in Bible study, Joseph Gray. Gray had given Ed a chance to help him launch a new online advertising venture after Joseph had found success in a related TV ad business.

Ed was eager to move on from Joseph's company, though, and before too long, he and Chris decided to leave their respective jobs and start a business together. They figured they could combine their skill sets to build their own ad company and stop making money for other people. In 2009, they started 800XChange, staking out a corner of the ad business known as lead generation. Think about the late-night commercials and online banner ads for things like debt consolidation, hair loss cures, or lowering monthly mortgage payments. The companies that design and place those ads don't necessarily work for businesses that provide those products or services. Instead, companies like 800XChange would run ads and collect information from people who responded—leads—and then sell that information to businesses they would contract with, giving them a list of people interested in their services who they could then call or email.

Lead generation is a robust subset of the advertising industry, and operations like 800XChange, which have the advertising and internet expertise to get people calling and clicking, can be incredibly lucrative. In their first year in business, Ed and Chris, each barely thirty years old, grossed over $12 million. The vast majority of the money the company took in was profit. All they needed was a little bit of office space, a few employees, and, of course, the cost of the advertising. Due to the payment formula for leads, and their low overhead, it was like they were printing money.

From the outside, Chris's life seemed close to perfect. He had a wildly successful business he had cofounded with a friend and was making the kind of money most people can only dream of. He had a gorgeous girlfriend, Erika, a professional dancer, to whom he was getting ready to propose. He was driving a new Range Rover and had moved into a luxury ocean-view apartment in Laguna. Business was going so well that he had offered his brother Paul a job, and Paul's family moved down to Laguna as well. Chris was spending most mornings on the water. He would head into the office after surfing and work late into the evenings on new ad campaigns. Ed was handling the business side, Chris was generating the creative product, and together they were absolutely killing it.

But things were not as idyllic as they seemed.

It turned out that Ed had moved on from his previous job not just because he was ready to start something for himself, but because he didn't want to hang around and wait for certain things to be discovered. Joseph Gray had helped Ed significantly—even assisting him with buying a house—impressed by Ed's intelligence, his devotion to his wife and kids, and his apparent love of the Lord. "I could tell that Ed was driven, and I had been in situations in my life where I helped certain people and they have risen above my expectations and I love it when that happens," Gray later told CNBC.

Joseph Gray had trusted Ed—perhaps too much. When Ed left Gray's company to start 800XChange, there were some irregularities in the books. Joseph did not yet realize just how significant those "irregularities" would become. Ed also took some lucrative advertising clients with him, without Gray's permission. When Chris first learned of the problems between Ed and Joseph, Shin assured him it was a routine business dispute and he would handle it.

But that wasn't how it played out. As Joseph Gray continued to investigate, it became clear that this was far more than a simple financial misunderstanding. Gray accused Ed of redirecting payments from the company into his own personal accounts. Gray filed a civil lawsuit and also a criminal complaint. After an investigation by the Riverside County District Attorney's Office, Ed was formally charged with criminal embezzlement.

Ed pled guilty, and to avoid jail time he agreed to pay $700,000 in restitution. The Riverside County Superior Court sentenced him to sixteen months in state prison, suspending the sentence pending successful payment of the ordered restitution "on time." The Court then placed Ed on formal probation. This meant that if Ed didn't pay within six months, he was going to state prison for a minimum of 240 days.

Chris suddenly found himself attached at the hip to a convicted felon and apparent thief. Even worse, as Shin's partner, Chris was soon named a defendant in one of the several civil lawsuits filed against Shin for what he had done in Riverside. Chris worried first about what this would do to his professional reputation in the advertising industry, and next about the impact this would have on their growing, successful business. Finally, Chris also worried about what business funds his partner might try to access to satisfy his debt.

Life for the surfer had suddenly become quite stressful.

The expectation, given the company's profits, was that Ed should have had several million dollars of his own money available to satisfy the restitution payments. After all, 800XChange's overhead was still low, and there had been no extravagant expenses. Chris, who also should have shared in the several million dollars of cash available in their business accounts, didn't want to share in the obligation; he wanted to make sure Ed paid out of money that was solely his. But Ed had handled all of the business accounts for 800XChange, and Chris didn't even have access. When Chris asked Ed to let him see the accounts, Ed resisted. There should have been plenty of money, and Chris didn't know why this suddenly seemed so complicated.

Chris became increasingly concerned and decided to consult with a lawyer—Ernesto Aldover—who specialized in business disputes. Chris wanted access to the account records, and to add some safeguards into the system, requiring both he and Ed to cosign any significant checks. The back-and-forth went on for weeks, and then months. Chris was getting more and more nervous as Ed seemed to become more and more slippery.

An installment of restitution funds was due the week of June 7, 2010.

On Friday, June 4, Chris sent an email to Ernesto Aldover around lunchtime, saying that he and Ed were meeting, and that Ed was going to give him the passwords to the accounts.

It appeared to Aldover that progress was finally being made. The next email the lawyer received from Chris was at 6:01 that evening, saying that he and Ed had agreed in principle for Ed to buy him out of the business, for half the assets that the company owned. According to the email, Ed was going to send a down payment in good faith and wire the rest in installments. A signed contract soon followed. Chris's stress, it seemed, was going to be over, and it looked as if he had managed to extricate himself from this painful mess. His brother Paul received an email from Ed saying that Chris had decided to let Ed buy him out, and he was headed to the Galápagos Islands to celebrate.

This all seemed odd to Ernesto Aldover, after having worked so hard with Chris over the preceding months to get more control over the business. They had never discussed a buyout before. But to his family and friends, it also didn't seem entirely out of character for Chris. He had always told those close to him that his endgame was to escape, maybe be a bartender on an island somewhere, enjoying the sun and the surf instead of the frustrations of the corporate world.

Like so many surfers, Chris dreamed of hanging it up, turning his back on the rat race, and living a simple life on the ocean. Chris had invested a fair bit of his wealth in South African gold coins called Krugerrands and therefore had some immediate liquidity. His dream of leaving it all behind was familiar to all who knew him.

Based on emails to his family over the following week, it appeared that Chris had decided to really do it. But it wasn't exactly the escape they had imagined. Chris's girlfriend, Erika—recall that his family believed he was getting ready to propose—received a text from Chris's phone saying he was in Las Vegas, and then, via a cold, heartless email, he broke up with her, harshly. He told her he didn't love her, and that he was running off to the Galápagos with a former Playboy Playmate named Tiffany Taylor.

Paul couldn't believe Chris would do such a thing and asked him to send a photo just to let him know he was okay. Paul soon received an email containing a photo of a stunning Tiffany Taylor getting out of a swimming pool—but no Chris. The photo irked Paul. He wanted a picture of the two of them, and this seemed to be more of a modeling shot than something Chris would have taken himself.

More troubling, Paul, and the rest of Chris's family, couldn't believe that he would dump Erika like that, and run away with no notice, no warning, and no goodbyes. It bugged Paul that Chris would sell his share of the company—a company he'd brought Paul in to work for—and not even tell him. (He found out from Ed.) Not to mention, Chris was supposed to pick Paul and his family up from the airport (they were returning from a vacation) and he never showed. He was already gone.

His family was torn between anger, concern and acceptance that sometimes this was just the way Chris was. He had been known to disappear before. He had checked out more than once for a few days to grab some waves and clear his head. Although Paul, Erika, and Chris's parents were all disappointed by Chris's sudden departure, they had to admit to themselves that it wasn't as shocking as it might have been if he didn't have this history, and the expressed desire to one day get away from it all.

Confusing emails continued from Chris to his family for several months. His vacation grew longer and longer. From the Galápagos, he went to Peru and then Argentina, and eventually crossed the ocean to Africa. His mood in the emails seemed to fluctuate. At one point, he emailed his parents that it had been a really rough year, and that he'd thought about doing "the unspeakable." He said he'd been reflecting on what he now thought had been a troubled childhood, and that someday in the future he'd share his thoughts with them.

The problem was that he didn't have a troubled childhood. In fact, with two loving parents, a brother for a best friend, and the ocean for his backyard, it was pretty close to ideal. This kind of talk didn't sound like Chris, and alarmed his family, who had never known him to have any kind of emotional drama while growing up. His father, Steve, was a firefighter, his mother, Debi, was a preschool teacher, and he grew up in a supportive, all-American family. This wasn't the Chris they knew.

As time went by, Steve, who had been a cop before switching to the fire department, began to develop a bad feeling about the whole situation. He sent an email asking Chris to confirm the name of the lake that he had grown up on, and the kind of boat they used to drive. Chris wrote back "Kelly Lake," and told his father to stop worrying so much.

Steve tried to relax and convince himself everything was okay. But the months kept on passing with barely any communication. Finally, as the end of the year approached—six months since Chris had left on his trip—it seemed like he was beginning to make new plans. Chris emailed Paul that they should meet in March in Costa Rica, and that he would share his ideas for a new business.

But the emails also described a trip that was getting more and more dangerous. Chris said he met a man in India who was sailing to North Africa, and that Chris was going to hitch a ride. He mentioned something about trying to sell some of his Krugerrands, going somewhere in Rwanda where he'd apparently heard about someone paying a 30 percent markup, which made no sense in its own right. Finally, he said he planned to go to the Congo and buy a conflict diamond. A young white man, loaded with gold coins, heading solo into one of the most dangerous areas of the world—this adventure was giving his mother fits. It sounded extremely dangerous—and the note about the trip further into Africa ended up being the last email the family ever received.

Steve and Debi were now starting to fear the worst. Weeks went by with no word at all. Debi was looking at every news report she could find about young Americans being kidnapped or murdered in Africa, even trying to find the village where Chris might have traveled and zooming in on Google Street View to see if she could happen to catch just a glimpse of her son. And Steve was trying to figure out where exactly his son had ended up. Desperate, he called the US State Department to find out the last place where Chris's passport had been used.

This is where things began to fall apart.

Chris's passport hadn't been used at all. As far as the government was concerned, he was still in the US. This was not good.

Concerning on a different front, Paul was still working at 800XChange, and Ed had taken the entire company to Las Vegas in order to host a party to impress potential new clients. There, he had engaged a Vegas host who hired a bunch of "atmosphere models," professionally gorgeous women to join the festivities to give the impression that the company was the coolest thing around. Surrounded by all the lights and bling and all things Vegas, Paul looked across the room and was suddenly shocked.

Looking stunning in a black cocktail dress, there was Tiffany Taylor, the former Playmate who had supposedly been on the trip with Chris. Chris's emails had stopped mentioning Tiffany a while back, and it had seemed like Chris might be on his own now, but he thought she would certainly have some answers. Paul beelined to her: "Aren't you supposed to be traveling with my brother?"

Paul wanted to know all about their trip and how his brother was doing. She looked up and appeared confused. "I'm sorry, but I have no idea what you are talking about," she said. "I have never been to the Galápagos, and I'm afraid I don't know your brother."

Paul looked over at Ed, who shook his head and tried to tell Paul that Chris had been with a *different* Tiffany Taylor.

The picture had definitely been of this woman.

Things were no longer making any sense at all.

Steve drove down from his home in Oregon to Laguna Beach to meet with Ed. He wanted answers, but Ed didn't have much to tell him. He insisted he didn't know any more than the family did, and that Chris was halfway around the world. Had Ed made payments to Chris, as their deal had specified? Ed insisted that Chris wanted him to wire the money to an account in the Cayman Islands. Steve asked about the passport, and Ed told him that he'd actually been with Chris when he got a fake passport in Vegas, wanting to be untraceable in his travels.

Ed gave Steve the name of his Vegas host/fixer, a man named John Koponen (known as "Johnny Vegas"), saying he had arranged for the fake passport. Steve did not know what to make of any of this, and he reported Chris missing to the Laguna Beach Police Department. At first they resisted taking the case, saying he needed to file back home in Oregon, but Steve pushed, and eventually they agreed.

Detectives from Laguna Beach arranged for an interview with Ed at the police department. Ed had paid off his restitution and was out of trouble with the law, or so it seemed. He was cooperative, relaxed, and charming with the detectives. Ed methodically laid out the same story he had given Steve: Chris had signed away his share of the company, gotten a fake passport, and decided to travel the world. Ed said he would be happy to produce proof of the wire transfers and copies of the emails he'd received. He complained that running the business had been hard without his partner, and that it had been a very stressful six months.

About halfway through the interview, it appeared that the detectives relaxed, persuaded by Ed that Chris was probably sitting on a beach somewhere. It occurred to me when I reviewed the interview tape that the detectives very likely believed his story. There was no obvious reason for them not to: Shin was incredibly smooth.

But Ed Shin had made a mistake—one of a few mistakes, as it would turn out. Ed had moved the company to a different office location several months earlier and had skipped out on the rent at the old building. Why he didn't think it would ever be pursued still isn't clear to me. Ed was a smart guy, with a lot to lose, and this was an unforced error. The property manager did eventually come looking for him and knocked on the door of local private detective Joe Dalu, who had recently moved into the same office complex. The property manager said he wanted to find Ed and Chris in order to get the back rent, and Joe didn't have much trouble finding Ed. Chris was another story. Joe reached out to Chris's father and heard the long saga of Chris's vacation and then disappearance. He was intrigued and volunteered, pro bono (for free), to help out and look into it a little further.

Joe was savvy and thorough, a solid investigator, and the Smiths were lucky he had landed in their lap. Joe reviewed the emails and noticed the email trap that Steve had attempted to set. He saw that "Chris" had told his father the name of the lake he grew up on, but never the type of boat. At the same time, as it turned out, "Chris" had emailed his brother Paul and asked, out of the blue, "What kind of boat did we have growing up?" He was fishing for the information their father had asked for. Suspicious, for sure.

It turned out that the old 800XChange offices were still vacant, having been completely abandoned by Shin, at this point a full ten months earlier. Joe asked the property manager if he could have a look around. Of course, why not? Shin was certainly in no position to object.

And here is where things went from suspicious to sinister. Before even entering the office, Joe looked through the glass front door and immediately noticed a stain on a light switch that appeared to be dark red. Based on his training and experience as a former police officer, he suspected it might be blood. Joe backed out carefully, recognizing the scene would need to be forensically processed.

/////Λ\\\\

Just as Joe Dalu was calling investigators to take a look at the old 800XChange offices, I was conducting a training session for new detectives at the sheriff's academy and was approached by Detective Julia Bowman from Laguna Beach. She was young and energetic, and wanted to discuss the Shin case. She didn't agree with her supervisor's apparent assessment that Shin was telling the truth, and she wanted to talk. Laguna Beach, where Chris had lived, was my jurisdiction. The 800XChange company was headquartered in nearby San Juan Capistrano, so it was patrolled by the sheriff's department, and therefore in the territory of my colleague Brahim Baytieh. Brahim had already fielded some phone calls regarding the case from Orange County Sheriff's Office investigators Sergeants Don Voght and Ray Wert. We decided that since it was a Laguna Beach missing person, I would take the case, but Don and Ray would conduct the investigation. They were real pros. As soon as it became clear there was more to the story, they began interviewing witnesses to put together a picture of what had happened in the days leading up to Chris's disappearance the previous June.

They compiled warrants to examine business records, financial statements, phone records, and even the furniture that had been used in Chris's office. They also, of course, wanted the Orange County Crime Lab to come in and forensically process the abandoned offices. They sprayed luminol—a chemical that reacts with the proteins in blood, turning old stains into an ironically dazzling fluorescent blue. When they got to Chris's old office, blood appeared to be everywhere. It had now been almost a year since Chris had last been seen, but evidence doesn't always vanish with time. They found additional specks of blood in areas that might be missed if someone tried to clean a crime scene: behind a doorjamb, behind the baseboards, and even on the ceiling. Then they pulled up the carpeting.

One of the most common mistakes among people who attempt to cover up a crime scene is not realizing that liquids will sink through a carpet right down to the padding at the bottom. You can clean the top layer of carpet perfectly well, but, as anyone who has ever attempted to housebreak a pet knows, if you get a carpet dirty enough, it will eventually have to be replaced no matter how thoroughly you clean the surface. When the crime lab lifted the carpeting in Chris's former office, any hope of him still being alive immediately vanished.

Large stains of a coagulated red substance were immediately recognized by the experienced forensics team. They knew it was blood before they even applied the luminol. The entire scene was a bloody mess. Using DNA samples from Chris's parents and Paul, they were able to determine all of the blood was from one source, and that source was Chris Smith.

Sergeants Voght and Wert began interviewing people who worked for the company. Their media buyer said that Ed had closed the office for the week after he supposedly bought Chris out of his partnership.

Ed explained to several employees that Chris had become drunk after they closed the deal, vomiting red wine all over the interior of his office, and that it needed to be cleaned before they could return to work. She recalled returning a week later and noticing a horrible smell emanating from the office.

Thinking back, the property manager also remembered a call from Ed around that time, asking... about cleaning. He told him he had cut his hand and wanted to know how to get blood out of the carpet. No employees remembered Ed having any injuries at all when they returned from the week at home. And, of course, the blood the investigators found all belonged to Chris.

As additional records trickled in pursuant to various warrants, it became starkly apparent that the financial gain component of this case was significant. The business 800XChange was hugely profitable. Ed Shin should have had the money to pay back Joseph Gray and avoid prison. But he didn't. Why not? As investigators dug deeper into Shin's life, all roads kept leading back to the same place: Las Vegas and the Wynn Hotel.

Chris had sent an email to his attorney about Ed renting a safe and storing almost $200,000 of gold coins without his permission... at the Wynn. Paul talked about meeting atmosphere model Tiffany Taylor... at the Wynn. Business junkets before and after Chris's disappearance... were all at the Wynn. Jennifer Matthews remembered Ed gambling feverishly on one of her business trips to Vegas... at the Wynn. It appeared that Mr. Bible Study was spending substantial time somewhere other than Disneyland with his kids.

More clues emerged when investigators went to Chris's apartment in Laguna Beach and found that a man named Kenny Kraft was now living there. They discovered he was also driving Chris's Range Rover (which, when forensically processed, was found to have more of Chris's blood in a crevice of the rear cargo compartment) and even wearing his clothes. Kraft had been hired by Ed, after Chris's disappearance, as a personal assistant. Kraft, though somewhat reluctantly, cooperated completely with investigators. He said that Shin had given him permission to move into Chris's apartment and drive his car, both of which were actually being paid for by the company. He said that all of Chris's stuff was still in the apartment when he moved in, including Chris's two favorite surfboards (a dispositive clue to any real surfer—if you're going on a surf trip, you definitely don't leave your boards behind). Ed told Kenny he could drive the car, wear the clothes, and sell the boards. Kraft said he had also gone to Vegas with Shin, and that they traveled in style. Not only had they flown by private jet, but in fact they had been picked up by the Wynn Hotel's very own private jet. Unbeknownst to the Wynn, Ed had filled the plane with booze and exotic dancers providing lap dances on the way out. Mr. Kraft didn't mention anything about Bible study on the plane.

As everyone knows, Las Vegas operates in a reality that has to be unique in all the world. An oasis of lights and false opportunity in the middle of one of the world's hottest and most desolate deserts, it's not a bad place to visit if you like to play golf or sit by the pool for a couple of days, but those fabulous buildings weren't built on the winning nights of amateur gamblers. The blinging sounds and cool air of those casinos supplement the complimentary cocktails that make it a little easier to buy just one more stack of chips and see what happens. Lurking under the thin veneer of fine dining, pretty lights, and just-one-more-roll success is a seedy underbelly that exists to fulfill the other name for Las Vegas: Sin City. This is the world of party hosts, pimps, and cocaine dealers. This is where a guy like Ed Shin can show up with embezzled money on a casino jet, get comped a fantasy room, gamble his guts out, and then get virtually anything else he wants from the legion of people, not employed by the hotel, who are all there to service his desires—for a negotiated price, of course.

Even though 800XChange was a hugely profitable business, Ed Shin didn't have the money to pay Joseph Gray, because in reality he was a degenerate gambler. Ed Shin lost literally millions of dollars at the tables of the Wynn Casino in Las Vegas—on trips that continued even after Chris's murder. One employee said that when he went to bed, he saw Shin at the tables with stacks of "purple chips." A purple chip at the Wynn is worth $500, and in Vegas a "stack" is usually twenty chips. He said when he got up the next morning, Ed was still gambling away at the same table. Ed's fancy parties, with the "atmosphere models," were held on trips that were being comped by the Wynn, arguably the nicest hotel in Vegas, with a two-story suite equipped with a private elevator, a pool table, and even twenty-four-hour butler service. The casinos fawned over Ed not because he was a great guy, but because he was one of the biggest losers they knew. Like Michael Corleone's brother Fredo famously "banging cocktail waitresses two at a time," Ed Shin—according to Kenny Kraft—regularly engaged the services of multiple sex workers in Las Vegas, sometimes at the same time. Kraft, who wasn't hired until after Chris was gone, claimed to have gone to Vegas with Shin no fewer than a dozen times. Family man, indeed.

The search warrant came back on Shin's phone records, and a new dimension in the investigation began to take shape. Ed Shin had rented a pickup truck at a U-Haul in San Clemente, and his cell phone had pinged near a transponder tower in the middle of the desert, just north of the Mexican border in east San Diego County. It was three in the morning. The records show his phone traveling from Orange County just two days after Chris went missing. Once detectives saw the phone evidence, they realized there was little chance they would ever find Chris's body, at least not without Ed's help.

There is a moment in the beginning of the movie *Casino* when Joe Pesci's character, based on the real-life Vegas mobster Anthony "the

Ant" Spilotro, informs the viewer about the intricacies of properly burying a body in the desert: "A lot of holes in the desert, and a lot of problems are buried in those holes. But you gotta do it right."

Delivered in a way that only Joe Pesci could make both chilling and funny, the comment is in fact based on real life. Over the last 120 years, there have been 141 bodies recovered in Riverside County alone that have defied identification. And those are only the bodies that have been found. Early in my time in Homicide, Larry Montgomery and I worked a case where a woman named Judy Valot had murdered her boyfriend (after incorrectly accusing him of cheating) and taken the body to Blythe, California, near the Arizona border. We knew she went off into the desert on an ATV early in the morning with a small attached trailer and returned several hours later.

When Larry informed one of the local sheriffs that he was thinking about bringing a cadaver dog out to look for the body, the sheriff laughed. "Oh, you can bring your dog," he said, "and I can almost guarantee you will find a body, but it won't be the one you're looking for."

Larry was taken aback. "You guys find that many bodies?" he asked. The sheriff answered with a chuckle. "Son, on Judgment Day, when the dead all rise, it's going to be standing room only out here."

Unless Shin confessed, there was almost no chance we would find Chris. If I filed charges, it was pretty clear this was going to have to be prosecuted as another no-body case. Many people assume the most difficult cases to prosecute are those where the victim has never been found—how, after all, do you really prove someone is dead when there is no dead body? Counterintuitively, such cases are actually easier in many ways. As a prosecutor in a homicide case, you need to prove that a human being was killed. The existence of a body satisfies that element most clearly. But without a body, you must first prove that death. You get to present evidence that might not otherwise be allowed about who the victim was as a human being. Or in the immortal words of Lew Rosenblum: "The jury sees the soul of your victim reflected in the eyes of those who loved them."

You get to call the person's best friend to say the victim never would have missed the big game, their grandma to say the victim never would have skipped Thanksgiving dinner, or their girlfriend to say he never would have left without his beloved dog. It is legally necessary, but also incredibly powerful testimony. The jury sees the visceral pain of the victim's loved ones, and what it's like for the family to never have a place to mourn. They end up understanding the emotional desire to believe emails that seem so obviously bogus with the benefit of hindsight.

It has a profound impact.

That's not to say you don't still have to do the work.

And that's not to say you don't still need evidence.

But it certainly appeared that Edward Shin was guilty as hell, whether we found Chris Smith's body or not.

Police were getting ready to reapproach Ed with all of this new evidence when they got an alert that he was about to take off on a flight to Canada. They immediately called me, and it was decision time. With no body, did we have enough to charge him?

Ray Wert reached out to Shin's probation officer to find out if he had travel restrictions, and if he needed permission to leave the country. The answers were yes and yes. Getting on a flight to Canada was a violation of Shin's probation on the embezzlement case. So, without tipping Ed off that they were really there to ask about Chris, detectives had him pulled off the plane just before takeoff. They were very polite, and asked him no questions, but on the ride back to the sheriff's department, Ed started talking. Flimflammers, snake oil salespeople, and con artists typically can't help themselves.

Once in the interview room, and after Shin had been properly Mirandized, Don Voght and Ray Wert led him to the real topic. They asked if he'd been in contact with the police since his embezzlement case, and he didn't volunteer that Laguna Beach detectives had talked to him about Chris's disappearance. When they brought up Chris, he told the very same story that had worked at Laguna Beach—Chris was a free spirit, a surfer, and had taken a round-the-world trip before his emails suddenly stopped.

After hours getting nowhere, Wert and Voght decided to confront Ed with the blood evidence. They told him that Chris's blood was found on the walls, in the doorjamb of his office, and on the ceiling. They asked him how it got there. Ed resisted—he said he had no idea what they were talking about. He asked for a lawyer, and the investigators immediately stopped the interview.

Just minutes later, no lawyer yet, Ed said he wanted them to come back in so he could set the record straight. He wanted assurance that if he told a sensible story, perhaps he wouldn't be charged with murder. Of course they couldn't promise that, but they told him they wanted to know what happened.

Suddenly, Ed's story completely changed.

He described an epic brawl in the office, where Chris, drunk and on sleeping pills, stressed over the embezzlement and worried Ed was going to implicate him in the scheme, attacked Ed viciously. Ed talked about how they both ended up in midair, Chris on his desk, launching himself toward Ed, like two fighting rams. Eventually, after much back-and-forth, Chris chased Ed into the hall, and then Ed, summoning new strength within him, threw Chris back into his office, and Chris's head hit the side of his desk. Suddenly, he was unconscious, and there was blood all over.

Ed didn't know what to do. He said he didn't believe that police would trust him, given the embezzlement charge, and so he didn't call 911. Instead, he said he drove around, confused and in a state of shock, and then came back, hoping Chris would still be alive. But the pool of blood was larger than before, and Chris wasn't moving. So he called someone who connected Ed to a guy who could clean everything up—the body and the office. Ed met this mystery man at a gas station—a young, strong, blond man, with a flattop-style haircut and a Russian accent—and gave him ten or fifteen thousand dollars. Ed claimed he never heard from him again. It wasn't murder, Ed said, it was self-defense, and he had no idea where the body was.

The emails, Ed admitted, were all invented by him to keep Chris's girlfriend and family from finding out the truth. Yes, he could have been kinder to Erika, he knew, and perhaps it was a bad call to try and blame Chris's parents for what seemed to be leading toward suicide at one point in the email chain. Ed said it got too hard pretending to be Chris, and so he stopped, though clearly he'd hoped the family would have concluded he'd died somewhere on that trip to sell his gold coins in Africa.

There was no body, no weapon, and with a good enough story, Shin figured he could talk his way out of it. It was pretty obvious while watching the recorded interview that this was exactly what Shin was still doing. The question was: Would it work? And although he did a reasonable job of inventing a story that explained a small portion of the forensics, there were a few critical problems. The first was Ed's puzzling lack of injuries. Not a drop of blood in that office belonged to Ed, and no one ever saw him with even a scratch on him. He told investigators at one point that he had trained himself not to bleed. Listening to the interview, I needed to rewind that part. *Did he really just say that?*

The second problem was the email to Chris's lawyer at 6:01 that evening. The last employee left the office that day at 5:00 p.m., so it was impossible for whatever happened that day to have started any sooner. Given that, it seems extraordinary that despite being overcome with shock and grief, and "driving around," as he claimed, the first thing Ed decided to do was draft a typo-free email to Chris's attorney saying that Chris was agreeing to sell his share of the company. The clearheadedness of that email—the coherent thoughts that would have been necessary to come up with that plan—did not track with anything Ed said about his state of mind. Not to mention—when would he have had time to write it? It seemed beyond clear to me that the email must have been prepared in advance. Ed did not go into Chris's office and get blindsided by an attack from a man with no history of violent behavior. This had to have been planned, and worse, the motive was clearly financial. As soon as Chris was dead, Ed was ready to press send.

Putting aside the murder of children, some of the most morally depraved cases involve killing for money. The killer or killers will often cook up elaborate plans that you as a prosecutor, along with your investigators, have to undo. They typically involve false leads and some sort of fake evidence to throw detectives off the scent. Here, of course, we had a whole book of fake emails. It was shocking to hear Ed reveal that he had spent literally months posing as the business partner he'd killed in cold blood, spinning tale after tale to his petrified family.

Perhaps the biggest problem with Shin's story came in the form of the smallest forensic evidence—those tiny, almost imperceptible blood specks all over the metal partition strips between the ceiling tiles. There is an entire discipline in the world of forensic science devoted completely to what is known as *blood spatter evidence*. It is essentially a detailed analysis of how blood is dispersed at a crime scene. Like the arterial spurting on the inside trunk lid of Cathy Torrez's red car, the findings can be hugely significant. In Shin's case, blood on the ceiling was consistent with what is known as *cast-off*, and pretty much only happens with repeated stab wounds or blows from a blunt object. Those tiny droplets of blood were far more consistent with Shin beating Chris to death with a baseball bat than him hitting his head on the corner of a desk.

Ed had some sort of an explanation for everything else, but not that. As far as his phone records, he claimed he was so distraught about the accidental death of his friend that he contemplated driving to Mexico to escape, but then had a change of heart and couldn't leave his family. And he thought his Mercedes wouldn't be able to handle the roads in Mexico, thus the rental truck...because apparently there are no paved roads south of the border?

Ed's story about not knowing the location of the body turned out to be a fairly critical component of the case. From a defense perspective, the body, if found, would have been able to prove or disprove Ed's story. If Ed was telling the truth, the skull would likely show a fracture consistent with Chris hitting his head on the side of the desk, as Ed had explained. Thus, if Ed was telling the truth, one would think he would have gone to any length possible to figure out where the body had been taken. That was the one piece of evidence he needed to corroborate his story. But he insisted he was entirely unable to get back in touch with the imaginary Russian man who had dumped the body. Terrible luck.

An interesting strategic element presented itself with Ed's recorded interview. We did have Ed admitting on tape that Chris was dead, but it was intertwined in Ed's ridiculous story, filled with excuses and explanations. I could use the interview to prove Chris's death, but that would allow Ed's attorneys to argue the truth of everything else he said in the interview—and then Ed wouldn't need to testify.

Alternatively, I could ignore the interview. A criminal defendant is not permitted to play their own statement at trial unless the prosecution somehow opens that door. If I didn't use his self-serving fairytale, Ed Shin would have to testify if he wanted to assert self-defense. This would mean a showdown where I would have the opportunity to cross-examine him. Every experienced trial lawyer wants a shot at the bad guy on the stand.

The problem is that this would mean that I had to prove Chris's around-the-world emails were fake without using Shin's admissions from the interview. In my mind, the best way to do that would be to call Tiffany Taylor to say she never went to the Galápagos. Could I get Tiffany? Would she cooperate? All roads kept leading us right back to Las Vegas. The question for me was, What part of the Vegas world did Tiffany Taylor occupy? What in the world was an "atmosphere model" anyway? If she was shady, there was no way she would ever expose herself to cross-examination at the hands of Shin's high-dollar defense team, especially not on a national media case with cameras in the courtroom every day. It's funny how the success or failure of an entire case can often turn strategically on the cooperation of a single witness. With Tiffany available, I would probably get Ed Shin on the stand. Without her, I would have to play Ed's statement to police—which I did not want to do.

Like so many of the other high-stakes murder cases that we've already examined, this case took several years to come to trial. As things proceeded, we had a very difficult time finding Tiffany Taylor. With out-of-state witnesses, the rules for subpoenas are very different. The cooperation of a local police department is required to effectuate service, and a local judge must sign off on it. It seemed like every time the officers from Vegas Metro went to Taylor's condo, they had just missed her. I didn't know if she was busy, traveling, or ducking us. As the trial got closer and closer, it looked as if I would have to proceed without her. That meant Chris's poor family would have to listen to Shin's interview without ever hearing him called out on his nonsense. It also meant I might lose the opportunity to call loved ones of Chris's for the purpose of proving he was dead. But it seemed like we might have no choice.

A couple of days before the trial began, I was walking out of my office when my investigator, the awesome Don Holford, stopped me in the hallway. Finally, he had heard from our key witness. Apologizing profusely for not getting back to us sooner, Tiffany Taylor explained that she had moved back with her parents in Virginia. And "Tiffany Taylor" did not actually exist. This was her modeling name, and that might have caused much of the confusion in trying to locate her. She said she felt horrible for Chris's family, and would of course do whatever she could to help. Bingo.

Now that I had Summer Hanson, aka Tiffany Taylor, I could try this case the way I wanted. And the truth in my eyes was pretty clear: In trying to legally protect his financial interests, Chris Smith became a significant obstacle for Ed Shin. Having converted millions of dollars of Chris's money into those purple chips in Vegas, Shin couldn't possibly let him see the actual books. With Chris's attorney involved, a lawsuit would have been filed, the accounts would have been frozen, and the criminal restitution would not have been paid. Shin would have been on his way to prison quicker than losing a hand of blackjack. Making Chris disappear, and taking all of his money, was the only way Ed could solve his problems—and, indeed, it did, for a while. Ed had settled his lawsuit as soon as he could, paid Joseph Gray back his money, kept his freedom, and avoided going to prison. But Ed was back at the Wynn in no time. It's also worth noting: No one in Chris's family ever saw a dime of Chris's money from the supposed agreement he and Ed had made about the company. The gold coins Chris kept at home—an estimated $60,000 worth—also magically disappeared at some point after Shin had visited the Laguna Beach apartment.

Thus, we had charged Shin with first-degree murder with the special circumstance of murder for financial gain, which carried a potential sentence of life without the possibility of parole.

For our looming trial, the stage was set. I had Summer Hanson,

I had the cell phone pings in the desert, I had the bloody office, and I had what I believed to be a strong motive. I also had Ed Shin's past in mind, backing up everything we had discovered. As we had delved deeper and deeper into Shin's history, we learned that none of this behavior was new. Ed had a history that Chris, and probably every-one else in Shin's life, never knew about. As a young man, Ed had faked his own kidnapping in an attempt to extort a million dollars from his father, sending fake emails in the process (sound familiar?). Prophetically, in Ed's embezzlement case, Joseph Gray had actually sent a victim-impact letter to the judge saying that Ed had no con-science, and predicted he'd be back in Court sooner rather than later, and that next time, people would be hurt.

So it was clear he did it. But we still had no weapon, no body, and a very slick defendant who would have to take the stand if he wanted to run his claim of self-defense. If he convinced a single juror, the case would hang; if he convinced *all* the jurors, he would go free. He also had two very fine and experienced attorneys in Ed Welbourn and Al Stokke, both of whom I had known and admired for years.

Shin had to decide: Did he think it was likely that he could convert at least one juror to vote his way by hearing and believing his version of the story, or was he worried his own presence on the stand would doom his case?

For a sociopath who thinks he is the world's greatest liar, I think it was probably an easy call. But first I had to get through my case. I went through the forensics, the employees of 800XChange, Joseph Gray, and Ernesto Aldover. I took the jury through all the emails, the plea agreements, and Ed's clear motive. Chris's brother Paul was especially powerful on the stand.

Then I played my ace, Summer Hanson. She had flown in, without being subpoenaed, just like she promised. A professional model, she had done nothing wrong and had nothing to hide. She brought her passport to show the jury she had never been to Ecuador (the Galápagos) and explained that she had never met Chris Smith. I had her on and off the stand in less than twenty minutes. I had established everything I needed for my no-body case without producing a single minute of Ed Shin's self-serving interviews with police. Now the ball was entirely in Shin's court.

As I had hoped he would, and in a designer suit—likely more expensive than my entire wardrobe—Ed Shin took the stand. His lawyer skillfully walked him through his story, which, as it turned out, had new details he'd never before described, including Chris grabbing him by the throat (no marks) and a new gem I had missed before: When asked who set him up with the mystery Russian body disposer, he said he went to his go-to guy for all things sketchy, his host, "Johnny Vegas" Koponen—the same person he had told Chris's father had given Chris the fake passport. He had denied to Chris's father that he had anything to do with Chris's disappearance and then sent him to the guy who he now claimed helped dispose of the body.

By this point, Shin had told so many lies he couldn't keep them all straight, and that oversight was huge.

On cross-examination, I spelled it out for the jury, and Ed didn't have much of a response. Not in a million years of murder has anyone been stupid enough to claim their innocence to a victim's family and then tell them to talk to the one person who could completely contradict the story. I had caught Ed Shin in a huge lie. Not a lie to me, or the judge, or his probation officer, but to the jury that would decide his fate. This is why experienced prosecutors *always* want a defendant to take the stand.

(It should be noted, Mr. Koponen was entirely cooperative with our investigation, he denied any of the nonsense Shin had claimed, and none of the investigators believed he had done anything wrong. I agreed.)

As the cross-examination continued, I tried my very best to get Shin to tell Chris's poor family where the body was. He wouldn't, of course, because that would prove his story a lie. But the line of questioning would also let the jury see him squirm, and stonewall, and continue to make absolutely no sense. At one point, as we went through his various efforts to cover up the death, Ed Shin choked up and looked as if he were about to shed some crocodile tears. I asked him if he needed a break.

"No sir, I'm okay."

"Are you sure, Mr. Shin?"

"Yes."

"Okay, just one quick question before we continue, when you were typing those emails to his mother suggesting Chris was suicidal because he had bad parents . . . were you crying then?"

I finished my cross-examination by putting up a topographical map of the area surrounding the desolate cell phone tower where Shin had spent an hour in the middle of the night. The area covered by that tower encompassed perhaps seventy-five square miles of desert, where everyone knew Chris's body was buried. "We have a search and rescue team out there right now." (We actually did.) "They have a cadaver dog named 'Karma.' Here is a marker, Mr. Shin. Please circle the area where Chris Smith's body is buried."

With Chris Smith's mother sitting in the front row, he looked at the map, paused, and refused to do it. "I don't know where it is."

It took the jury forty minutes to come back with a guilty verdict. Nine years of waiting, nine days of trial, and then forty minutes. We had a great jury, and not one of them believed Ed Shin.

The Chris Smith case is so interesting in part because of how long it took to even know there had been a crime committed, especially a murder. Chris Smith may have been the perfect person to go missing, because he had often told people he dreamed of disappearing. And Ed Shin was as close to a perfect murderer as I've seen, because—unlike Eric Naposki, Sam Lopez, and especially Daniel Wozniak in their early interviews—Ed performed almost perfectly when questioned by detectives. Naposki, Lopez, and Wozniak all behaved in ways that absolutely doomed their cases, but Ed Shin was different. Ed Shin came off as a guy who had nothing to do with Chris's disappearance. Had he not made a few mistakes—the rent, the Vegas fixer, Tiffany Taylor—he may have never been caught at all.

There was a moment after the verdict that I will never forget. Paul Smith, a surfer who had lost his beloved brother to a lying, thieving, greedy killer, came over with tears of relief and gave me a bear hug. I can still feel the stubble of his face rubbing against my cheek, mixing with tears as he thanked me. His gratitude, and the gratitude from his wife, Leah, as well as from Steve and Debi Smith, was exactly what Lew was talking about years earlier when he told me about sympathy for victims who were worthy of it. These were exactly the kind of people I wanted to help when I decided to dedicate myself to this work—a decision I made so long ago at a picturesque surf spot producing the near-perfect waves that I just know Chris Smith would have loved.

I was at a Christmas party a few days after the verdict at the home of some mutual friends when I ran into Ed Welbourn. He is an excellent trial lawyer, and a fundamentally good guy. He also has a wicked sense of humor. An elegant older woman came over to me and said, "Thank God you convicted him. That poor family."

"C'mon, Mom . . ." Ed said, standing next to me. "I'm literally right here."

The unpublished opinion by the Court of Appeal weighs in forcefully on Shin's credibility:

We agree with Shin this was a credibility case. Simply put, he had none. His conduct both on and after June 4, 2010, evinced a callous and depraved mind. . . . He embezzled from LGT and devised and executed a sophisticated plot to conceal Chris's death for nearly a year. Shin's admission he was "'battling against the odds in terms of credibility'" is an understatement. The odds were insurmountable. . . . This was not a close case concerning whether Shin intended to kill Chris for financial gain. Where we have assumed error, Shin was not prejudiced. Based on the overwhelming evidence of Shin's guilt, we conclude there was no substantial error and the cumulative effect of any possible errors does not warrant reversal of the judgment. (*People v. Shin*, G058082, 26–27 [Cal. Ct. App. Apr. 14, 2021])

They affirmed the conviction.

We still haven't found Chris's remains. Despite cadaver dogs and hundreds of people-hours combing the area around where Ed's cell phone pinged in the desert, there's been nothing. They did eventually do a memorial service—a "paddle out" on the water, which is a traditional send-off in West Coast surf culture—attended by about twenty-five of Chris's closest friends, everyone joining hands on their surfboards and forming a wreath to commemorate Chris's life. They took some photos of the event and Paul had them embossed on a metal plate with a photo of a smiling Chris, along with a personal message of thanks for all our hard work. Honored and humbled, I hung it on the wall of my office, where it remains to this day.

CHAPTER

10

THE HUNT

ERNEST HEMINGWAY'S 1936 short story "On the Blue Water" begins like this:

> Certainly there is no hunting like the hunting of man and those who have hunted armed men long enough and liked it, never really care for anything else thereafter. You will meet them doing various things with resolve, but their interest rarely holds because after the other thing ordinary life is as flat as the taste of wine when the taste buds have been burned off your tongue.

Reading the passage, I can't help but imagine some of my favorite Homicide detectives sitting down with Hemingway in a Cuban bar in the 1930s, drinking whiskey and adding their own perspective on the thrill of the hunt. When it comes to murder investigations, after all, the men and women I worked with were hunters in the truest sense. And, in my biased view, they were the very best. From what I observed throughout my career, when it comes to the hunter-detectives, Hemingway absolutely nailed it.

The single greatest pursuit I ever witnessed came toward the end of my long tenure in the Homicide Unit. In fact, this case ended up as my final trial as a Deputy DA, taking the verdict on my very last day. After seventeen years in Homicide, and 131 jury trials over my career as a prosecutor—through murders for love, for money, for sexual satisfaction, and for the perverse desires of those who hurt innocent children—I thought I'd seen just about everything a sadistic human being could dish out. But one of the cruelest crimes, and greatest hunts I ever witnessed, wasn't even part of a murder case—though it came awfully close.

The investigation that followed in this case demonstrated the power of a well-run DA's Office to not just hold people accountable for the horrible acts they committed but help save the lives of the redeemable, and give good people a second chance.

It started with a woman in black pajamas, running barefoot through the Mojave Desert, hands bound behind her back with a plastic zip tie, crying and screaming for help at the first light of dawn on October 3, 2012. In one of those moments of either divine intervention or just crazy good luck, the very first car she encountered on the dark desert highway was a police officer on his way to work. As soon as he saw her, Kern County Sheriff's Deputy Steve Williams immediately knew this woman needed help, and that whatever this was, it was going to be bad.

As he pulled his car over and quickly tried to comprehend her story, Williams—like a smart officer—began photographing everything to properly document every detail. The woman told Williams her name, Mary Barnes, and that she and her boyfriend's roommate had been woken up in the middle of the night, bound and gagged, shoved into the back of a van, and driven into the desert.

The boyfriend's roommate, a man whose identity has never been made public, is referred to in Court filings as Michael S., and Mary said he was still on the ground, and desperately needed medical assistance.

Williams cut the bindings off Mary's hands, and she led him toward the site where she'd left Michael. They found the dirt road where the two of them had been dumped, and soon located him. Deputy Williams was immediately hit with the powerful smell of bleach as they approached him. Michael was tied up, bleeding, his jeans pulled down around his knees. He was in shock and bore the unmistakable signs of having been beaten and tortured. And one more thing: His penis had been severed from his body.

Paramedics were called immediately, backup was summoned, and Michael was transported to the hospital. Deputy Williams then participated in a grid search with various personnel at the scene, hoping to find Michael's severed penis, knowing that if they found it, there would at least be some hope it could be reattached. Incredibly, they soon realized the kidnappers must have taken it with them.

As Michael was being treated, Mary filled in some more of the story. She had recently moved to California from Florida to live with her boyfriend, who shared a house in Newport Beach with Michael, a friendly twenty-eight-year-old businessman who owned a legal marijuana dispensary in Orange County. Medical marijuana, as it is known, had been legalized in California, and the industry was growing. Michael was fully licensed and operating legitimately, but the marijuana world in California was, and still remains, a little like the Wild West.

Legitimate business owners like Michael have been squeezing

out much of the criminal element that controlled the industry for decades—but not without resistance. Very much related to this, since marijuana cultivation is still a federal crime, it means that proceeds of even the legitimate businesses cannot be deposited into traditional banks. The *F* in FDIC that we see on the window of every retail bank stands for "Federal." In 2012, that meant that in a typical marijuana dispensary there were no credit cards, and no electronic debits. Instead, at the end of each business day, there was a stack of good old-fashioned cash. Mix that with the ruthless criminals still involved in the business, who all seemed to know which operations were doing well, and it was—and largely remains—a recipe for calculated disaster.

On the night in question, masked intruders appeared seemingly out of nowhere inside of Michael's house. They found Mary asleep in the primary suite, and Michael sleeping on the couch in a TV room down the hall. Mary awoke to find a gun pressed to her neck. A man whispered to her, "Don't worry, this is not about you." Her mouth was taped shut, her hands and feet were zip-tied, and she was dragged into the back of a waiting van. Michael was awoken far more violently, with the intruders beating him in the face with a pump-action shotgun and then demanding to know where "the money" was. He pointed them to $2,000 hidden in his sock drawer, but they said they wanted "the million bucks"—which he insisted he didn't have.

After binding him, they dragged Michael down the steps of the townhome, feet first, his head bouncing off each step on the way down, before loading him into what he believed to be a white truck or possibly a panel van. Mary and Michael could tell that there were three men: a driver, and two in the back, one of whom spent the ride beating Michael with a rubber hose, burning him with a blowtorch, and shocking him with a stun gun.

Michael is not a large man, and he offered no resistance. The men appeared to be speaking with fake Mexican accents, and the radio played Latin music the entire time. They told Michael they knew his girlfriend's name, and correctly identified her hair color and what kind of car she drove. They also told him that they knew where his parents lived, and they threatened to hurt "his lady friend" if he did not tell them where the money was. They kept demanding he give up the "million bucks," and he kept insisting he had no idea what they were talking about. He admitted to a safety deposit box with $100,000 and told the men he could get them access in the morning, but they responded with more beating and burning.

The van drove for hours, and Michael was tortured the entire way. Then the driver turned off the main road onto a gravel path, and finally onto one of the countless dirt roads of the California desert. Mary was certain they were about to die. The van stopped, and the two of them were pulled out and dropped on the desert floor. It was dark and completely deserted. The men demanded the money one last time.

"Fuck you, we know it's here," one of the men said.

For the last time, Michael offered to take them back to the office and open the safe for them. Suddenly they pulled down his pants and attached a black zip tie to the base of his penis. While one of the men stood on his torso with enough weight to leave boot imprints on Michael's shoulder, one of the others began to laugh as he sang "back and forth, back and forth." Michael could feel as they began to cut his penis. Mary remained on the ground next to him, still blindfolded and gagged.

Michael was silent—presumably he passed out at some point—and Mary heard the *glug-glug-glug* of liquid being poured on him. She assumed it was lighter fluid and they were about to be burned to death. Instead, she soon smelled the overpowering odor of bleach. This was significant. In the forensic world, nothing destroys DNA more efficiently than simple Clorox. In fact, it is what the crime labs use to clean their equipment to ensure there is no cross contamination.

One of the men then tossed something onto the ground near Mary's feet and said that if she could find it, she could free herself . . . or otherwise she could just die. She heard the doors slam, and the van drive away. Once there was silence, she managed to push her blindfold up high enough on her forehead to be able to see, and to find the knife that had been thrown to the ground. Still bound, she somehow managed to grab it with her feet and cut off the plastic zip ties around her ankles.

She still couldn't get her hands free, so, moving over to Michael, she attempted to cut the bindings on his wrists. She inadvertently cut the palm of his hand (quite severely) instead. This wasn't working. Mary wriggled her way off the ground and could see lights in the distance. Perhaps it was another road, she thought. She took off running through the open desert—hands still bound, and barefoot—knowing she was Michael's only hope. And then she found the highway, and Deputy Williams.

Meanwhile, Michael waited by himself in the cold. He was still bound and covered in bleach (which was burning his tortured skin), and he was terrified that his penis was gone. As he lay there alone, he contemplated whether he even hoped to be rescued or if it would be better to simply die.

There were precious few clues at first. Michael was being treated, and from his hospital bed he explained that he had no enemies he could imagine. He had never been in trouble with the law, he honored his contracts, he remained fastidious about his licensing, and he never slept with anyone's wife. In fact, although he owned a marijuana business, he didn't even personally use it.

Police entered his Newport Beach home and found a bloody pillow where Michael had been sleeping, but little in the way of helpful fingerprints or other forensics. At that point, there was essentially nothing to go on.

Investigators then decided to perform what is known as a *canvas*. This is when they go door-to-door through the immediate neighborhood, hoping against hope that someone might have seen something useful. Neighborhood canvassing is historically not a terribly useful tool. All sorts of well-meaning people come out of the woodwork offering potential leads, which typically have nothing to do with the crime police are investigating.

"I did hear a noise, but it could be those damn raccoons again. . . ."

"I heard a woman screaming, but it might have been from my neighbor's loud wife. . . ."

You often end up chasing well-intended hypotheses that don't add up to much, other than expended resources and wasted time. But every once in a while, you get lucky. For those old enough to remember the 1960s television show *Bewitched*, you might recall the busybody neighbor, Mrs. Kravitz, who knew there were witches in the house, but nobody would believe her.

To a college student, observant, record-keeping neighbors like Mrs. Kravitz can be a nightmare, but to a detective working a brutal crime, these people are nothing short of pure gold. As detectives knocked on door after door with nothing of value to show for their efforts, they made their way to a home across the back alley from where the kidnapping took place.

A kind woman answered the door. "As a matter of fact, I did see something odd," she said. "I saw three boys in a white truck that didn't look right. They were wearing yellow hard hats that looked too clean, and they put a ladder up against the house. I saw a couple of them go up the ladder, but I didn't see them come out."

She recalled this happening less than twenty-four hours before the kidnapping. Detectives were praying she might be able to provide perhaps a description of the truck. . . but she floored them.

"Well, I wrote down the license plate. . . . Will that do?"

Investigators ran the plate and discovered the truck was registered to someone named Kyle Handley. They brought that name to Michael—and it turned out that Michael knew him. He was also in the marijuana business, and he had sold some product to Michael earlier in the year for his dispensary—as many as nine transactions of up to five pounds of product each time, perhaps in the range of $100,000 in sales. Michael and Kyle became friendly, and even when the transactions stopped, they continued to hang out. Michael invited Kyle and some others on a pair of trips to Las Vegas, where Michael perhaps spent beyond his means, paying for the penthouse at one hotel and gambling at high-stakes tables. Always, of course, in cash.

Michael had trouble reaching Kyle after that, but didn't think much of it in the fairly unstable world of marijuana growing and selling. He didn't imagine that Kyle was plotting to rob him, or that the trip had made his friend think he was flush with a million dollars in hidden cash.

I soon had warrants on my desk for a search of Handley's house—and detectives were eager to see what they could find. Unsurprisingly, the house provided critical clues, but also some additional questions. First, police found zip ties in the laundry room that looked very similar to the ones used to bind Mary and Michael. Not exactly a forensic home run, but a solid piece of the puzzle. They also discovered a trash bag in the backyard with a single white zip tie lying on top. When they opened the camper shell covering the bed of Kyle Handley's white pickup truck, police noticed the unmistakable odor of bleach. Under the driver's seat, they also located a single blue nitrile glove.

It had been three days since the investigation started, and police were ready to make their first arrest. They took Handley into custody and sent the glove and zip tie to the crime lab for DNA analysis. At this point, Kyle Handley was in big trouble. In the state of California, the penalty for aggravated kidnapping—a kidnapping with the motive of robbery when the intended victim suffers great bodily injury—carries a maximum sentence of life in state prison without the possibility of parole. Hoping Kyle would roll on his crime partners, we were disappointed to learn that he immediately invoked his right to silence. But catching Kyle himself was obviously a huge first step.

Kyle Handley had grown up in Fresno, California, and went to Clovis West High School, where he excelled at...pretty much nothing. He had a close-knit group of friends, smoked a lot of weed, and seemed to have almost no ambition for anything. Despite being clearly up to his eyeballs in this, it did not appear that Kyle was a violent person, and, frankly, he did not seem clever enough to have put together a crime this complex. We believed the mastermind was still on the loose.

As detectives continued to work on the case, the glove and the zip tie were slowly proceeding through crime lab analysis. At this point, I had done everything I could to assist the investigation, but it was also the case that Michael—fortunately—had lived, meaning this wasn't a homicide.

I had perhaps thirty pending homicides on my caseload at the time. In addition, I was responsible for any new murder committed in my four assigned cities, I had several pending cold case investigations, and I had to keep up with my responsibilities for the Special Circumstance Committee. In other words, I was buried. By this time, my dear friend Dennis Conway had rotated out of the Unit. Dennis had gotten married a year or so earlier, and he realized that he needed to rotate out of Homicide to live the balanced lifestyle more appropriate for the devoted husband he wanted to be. He moved into management, much more of a nine-to-five job, and was soon put in charge of the Felony Panel, where the non-homicide prosecution of Kyle Handley would logically land. His Assistant Head of Court, Heather

Brown, also a good friend of mine, would be set to prosecute Handley. I gave the file to Dennis and figured that would mark the end of my involvement in this horrible yet interesting case. That plan worked for about three weeks.

Detectives in Newport—*my* detectives in Newport—were soon notified the lab had recovered DNA from both the zip tie found in the backyard and the blue nitrile glove found in the cab of Handley's truck. The zip tie returned only a partial profile, from a male individual, who did not appear to be in the CODIS system. The DNA on the blue nitrile glove, on the other hand, came back with a perfect match to someone named Hossein Nayeri. So we had three kidnappers and three DNA profiles: Handley, this Nayeri guy, and a mystery man with a partial profile found on one of the instrumentalities to the crime. This was looking hopeful, but also increasingly complex. Michael did not recognize the name Nayeri, and neither did the police. That was about to change.

Detectives quickly learned that the Newport Beach Police Department happened to have Hossein Nayeri's Chevy Tahoe—or, to be more precise, his wife's—in their possession. Less than a week before the kidnapping, Nayeri's wife Cortney Shegerian's car was involved in a high-speed police chase after the driver refused to pull over. Driving like a madman, attempting to evade the motor officer behind him, the driver—whoever he was—ended up abandoning the vehicle on Balboa Island and apparently swam out of sight. He ended up escaping. The Tahoe was taken to the impound lot, and police contacted the registered owner, Cortney, who first claimed she had no knowledge and then filed a police report saying the car had been stolen. The vehicle was still sitting in the lot weeks later, so as soon as detectives connected the dots, they applied for a warrant to search the car.

This was getting more complicated, and I got a call from Dennis asking me to take the case back. He explained that Heather's caseload was even heavier than mine, and it looked like this would need a lot of time and resources to put together. Besides, I knew all the detectives from Newport, and I dealt with them on a daily basis. Thirty murders plus this mess . . . Why not? I agreed only on the condition that Dennis would continue to help, and Heather and I could work the case together. Dennis agreed.

When detectives searched the Chevy Tahoe, they discovered a treasure trove of evidence. The SUV was filled with cameras, GPS trackers, and strong magnets to attach the trackers to a vehicle. When the data from the cameras was downloaded, the very first image to pop up was footage taken from outside of Michael's Newport home. Bingo. In fact, there were hundreds of hours of surveillance footage. There was also a "burner" cell phone with email receipts for the purchase of various items of surveillance equipment, going all the way back to March, soon after the trip to Vegas when Michael had paid for Kyle's room. It appeared this crime had been in the works for seven long months before the kidnapping. It was all starting to make sense.

The trackers had been purchased by someone using the name Michelle Hong, who opened a Yahoo account used solely for the purpose of buying gear for this crime. The surveillance cameras were linked to the same name and Yahoo email address, and all of the supplies had been delivered to . . . Kyle's house. Oops.

When detectives obtained the IP address used to place the orders, it could be traced back to a hydroponic supply store in Fresno called Agriglobe. Hydroponic grows are a huge part of the modern marijuana business. They essentially allow marijuana to be grown indoors, away from pests, rivals, and prying eyes.

There was nobody at Agriglobe named Michelle Hong, but there was an employee named Naomi Rhodus who had gone to Clovis West High School with Kyle. She had also recently purchased a 9mm pistol and a 12-gauge pump-action shotgun.

As detectives dug deeper into the background of Hossein Nayeri, they learned he had been born in Iran, immigrated to Fresno after middle school, and joined the Marine Corps for a brief time. They also learned that he had been convicted of manslaughter following a car accident involving a former friend and business partner, Ehsan Tousi, who died in the wreck. It was determined that Nayeri had been intoxicated at the time. Nayeri was charged, made bail, and then fled to perhaps the single most difficult nation in the world when it comes to extradition back to the US: his native country of Iran. A judge issued an arrest warrant, but Nayeri was gone. He stayed in Iran for a year, living with his mother, before sneaking back into the US. Somehow, Nayeri managed to escape any significant legal consequences in that case and only did minimal custody time (a shocking example of how he was able to work the system to his advantage).

But how was Nayeri connected to Kyle and Naomi? He had been a varsity wrestler at the very same Clovis West High School—and things started to make more sense. Nayeri was big, athletic, highly intelligent, and had zero respect for authority or empathy for other people. Unlike the stoned, doughy Kyle Handley, this guy appeared to have all the makings of a ruthless mastermind. Detectives immediately attempted to find Hossein Nayeri, but couldn't. It was as if he had fallen off the face of the earth, and he may as well have. Nayeri had once again escaped to Iran. He was long gone weeks before detectives even knew his name, fleeing as soon as Kyle Handley was arrested.

Now what? We had a truly horrific crime. A young man had been sexually brutalized by someone who laughed and sang a song while severing his penis and taking it with him. It was beyond cruel. But Kyle was not talking, we had no idea whose DNA was on the zip tie in his backyard, and Hossein Nayeri was in a country that would absolutely never extradite him. We appeared to be stuck. It would have been very easy at this point to put out a warrant for Nayeri, prosecute Handley, and call it a day.

But when it comes to the investigation and prosecution of conspiracy cases, there are always weak links in the chain. Sometimes, you may even have a good person somewhere on the periphery who is in over their head and wants to do the right thing. We didn't have Hossein Nayeri, but we did have his wife. . . .

Cortney Shegerian also grew up in Fresno and had known Nayeri since she was sixteen—and he was twenty-four. She was having lunch with her cousin one day at Mimi's Café and met a waiter who she thought was cute. They dated for years, and her parents couldn't stand him—but they were married on June 5, 2010. By all accounts, Hossein Nayeri had been horribly controlling and abusive. At the time of the kidnapping, Cortney and Nayeri had been living in a condominium in Irvine, which had been visited at least twice by police for reported instances of domestic violence. In one of those incidents, Cortney had called the police after Nayeri threw her to the ground and threatened her with a box cutter. The case was, in fact, filed—but Nayeri received an offer of what is called *deferred entry of judgment*, by which the case was dismissed after he completed an anger management class.

We then learned something else: The certainly abused, certainly terrified, certainly knowledgeable wife of Hossein Nayeri was also a student at Whittier Law School. Cortney Shegerian was about to become an attorney.

Not long after Nayeri fled, Cortney called Newport Police inquiring about how she could get the Tahoe out of impound. Dennis and Heather decided to see what she knew. The return of property form required Cortney to acknowledge that the vehicle, along with all of its contents, belonged to her. This included all the electronic devices and tracking equipment found inside. Detective Ryan Peters let Cortney know that she could come get her car. When she arrived at Newport PD, detectives started asking questions. Cortney was obviously scared . . . and initially not very cooperative. She signed the paper they placed in front of her, but only after they insisted she read it first. It's not clear how closely she examined the document—despite being a law student—but by signing it, she implicated herself as an accessory to all of the crimes that had been committed. She was now in huge trouble.

We didn't believe that Cortney was behind her husband's horrific act, especially once we realized the degree of abuse she had likely suffered. As I mentioned, domestic violence cases are the sad bread and butter of so much of the criminal justice system. Detective Peters believed Cortney was scared to talk—terrified of her husband, even with him halfway around the world in Iran.

We had evidence at that point that Cortney had aided and abetted in a horrific crime, and this could have exposed her to the same potential sentence as Kyle Handley. But Peters was also a father, and he believed Cortney might have been a decent young woman who was just in way over her head. He decided to do something fairly unorthodox. He called Cortney's father. Cortney was twenty-six years old, not a minor, but Peters had a feeling. Sure enough, her father, a wealthy businessman, didn't even know that Cortney and Nayeri were married—it was a secret she'd been keeping from her family, since she knew they wouldn't approve—and he was shocked to hear about what Cortney had gotten involved in.

I was playing golf with some of my friends on a Saturday when I got a call from an attorney who had just been retained by Cortney's father. "She's a nice young woman who has been terribly abused by her psycho husband," the lawyer said. "Let me bring her in for a proffer [an interview in exchange for a grant of use immunity] and she will tell you everything. I think she has information that may really help."

Normally, I wouldn't have believed that anything was going to get Hossein Nayeri out of Iran. His crime partners might go down for this, but what did he care? He had made it out. He was safe in his native country, which would never honor an extradition request. Under normal circumstances, we would have been done. But Cortney's lawyer was perhaps the only lawyer I knew who could potentially pull off the impossible: once again, my former boss and mentor, Lew Rosenblum.

It would not be unfair to ask why we were so open to hearing what Cortney had to say, but the reality is that a good prosecutor needs to have an open mind, and a good prosecutor needs to listen. Besides, at that point we had absolutely nothing to lose. At first glance, Cortney seemed like she might be as guilty as the rest of them, helping her husband at significant moments. After our interview, we alerted the State Bar regarding her possible involvement. But the more we learned about her, the more we all came to doubt that initial appearance. Over time, we all began to believe that Cortney was far more a victim than a villain. It became obvious that she had been abused and tormented by Nayeri for years. We had the unrelated police reports, from other departments, that certainly corroborated at least some of Nayeri's abuse. She undoubtedly believed he was going to kill her, and I have no doubt that if he ever gets the chance, he will. She was not Jennifer Deleon, scheming and smiling. But to get out of this mess, she was going to have to come completely clean, and work with us to deliver justice to her husband.

We sat down in the very same Newport Beach Police Department conference room where Alonso Machain had broken down the murder of Tom and Jackie Hawks. Cortney sat with Lew on one side of the table, and I sat with Heather Brown and Ryan Peters on the other. I am certain that Lew explained to Cortney the stakes of what was about to happen. He knew that the only reason we ever spoke to Alonso—and offered him a plea deal that cut his sentence from life without parole to twenty years—was because Jennifer Deleon let young love prevail and had refused to accept my offer of immunity. She is, of course, now serving two consecutive sentences of life without parole.

Lew also knew that in the Cathy Torrez trial, I made the decision not to use Xavier Lopez as a witness against his client, Sam, because I believed Xavier was dishonest during his proffer. If Cortney lied, or attempted to assist Nayeri in any way, Lew knew that she would lose all value as a witness and that we would not hesitate to prosecute her to the fullest extent of the law. Depending on what happened next, she might never again see freedom. This was the most important interview of her life.

Cortney, obviously terrified, proceeded to walk us through everything she knew. Over the next couple of hours, she told us things we were already aware of, and things we weren't. She gave us the names of most of the people involved, what happened, and why—and the ruthlessness of her husband was shocking to hear. As we had suspected, the plan to kidnap Michael was purely about money, and months in the making. Hossein Nayeri's descent into this kind of evil was pretty consistent with the story of his life. Nayeri's father was a doctor and his mother a lawyer, both in Iran—but despite growing up in an upper-middle-class environment, he couldn't escape trouble. He got in fights at school, had issues with authority, and ended up enlisting in the Marines, saying he wanted structure in his life. He was highly intelligent and spoke multiple languages, so he rose to a specialist role, though he didn't last more than a couple of years. He was involved in an altercation, went AWOL for a time, and was eventually given a dishonorable discharge. He contested it, and was able to get it changed to a general discharge, perhaps the first example we have of Nayeri being able to manipulate his way out of trouble.

He ended up back in Fresno working as a waiter, where he met sixteen-year-old Cortney. They began seeing each other—and she quickly found herself under the spell of Hossein Nayeri, an attractive guy with lots of charm.

We knew Nayeri had gone to high school with Kyle Handley, but what we did not know until Cortney's proffer was that Nayeri was also close to Naomi Rhodus. In fact, Naomi had previously been married to a man named Ryan Kevorkian, who happened to be one of Nayeri's closest friends.

Cortney also told us about Nayeri's previous escape to Iran—leaving Cortney behind—and, a year later, his return. He and Cortney soon got back together—she was in college at this point, on her way to law school—and he became more and more controlling and abusive. Cortney hid the relationship from family and friends, who did not approve. She later described that she felt as if she was living a double life—composed student during the day, secretly abused wife at night.

"There was the nice, charming, manipulative, draw-you-in part," Cortney ended up testifying about Nayeri. "And then there was this angry, crazy, temper-driven, scary part. And it could go from zero to a thousand in a minute. . . . Of course, I was in love with him."

In filing for a protective order against Nayeri, Cortney described an incident where he had knocked her over in a chair, stood on her neck and chest as he slapped her face, and then put her in a choke hold and punched her in the thigh when she attempted to get away.

And yet, she stayed—whether out of fear that he would hurt her if she tried to leave, or the kind of psychological manipulation that can happen when you've been with someone since you were really just a child yourself. In fact, when Nayeri and Kyle Handley started a brand-new marijuana growing business in 2011, Cortney funded it with her parents' money, using the credit card they gave her to pay for school expenses—$150,000 in all. Her parents didn't realize any of it—at least not until Ryan Peters gave Cortney's father a call.

Once Cortney was cooperating, the truth came out. She told police that she had lied about her SUV being stolen and, in fact, knew that Nayeri had been driving it. She filed the police report at Nayeri's direction after the chase. She described how he came home that night—or really the next morning—still wet from his swim and told her he'd abandoned the car and been hiding under a bridge.

She revealed that Nayeri had been stalking Michael's movements for months, convinced he had hidden away massive amounts of cash from his successful marijuana business. She admitted Nayeri told her to go online and gather as much information about Michael as she could. She also admitted she was with Nayeri on multiple occasions as he set up cameras all around the area, and watched as he secretly attached a GPS device to Michael's truck.

At first, Nayeri thought Michael was hiding his cash at his parents' house, and he set up a camera there. But Nayeri was worried he'd never be able to break in. The parents had a dog that would constantly bark whenever he approached—and the camera batteries needed to be replaced on a regular basis. Cortney then dropped a minor bombshell, at which point we knew she was being completely honest. She admitted that she helped her husband make poisoned meat, which Nayeri planned to feed to the dog. She bought the ground beef and watched him wear gloves as he mixed in some unknown toxin. He then told Cortney to throw away the pan when he was done cooking. Nayeri fed it to the dog—who happily gobbled it up, shrugged it off, and, thankfully, never even got sick.

The suspected location of the money soon shifted in Nayeri's mind. The GPS trackers revealed that Michael's car drove into the Mojave Desert one day, and Nayeri convinced himself that this was the clue he'd been waiting for: Like a pirate's treasure, the cash must be buried in the desert!

In reality, Michael was accompanying a friend to look at some real estate, an innocent and meaningless trip—but Nayeri imagined something entirely different.

Cortney explained that Nayeri had purchased a burner laptop to download all the GPS tracking information. In other words, he could do all the internet searches he wanted, download all the incriminating data, and then dump the computer. If anyone ever looked, all the other computers and electronic devices at his home would be totally clean. That was extremely clever, and something I had never seen before. Burner phones are common, but a burner computer?

Cortney went on to explain that the week before the kidnapping, Nayeri asked her to buy him four burner phones. She said she saw Nayeri and Kyle Handley playing with a blowtorch in their garage. She saw Nayeri try to scuff up a hard hat to make it look used, and she watched him pack up her pink stun gun. She knew he was up to something really bad, but didn't know exactly what. Whether to protect her, or simply to exercise more dominion and control, Nayeri never told her the plan.

The day of the kidnapping, he asked Cortney for four more burner phones and had her throw the other ones away. Ironically, the kidnapping was set to happen on the same day as their anniversary. After he left, Nayeri called Cortney and asked her to put money in the meter for Kyle's truck. She drove down to Balboa Peninsula and found the truck, parked very close to Michael's house.

After the event, she said Nayeri's socks were bloody, and she threw them away. She said he seemed frantic, especially after learning that Kyle had been arrested. He sent Cortney to Kyle's arraignment; when she came home reporting that he'd been charged with kidnapping, Nayeri panicked.

He got rid of every piece of electronic equipment in their house, and cleaned out Handley's house as well. From Kyle's house Nayeri took anything valuable and instructed Cortney to sell it all and send him the money. No honor among thieves. Less than two weeks after the kidnapping, Nayeri was on a one-way flight to Iran.

Cortney told us that Nayeri was closely monitoring the publicly accessible courthouse computer system in order to find out if we were on to him. The conventional move after a DNA hit would have been to file a case, get a warrant, and start looking for him. That would have meant a computer entry, and he would know he had been identified. But conventional was never going to be the best approach here. If we wanted any chance of catching this guy, we would have to be really smart.

Before computers, there were ways to file criminal charges using good old-fashioned paper pleadings. There is nothing in the law to say you cannot still do that. We very carefully let the Court know that we intended to use the ancient system. Court Clerks can be wonderful if you are nice to them, and, although this was highly unusual, they were more than happy to help us. Cortney had just handed us her first save.

Cortney went on to explain that she knew Naomi Rhodus was involved in the kidnapping, but she did not know her exact role. Cortney explained that Naomi's ex-husband, Ryan, had a falling out with Nayeri when Hossein beat him up over some sort of alleged spousal abuse. Although that may sound noble, it was more complicated than that. Nayeri's relationship with Naomi had apparently at some point become sexual. He was cheating on Cortney with his best friend's wife. We would eventually learn that Naomi had planned at least one trip to go see Nayeri while he was on the run and out of the country. This made it even more obvious: Nayeri was never hesitant to do what suited him.

With Cortney's interview complete, we had new evidence, new suspects, and a far clearer picture of what took place. As we suspected, Handley was as weak as he appeared, and Nayeri was the heavy in this whole thing. He had managed to persuade, cajole, and manipulate a bunch of people into helping him carry out his scheme. We had a brutalized victim, we knew exactly who the ringleader was, but we also knew there was no way to get him out of Iran—which meant that Nayeri would likely get away with it.

Unless he didn't.

Cortney's family made the best decision possible when they decided to bring in Lew Rosenblum. When Lew left the DA's Office, he told me there were three kinds of cases he'd be willing to take on: those too interesting to turn down, those offering too much money to turn down, and those where he really wanted to help someone who deserved a second chance. This case appeared to involve all three. Lew correctly saw Cortney as a victim of Hossein Nayeri, and someone who didn't deserve the potential life sentence she'd be facing for aiding and abetting. In his heart, even as a defense attorney, Lew would always have a fundamental drive to make sure the right thing happened. He would have certainly expressed to Cortney the critical importance of owning up to everything she had done, explaining to her that she had to be honest and forthright, even when it was embarrassing. In return, he hoped that we would eventually recognize that justice would not be served by sending her to prison for life.

Lew Rosenblum wasn't just a fierce advocate for his clients. He wasn't just a former Homicide guru making money on the private side. Like Detective Peters, Dave Byington, Larry Montgomery, Ernest Hemingway, and so many fine police officers and prosecutors I worked with over the years, Lew Rosenblum was a true hunter. We sat down and had a chat. I wanted Nayeri. Lew also wanted Nayeri to pay for what he had done, but above all, he wanted to save his client.

Years before, Lew Rosenblum taught me about the paramount importance of doing justice when invested with the awesome power of a criminal prosecutor. This is a man I trusted completely, and he trusted me back. Could Lew come up with a plan? What if Cortney were willing to help us bring Hossein Nayeri to justice? What would that look like? Lew must have hoped that if she could somehow lure Nayeri out of Iran—to a place where we could extradite him to the US and try him for these charges—then I would do the right thing, and eventually grant her full immunity.

This was not a formal agreement yet, and no promises were made. We would give Cortney the opportunity to do the right thing, reclaim her life, and at the same time lure a true psycho out of one country in the world that would certainly never give him back. Nothing like this had ever been done before, at least not in Orange County, and I think we both relished the challenge. But if we were really going to pull this off, it was going to take an insane amount of work, and no shortage of good luck. It would also be the last time Heather and I would be able to speak directly to Cortney. In order to ensure the integrity of the discovery process, all communication from that point forward would have to go through her attorney and Detective Peters.

Heather and I had more than a few doubts that Cortney wouldn't warn Nayeri. There is a scene in the movie *Heat* when Val Kilmer's character returns to his girlfriend (played by Ashley Judd) after a big heist. Behind the scenes, her place is filled with police ready to ambush him as soon as he walks in the door. They tell her to stand on the balcony so he knows she is home. With her hands on the railing, she makes the slightest motion with her finger, telling him to keep driving. He sees the signal and gets away. A single moment of weakness on Cortney's part, one second of emotional hesitation, and Nayeri would dig himself into the Islamic Republic of Iran like a tick.

We would never catch him. (And, depending on Cortney's actions, she might end up put away for life.)

A year earlier, Cortney had been talking to Nayeri's sister about taking a trip to Spain after she completed the California bar exam. It had been a while since they had spoken, but Lew saw an opportunity. What if police used that as a trap? Cortney was understandably petrified that Nayeri would find out she was cooperating and either find someone to come after her or do it himself. But she was even more scared of prison, and of sacrificing the rest of her life for a man she now realized was a sadistic, abusive psycho. And, as we would come to understand, she was actually a good person who felt horrible for what her husband did to that poor innocent man.

I knew we would need more help putting this together, so I reached out to my friend Erin Rowe, who was responsible for all international extraditions into Orange County. She loved the developing plan and immediately went to work. We wanted to know which country would be best to extradite from. If we were going to buy Nayeri a ticket to Spain, we could route him through any nation we wanted. If we did this right, his layover would be his last stop before getting him back to Orange County.

Each country has its own extradition treaty with the US and various levels of cooperation. The consensus pick for the most extradition-friendly country in Europe was, interestingly, the Czech Republic. Apparently, all countries from the former Soviet bloc have a great deal of respect for the American system of justice and trust the fairness and due process afforded criminal defendants here. Counterintuitively, some of the worst nations for extradition are the UK, France, and, not far behind them, Spain. They are often very difficult to work with. Erin set up a call with the special agent in charge of the FBI in Prague.

He explained that the Czechs were very cooperative with extradition requests but also extremely meticulous. (We would end up seeing how meticulous soon after.)

By the time we had an idea of how this crazy plan would be enacted, Cortney hadn't spoken to her husband in months. Looking for an opening, Ryan and Lew sent her to Nayeri's uncle's funeral, trusting word would get back to him, and that he might reach out. He did—and she worked to get back into his good graces. She told him she missed him, and casually mentioned the long-discussed trip to Spain and suggested they could rendezvous there. Cortney had run into Nayeri's sister at the funeral (she was, of course, completely in the dark about our plans), and they began talking again about the trip. The idea was to buy Nayeri a ticket to Barcelona on a flight with a stopover in Prague, where authorities there would nab him.

Meanwhile, detectives dug further into the involvement of Naomi Rhodus. They learned that Ryan Kevorkian was a former California Department of Corrections prison guard who had lost his job because he had apparently impregnated a female prisoner during one of his shifts. It turns out, this is frowned upon by the Department of Corrections. He was unemployed and needed money . . . and so he was the perfect accomplice for Nayeri. It seemed like everyone close to Nayeri was either dead or somehow involved in this crime.

Detectives began kicking around the idea that Kevorkian might have been the third guy in the van. They sent a team to his home in Lancaster, California, to perform some surveillance, and perhaps even get a DNA sample to compare with the partial profile found on the zip tie in Kyle Handley's backyard. It didn't take too long before two Newport detectives watched Kevorkian go into a 24 Hour Fitness for a workout. One of the officers was actually a member of the gym chain, so he strutted inside, tried to look like he was working out, and promptly stole Kevorkian's unattended gym towel. (Just like the trash you put outside for collection, there is no reasonable expectation of privacy when it comes to a towel you drop at the gym. Constitutionally, it is fair game.) When the towel was tested, there was no longer a question that the DNA on the zip tie belonged to Ryan Kevorkian. So we had the third guy, but we also knew he was just another role player in Nayeri's unholy scheme. We were still on the hunt for Nayeri.

As Cortney went to work, every call felt like a high-wire act. She worked to re-ingratiate herself into his family, spoke to him whenever he wished, and did everything Lew instructed her to do. She was utterly convinced Nayeri would eventually catch on, realize she was cooperating with police, and kill her. Lew Rosenblum must have felt as if he was deprogramming her from a cult of one.

Despite our doubts, she performed her role perfectly. It also took time. We didn't want to spook Nayeri, and knew he would have balked if she tried to force anything too early. Besides, she still had to study for, and take, the California bar exam. Among about a thousand ridiculous demands from Nayeri, he instructed Cortney to send him fake travel documents to enter the EU. Cortney checked in with Lew daily, and he provided regular updates to Detective Peters, who would in turn inform me and Heather. Days turned into weeks, and weeks into months.

I would love to take credit for the brilliant decisions that were made during this time, but the grunt work was truly all done by Erin Rowe, Detective Peters, Lew, and of course Cortney. There were literally a thousand different things that could have gone wrong and thwarted all of our efforts, but the crew was amazing, and Lew, in particular, was single-minded. This was a man with exactly one trial loss in his entire career, and it was to me. It was like being recruited and coached by Michael Jordan to play in the NBA, and then having him pass you the ball in game seven of the championships.

Of course, I was still balancing all of this with the thirty homicides on my caseload. As we waited for Cortney's trip, I tried the case of Stanwood Elkus, a crazy hypochondriac who stalked his former urologist before setting up an appointment under an assumed name and ambushing him in his medical office. I tried a serial killer named Andrew Urdiales, a former Marine whose hobby became the rape and murder of innocent college students, and also of sex workers in Southern California—before moving to Chicago, where he continued to kill.

Finally, the day came. Cortney packed thousands of dollars in cash that she promised she'd deliver to Nayeri, she had the tickets ready, and she planned to meet Nayeri's sister at the airport. The plane would be loaded with detectives, and the FBI would be waiting in Spain just in case Nayeri somehow got through the Czech Border Police.

Then . . . apparent disaster: The night before he was supposed to leave, Nayeri suddenly wasn't answering Cortney's calls or texts. Had he figured it out? Did his sister notice something we'd missed and tip him off? This would have crushed us all. Finally, at the very last minute, just as Cortney was giving up hope, Nayeri called and said he had overslept but he was leaving for the airport.

He made the flight. And more than a year after Michael and Mary's abduction, Hossein Nayeri landed at Prague's Václav Havel Airport. As he raced to make his connection to Barcelona, the Czech Border Police surrounded him in force. Instead of a rendezvous with his wife, he met a group of stern, no-nonsense Czechs, all of whom knew that Nayeri had allegedly cut off a man's penis during a robbery attempt. They brought a fierce police dog, and I'm sure more than one of those officers hoped Nayeri would fight and end up attacked. Nayeri was blindsided. He couldn't believe it.

It was victory.

Or so it seemed.

Nayeri spent almost a year in Prague as the government processed the extradition request, in an Eastern European gulag-type prison that was actually constructed by the Nazis during World War II. It was not designed with prisoner comfort in mind. Erin Rowe went to work on the extradition. Cortney went into hiding, thinking Nayeri would find a way to come after her, especially after she sent him divorce papers arguing their marriage actually qualified for an annulment. It turns out, in addition to everything else, when Nayeri originally fled back to Iran after the manslaughter charge, he apparently married another woman. (A California Court ended up dissolving the marriage, confirming the bigamy claim.)

Finally, we received approval from the Czech government and Nayeri was flown back to the US. At long last, Detective Ryan Peters placed handcuffs on Hossein Nayeri at JFK Airport in New York City. Nobody could believe we actually pulled this off, and we toasted our success.

We were a tad premature.

The Orange County Men's Central Jail uses a banded inmate classification system. This means that when a new inmate enters the jail, a custodial officer conducts a review of the person's background, criminal record, gang affiliation, and risk of dangerousness to other inmates or staff. "Dangerousness" is also supposed to include danger to the community should the inmate, crazy as it might sound, try to escape. They then assign a band color from worst to best—blue (medically contagious), red, orange, yellow, or white, white being for the majority of inmates, who are of least concern. The inmates have to wear the assigned band on their wrists at all times. Part of the process involves an in-person interview during which inmates are checked for tattoos. These can tell officers almost everything from prior prison terms (convicts love to tattoo themselves) to aliases. This process works well when dealing with a gangster with "13" tattooed on his face, but not so well when it comes to a smart, charming, and highly manipulative guy like Nayeri.

Somehow, despite a felony conviction for manslaughter, a known history of working in the illegal underworld of the marijuana business, two previous trips to Iran to escape justice, and a shocking crime for which he now faced life without the possibility of parole, Nayeri convinced the classification officer to give him a white band. He was assigned to a dormitory filled with DUI defendants, wife beaters, and strung-out druggies too broke to make bail. Can you imagine what's coming next?

Nayeri was soon the king of his dormitory, an overcrowded, bunk bed–filled room. Despite growing up in California and speaking perfect, unaccented English, he was permitted to enroll in the jail's English as a second language class, taught by a single, lonely Persian woman in her late forties with a bunch of small dogs. Nayeri naturally turned on the charm. He convinced her to bring a satellite photo that showed the roof of the jail, complaining that his lawyer, whose office was across the street, wasn't visiting him often enough. Just like Cortney and Naomi, the ESL teacher was soon head over heels in love with him, and completely under his spell.

Meanwhile, we charged Naomi and Ryan. We offered a proffer agreement to Naomi, and her interview made it clear she had been a key player in Nayeri's scheme. She purchased the firearms used in the kidnapping, but she wasn't smart enough to admit her full involvement. She came up with some story about the guns, claiming she did a bunch of stuff for Nayeri but had no idea what he was up to and was shocked to find out the full story. Shocked!

There were three fundamental differences between her and Cortney: First, Naomi presented as a thoroughly pathetic figure. She was not particularly bright, loaded down with children with a soon-to-be-convict father, and had no career. Next, she wasn't completely honest, and trying to convince us she didn't know the plan made her useless as a potential witness. Finally, she was not going to be able to help us get Nayeri. She wasn't smart enough to pull it off, and we had absolutely no faith she would actually do the right thing.

On the other hand, she did explain how she got a friend to go to Enterprise and rent the infamous white van, and thus filled in one more connection between the instrumentalities of the crime and Nayeri.

At the very end of the hours-long interview, she added as an afterthought, "Oh yeah, I also have some stuff in storage." When police searched, they found the shotgun used to beat Michael and the laptop Nayeri used to download all the information from the GPS trackers. Afterthought, indeed. The case was really coming together, and we had every player in this terrible crime safely locked up in jail. Or so we thought.

On the afternoon of January 22, 2016, the Orange County Sheriff's Department conducted a count of the white-banded inmates. Then... a recount, followed immediately by another recount. To the great surprise of jail staff, there were three missing prisoners: Jonathan Tieu, Bac Duong... and Hossein Nayeri. Like some nightmare combination of *The Shawshank Redemption* and *Escape from Alcatraz*, sheriff's deputies soon discovered that a small wall vent near Nayeri's bunk had been cut away, creating a false front. This led into a passageway behind the wall that was used to access plumbing behind the jail cells. They found that a series of barred metal gates within the passageway had also meticulously been cut away. The cuts were clean and appeared to have been made with a hacksaw—because that's exactly what had happened. The opened gates led to a series of jerry-rigged ladders made from braided bedsheets leading to the roof.

So, after an international manhunt involving the FBI, the United States Marshal's Service, the Czech Border Police, and more hours and hard work than I can possibly describe, Hossein Nayeri was in the wind. Cortney, having warned us repeatedly that he would kill her if he ever got the chance, was immediately whisked away to an undisclosed location where she would be held under twenty-four-hour police protection. But "immediately" is relative. It had been fifteen hours since the last count, and these guys could be anywhere. Naturally, nobody in the crowded dorm knew or saw a thing. . . .

One more detail: Nayeri had left two printed photographs on his empty bunk, one of Heather Brown . . . and one of me. A clear threat. The sheriff notified Heather first, who called me swearing up a storm. "It's like they released Hannibal Lecter! How in God's name did they classify him so low?!"

Sheriff's deputies were immediately assigned to guard Heather's home, where she lived with her husband and young son.

My dear friend and assigned Homicide investigator Don Holford met me at my house with some Manhattan Beach Police officers to check the inside of my house, just in case Nayeri was waiting for me there. He wasn't. But as they cleared the house, I wondered if any of the Manhattan Beach officers had been in the police car I threw the newspaper at the night before the Wozniak trial. If they were, they didn't say anything. I looked for a dent on the patrol car door. All clear.

Growing up as a surfer in Southern California, I spent a lot of time surfing in northern Mexico and developed a pretty good understanding of just how easy it is to cross the border. Having studied international law for a summer, I also knew that Mexico and Iran enjoy surprisingly warm diplomatic relations. So Hossein Nayeri, a citizen of Iran, had a fifteen-hour head start to get to a border less than three hours away. The Iranian Embassy in Tijuana is located just a few short minutes from the point of entry. All he needed to do was head south, and walk in, and he would enjoy full diplomatic sanctuary and a ticket home. There was little doubt in my mind that the clever guy we had so meticulously outsmarted had just outsmarted us. The word *disappointment* fails to describe my feelings at that moment.

A new manhunt was launched. The FBI and US Marshal's Office were notified, the Newport Beach Police Department went to work, and we hoped to get lucky . . . again. Lew was understandably losing his mind. "How did they manage to screw that up?!"

The following day, I met with Orange County Sheriff Sandra Hutchens, her command staff, the FBI, Newport, and everyone else, attempting to figure out what to do next. Investigators had recovered a series of personal letters in Nayeri's abandoned possessions that appeared to be from the ESL teacher. The letters were written in the first person, as if authored by her, indicating very clear involvement in the escape plan. She wrote about the likelihood of her getting caught, or him getting caught, and ruining the life they planned together. The content of the letters was damning and incredibly convincing. The sheriffs wanted charges filed against her as soon as possible. I took copies of the letters home in order to thoroughly read them before making any filing decisions.

As I went through them there was something oddly familiar about some of the phrases used, as well as the handwriting. Among the items recovered from Naomi Rhodus were multiple documents that contained Nayeri's handwriting. When I checked those against the letters purported to be from the ESL teacher, they had clearly been written by the same person. Incredibly, after having had some sort of falling out, Nayeri's parting gift to that sad, lonely woman was to set her up for potentially far greater involvement in the escape than she ever really had. He deliberately wrote those letters and left them to be discovered. Astounding.

The following day, we were hit with another blow. Somehow, Nayeri had managed to get a cell phone smuggled into the jail. He used the phone to video his entire escape and had the unmitigated bravado to post it online. In the video, you see him smiling, relaxed, removing the air grate, and even throwing a thumbs-up to the camera. It shows him and his fellow escapees using the bedsheets to propel themselves up the ventilation system to the roof. He even added the *Mission: Impossible* soundtrack. I fully expected the next posted download to come from Iran, Nayeri with a smile on his face and an extended middle finger to me and my whole team. But one day turned into two, and then three—with no word.

I was worried for Cortney, of course—but I was also at least a little concerned for Heather and the rest of our team. (I was less worried about myself, mostly because I was personally confident Nayeri wasn't sticking around in California and was already across the border in Mexico.) While waiting for his case to come to trial, Nayeri had been provided all the police reports and investigative materials as part of the discovery process. This means he had answers to all of the questions that had to have been plaguing him as he sat and waited for his yearlong extradition in Prague. As soon as he got those reports after having been arraigned in Orange County Superior Court, Nayeri would have learned how we turned his wife against him, sent her to his uncle's funeral, and used his sister to further assure him that his trip to Spain was safe. He would have read all about our work with the different agencies and the complexities that went into the planning of his recapture.

He had to have been more than a little surprised at the lengths we were willing to go to get justice for Michael and Mary. Mostly, I knew he would have hated the fact that we had been smarter than him. Unlike some little gangster trying to sound tough in Court, when threatened by a guy like this, motivated by no small amount of personal animus, you really do have to look over your shoulder.

Seven days into the manhunt, with no leads, we suddenly got a huge break. Bac Duong showed up at an auto repair shop in Santa Ana and asked them to call 911 so he could turn himself back in. He was with a Vietnamese taxi driver who claimed he had been kidnapped by the escaped trio. Duong explained that they had rappelled off the roof of the jail and met a waiting taxi. Nayeri and the others somehow managed to get a gun, and they allegedly used it to take the taxi driver hostage.

The day after the escape, Duong arranged to test-drive a white GMC van that had been advertised on Craigslist. Instead of returning it, he picked up his fellow escapees, along with the taxi driver, and headed north . . . not south as I had expected. While recording all of it, they traveled up the California coast, with stops at the beach along the way (where they posed for pictures), and eventually to San Francisco. At one point, Nayeri and Duong ended up in an argument—according to Duong—over the question of whether or not to kill the cab driver. The argument soon became physical, and from there it got violent. Duong ended up leaving with the taxi driver when Nayeri and Tieu were gone. He had weighed his options, and he preferred the relative safety of life behind bars to being with the unpredictable and very dangerous Nayeri.

On the morning of January 29, a homeowner in the Bay Area near San Francisco reported the disturbing image of a man walking along the side of her house at three in the morning. The video was captured on her home surveillance camera, and the man was unmistakably Hossein Nayeri. The homeowner was listed as "N. Kevorkian," the former name of Naomi Rhodus. It has never been clear if he was looking for Naomi in order to seek help, or to seek revenge for her cooperation. Whatever his reason for being there, he soon left.

Nayeri and the inmate who remained with him ended up in Golden

Gate Park in San Francisco, where they videoed themselves inside the van smoking pot and eating bananas. At this point, the story of the escape was all over the news, with Nayeri being compared to Hannibal Lecter (by Heather) for the gratuitous brutality of his actions. Nayeri popped out of the van for a minute and was spotted by a local homeless man who, as it turned out, was a news junkie. He had read about Nayeri in the *San Francisco Chronicle* and recognized him. He called the police and reported "that Hannibal Lecter guy you're looking for is here right now." Police soon arrived, and they apprehended the two men. Finally, after eight days, Hossein Nayeri was back in custody, and Cortney (and the rest of us) could breathe again.

With national media focused on the escape, the sheriff's department decided not to repeat the classification error they had made before. Nayeri exchanged his white bracelet for a red one, meaning he had constant surveillance within the jail. They shackled his hands and feet for each Court appearance, and housed him with twenty-four-hour video cameras to ensure this didn't happen again.

Finally, in 2019, seven years after the abduction, the trial of Hossein Nayeri began. Kyle Handley had already been convicted and sentenced to two life terms without the possibility of parole for kidnapping Mary and torturing and mutilating Michael. Now, Nayeri was doing his best to put all the blame on Kyle. He insisted the glove was planted by police (sound familiar?) and that he had nothing to do with this terrible crime. There was no physical proof he was at the scene.

Cortney became a key witness, and was mercilessly attacked by Nayeri's lawyer for purportedly lying about him to save herself. And then, the moment we had all been waiting for—Nayeri decided to take the stand in his own defense. He was perfect during the direct questioning from his own attorney, controlled, soft-spoken, even getting emotional at times, and probably leaving the jury wondering if he was actually capable of doing something like this. He had crafted his own bizarre tale, insisting he had almost $2 million in marijuana profits of his own hidden away, and that he planned on getting out of the business and starting a family with Cortney. He claimed the surveillance was a favor to Kyle, who had paid him to watch Michael, who supposedly owed Kyle $300,000 (he didn't).

And then it was my turn. The goal in a case like this is always to see if you can get the defendant to "flash." You are searching for some subtle moment of weakness, usually hours into cross-examination, when you can get the jury to see the true personality of the person testifying. In crimes of violence, you always hope for a moment of anger where the true colors of the defendant come out. Hossein "Adam" Nayeri required no such subtlety or skill. With my very first question on cross-examination, it was immediately apparent to everyone in the courtroom that the man absolutely hated me. He was instantly combative, interrupted, answered questions with questions of his own, and snapped at me repeatedly. At one point, the judge had to stop the proceedings, excuse the jury, and instruct Nayeri to simply answer the pending question.

Among the many things Nayeri claimed on direct examination was that he had never been inside Michael's place of business. But we had a series of photographs recovered from the original burner phone found in the Chevy Tahoe. Those images showed the business directory for Michael's building, one of those glass boxes you typically find on the bottom floor of an office building with those white plastic letters indicating which suite corresponds with which business.

This was an odd denial, and potentially a huge mistake. I showed him the first image of the directory and asked if he had taken that photo. He adamantly denied it. I then moved on to other questions and topics before returning and asking again if he went inside the office building, which he again denied. I showed him another photo from the burner phone that again depicted the same directory, followed by another adamant denial. I did three or four rounds of that, getting Nayeri to insist to the jury, quite convincingly, over and over again, that he never took any of those photos.

Finally, I hit him with our zinger. The final photograph in the sequence was taken at an angle creating a reflection in the glass. This reflection very clearly depicted the photographer, who, complete with trendy aviator shades, was undoubtedly Hossein Nayeri. If he didn't hate me before, he certainly hated me then. The home run of all cross-examinations is to catch the witness in a lie. When it comes to criminal defendants testifying on their own behalf, it is one thing to lie to the police or the judge or a prosecutor, but it is an entirely different thing when they lie to the jury that will decide their fate. I had him, and he knew it.

As I wrapped up my cross-examination, I just had one more question, something that I had been wondering about ever since I got the first call from Newport Beach detectives alerting me about the kidnapping. "When you were out in the desert with Michael, and you cut off his penis, why couldn't you just leave it there in the hope it could be reattached?" I asked him.

"I'm going to give you an answer for that," Nayeri said. "Personally."

He followed by saying, "You're done!"

"What do you mean I'm done?" I asked. "What does that mean, Mr. Nayeri?" Although he was menacing and full of hate, I loved that moment. A criminal defendant hitting you with a not-so-veiled threat on the stand is about as good as it gets for setting up a closing argument. Nayeri finally got the duel he wanted. It was a battle of wits that brought him from a place of safety into potentially spending the rest of his life in a level four prison. He came out swinging from the first bell and by the end found himself flat on the canvas. Or so I thought.

During the closing argument, we used the jailbreak to show the jury who the true mastermind of this plan really was. Kyle Handley was an idiot, wrapped around Nayeri's finger. Ryan Kevorkian was a slightly smarter version of the same thing, as was everyone else in this twisted scheme. Of this group of definitive knuckleheads, there was only one with the mental wattage to put this together. Hossein Nayeri. Nayeri came up with the plan. Nayeri had the manipulative ability to bring all these people together. And Nayeri possessed the cruelty, malice, and singular drive to make it all happen.

I had shown the jury that even in a controlled environment, Nayeri was angry, menacing, and dangerous. This was a guy who literally threatened a Deputy District Attorney in open court, while surrounded by armed police, a Superior Court Judge, and the jury that would decide his fate. Just imagine what he was willing to do in a van in the middle of nowhere when he was frustrated and not getting what he wanted. I had eleven of the twelve jurors nodding along with enthusiasm. The twelfth juror, however, a young woman working as a food server, wouldn't make eye contact. I was concerned we had a problem.

The jury for Kyle Handley had come back with a verdict quickly, so I was hoping for the same here. This was to be my final trial as a prosecutor, and the case went off to the jury on my very last week. As I packed up my office and said goodbye to all of the wonderful people I had worked with over the years, I was beginning to lose my mind. How could I have been dumb enough to leave someone on the jury who fit the one demographic most likely to fall for Nayeri's manipulative voodoo? A young, single female . . .

The jury continued to deliberate through Tuesday, Wednesday, and all-day Thursday, my very last day. After twenty-six years, I was leaving the office and heading into private practice. I turned in my key card and ID, and walked out of the office for the last time. I headed to a retirement party at a local restaurant that some of my buddies were

THE BOOK OF MURDER

nice enough to throw for me. As I was parking my car, thinking I had managed to hang my last jury trial as a prosecutor, I got a call from Sal Ciulla, Nayeri's defense lawyer.

Sal was a class act and a tremendous trial lawyer I had known and respected for years. He left me a very nice voicemail congratulating me, I thought, on my retirement. I walked into the party, and my team seemed surprisingly happy. My paralegal, Dena Basham, and my investigator, Don Holford, were downright joyous. "Congratulations!" they shouted together.

"Thanks, guys. I'm really going to miss you. . . ."

"No, idiot!" Dena said, as everyone else laughed. "You have a verdict!"

It turned out that the young woman I was so worried about wasn't the problem I imagined. They apparently just needed to talk through the entire case. The following day, I had to be re-sworn in as a Deputy DA in order to take the verdict.

Nayeri was found guilty on the kidnapping and torture counts, but not the mayhem charge, which required the jury to be convinced that he personally cut off the penis. It was a compromise verdict, perhaps, but that didn't bother me in the least. Nayeri had been outsmarted, outplayed, and was now convicted. He would soon be sentenced to two consecutive life terms without the possibility of parole. In the end, for the sake of Michael S. and Mary Barnes, I felt like justice had finally been served.

We were not quite done. Lew worked as hard as he could to ensure justice for his client, Cortney Shegerian. As the State Bar looked into Cortney—recall, we had alerted them to the situation—Lew hoped they would be convinced that she deserved a second chance—and to get to keep her law license. Finally, after years of process, they agreed with Lew and Cortney's fine State Bar attorney that Cortney was another victim of Hossein Nayeri. She now spends much of her time doing pro bono work for the Los Angeles County Bar Association's Domestic Violence Program and the Sojourn Battered Women's Shelter, in addition to doing trials of her own for the law firm she cofounded.

Michael is still in the marijuana business.

For the last trial of my prosecutorial career, it was a doozy. Hossein Nayeri is among the cruelest, most devious, and dangerous criminal defendants I ever encountered, right up there with Rodney Alcala, Skylar Deleon, and Daniel Wozniak, each as manipulative and vicious as they were devoid of any human remorse. All young men when they entered California State Prison, each will spend richly deserved decades of their fleeting lives withering away in maximum security lockdown, incapable, God willing, of hurting anyone ever again.

CONCLUSION

IN THE END, I completed fifty-two jury trials during my time in Homicide. Throughout the seventeen years I spent in that Unit, I had wonderful investigators, a phenomenal paralegal, and support- ive bosses—without whom we never would have achieved justice for any of my victims' families. Some of the cases were sensational, while some had no media whatsoever, but the overwhelming major- ity of trials involved at least one person who loved the victim or—far too often—victims. I was very careful about the charges I filed, but on more than one occasion I dismissed entire cases when new evidence caused me to entertain doubts about a defendant's guilt. The sacro- sanct obligation of a prosecutor, after all, is to achieve justice, not convictions.

By the time my cases reached a jury, I never argued a single point against a single defendant that I did not earnestly and passionately believe to be true. Despite my maddening talent to screw things up in my personal life, when it came to my jury trials—in one form or another—I'm humbled to say that we won them all.

I can see now that perhaps I paid a steep personal price for my long-ago decision to go all in. The dedication and work required to achieve success at that level meant big sacrifices in my personal time, and even more in my personal relationships. Looking back, I was a terrible romantic partner for much of the time I was in the Homicide Unit. I never married, never had kids, and I have no small amount of regret (and even some shame) for the way I prioritized work over some of the relationships I was in at the time. One, in particular, haunts me even now.

That said, looking back at my time as a Homicide prosecutor, I miss the job, and my wonderful team, every single day.

After leaving the DA's Office, I signed a deal with ABC News to help them navigate some of the more interesting crime stories covered by their network. My dear friend Lisa Soloway, a senior editorial producer for *20/20*, wound up airing several episodes about some of the cases covered in this book. One of them, "The *Dating Game* Killer," caught the attention of actor (and now director) Anna Kendrick. She decided to produce a feature film about Rodney Alcala for her directorial debut, and she reached out to me to learn more about the case. Anna wanted to know about the history, the various players, and what it was like to deal with Rodney on an interpersonal—face-to-face—basis.

As we spoke, it quickly became clear that she was as captivated as I was in trying to understand the dark mind of a true serial killer. I was thoroughly impressed with her intelligence, sensitivity to the victims, and clear desire to better understand one of the most prolific murderers of our time. Of course, I was happy to help. Over the course of a few meetings, I grew to really like her. She is funny, super smart, and as dedicated to her craft as I have been to mine.

Anna invited me to the set one day to watch the filming of a scene where Rodney Alcala approached a group of girls on the beach. Not far from where I grew up, the location was one of a handful of spots where I had learned to surf as a kid. It was also one of the actual beaches where Alcala hunted for his victims.

Arriving in the late afternoon, I was walking through the parking lot toward the lights and cameras on the sand when I experienced one of the most surreal moments of my life. Looking for Anna, I accidentally bumped into a young man with long hair and bell-bottoms who was talking to a member of the crew. We both did a quick double take, and I suddenly found myself face-to-face with a young Rodney Alcala. Instantly recognizable, the actor who had studied the role was a true pro—and he realized that I was one of the prosecutors of the killer he was portraying. I had a strange and totally inappropriate desire to hug him. He, along with the rest of the crew, could not have possibly been nicer, more professional, or more gracious.

As I watched this young actor do his thing, directed by one of the most talented artists in Hollywood, I felt as if I was actually watching Rodney in full predator mode as he charmed a group of young women sitting around a campfire near the water. It gave me chills.

Knowing what the real Rodney would have done next also reminded me of the true heroes I was so deeply privileged to work with over the years: the dedicated professionals who show up in the middle of the night, in the rain and the cold, with empty stomachs and open minds, all without a single complaint. It occurred to me in that bizarre, full-circle moment that I felt a great sense of satisfaction (and maybe even a little pride) about my chosen profession and the wonderful people I met along the way. I didn't have to run in there to save those girls because, in real life, my friend Craig Robison already had. He caught that monster, and saved God-only-knows-how-many lives by doing so. Then Gina and I had the honor of putting Alcala away for good.

I had learned to surf on that beach the very same summer Alcala kidnapped and murdered that poor girl, sporting my own pair of personalized Vans skateboarding shoes, so similar to Robin Samsoe's. And there I was, no longer a skinny kid with a beat-up old surfboard, but the director's guest on the set of a movie dramatizing one of my cases. What a strange journey it all turned out to be, and how incredibly lucky I felt, even with the struggles.

As the sun was setting behind Rodney by the water, something else caught my eye. A fun-looking right-hander started to peel onto the sandbar just over the actor's shoulder. A new swell was just starting to fill in, and it looked like the weather the next day was going to be perfect. I needed to get home and go to bed. The waves in the morning were going to be great, and I was going surfing.

ACKNOWLEDGMENTS

It was my profound honor to serve the people of Orange County for twenty-six years, and to bring justice to the families who went through the unimaginable. In doing so, it was a privilege to work with some of the greatest police officers, detectives, prosecutors, and people on the planet, some of whom I've mentioned in these pages and some of whom I haven't. My gratitude for your hard work and dedication cannot properly be expressed with words. I would like to call particular attention to a group of true heroes, my wonderful investigators, who kept me on track—and relatively sane—case after case, and trial after trial. My most heartfelt thanks to OCDA investigators Candice Boyd, Kathy Tomlinson, Carol Mona, Larry Montgomery, Lisa Hunter, Susan Frasier, and Sergeant Don Holford. I love you all and miss you every day.

I want to thank Senior Assistant District Attorney Kathy Harper for giving me a shot as a Law Clerk in 1992, and DA Supervisors Bruce Patterson, Rosanne Froeberg, Jack Sullens, and Bryan Brown for tolerating me in Misdemeanor Court. I especially want to thank the Honorable Rick King for teaching me how to navigate the complex ethics of sexual assault cases, the Honorable Chris Evans for instructing me to never fear the tough case, and Assistant District Attorney

Lew Rosenblum for bringing me into Homicide, mentoring me, and teaching me how to be the best lawyer (and person) I could be.

Thank you to my wonderful teammate and paralegal Dena Basham . . . yes, the struggle is real. A huge thanks as well to Homicide supervisors Dave Brent, Dan Wagner, and Allison Gyves for your friendship and the support I needed to seek justice. I also want to thank the many wonderful detectives who stood by me (figuratively) and sat by me (literally) as we prosecuted some of the worst killers in the country. Special thanks to Newport Beach Detective Dave Byington, and Chief Joe Cartwright, Detectives Jay Short, Dave White, Ryan Peters, Brad Peters, and Keith Krallman, and Costa Mesa Detectives Lieutenant Ed Everett, Jose Morales, Stephanie Salinski, Carlos Diaz, Julian Trevino, Pat Wessel, Scott Stafford, Mike Cohen, and Mike Delgadillo (RIP). Thank you to Sheriffs' Sergeants Don Voght, Gary Jones, and Ray Wert; Irvine Police Detectives Mike Hamel, Tracy Jacobson, and Chief Michael Kent; Huntington Beach Detectives Pat Ellis, Dave Dierking, and the legendary Ed Duel. Thank you to Laguna Beach's venerable Captain Jason Kravitz. You are all some of the best humans I have ever met, and it was truly an honor to work with each and every one of you.

Tremendous thanks to my crew of fellow prosecutors in the Homicide Unit: Senior Deputy District Attorneys Jim Mulgrew (not a misfit), Dennis Conway (definitely a misfit), Howard Gundy, the Honorable Mike Murray, Scott Simmons, the Honorable Ebrahim Baytieh, the Honorable Kevin Haskins, Suzie Price, Troy Pino, Colonel Jim Mendelson, Mary Ann McCauley, Ed Flores, Brian Gurwitz, Eric Scarborough, Seaton Hunt, Cameron Talley, Jen Walker, the Honorable Cynthia Herrera, Bruce Moore, the Honorable Walter Schwarm, the Honorable Tom Glazier, Sonia Balleste, Sharron Tekolian, Keith Bogardus, the Honorable Steve McGreevey, and the

Honorable Larry Yellin. Your collective fellowship meant the world to me.

I owe a tremendous debt to a group of Superior Court Judges who had the courage to make the right decisions and do the right thing, and who always managed to strike a balance between scrupulous fairness to the accused and dignity for the victims. Thank you to Gregg Prickett, Frank Fasel, Fransico Briseno (RIP), Kazuharu Makino, William Froeberg, Cory Cramin, Mike McCartin, David Thompson, David O. Carter (aka God), Tom Goethals, Dan McNerney, William Bedsworth, Sheila Hanson, Charles Margines, Greg Jones, Brett London, James Rogan, Matt Anderson, Art Kholle, and Nancy Wieben Stock, Patrick Donahue, and Commissioners Clancy Haynes, Marty Enquist, Matt McCormick, and Joe Dane.

I would also like to thank elected District Attorneys Tony Rackauckas, Steve Cooley, and Jackie Lacy for their steady and fair approach to criminal justice.

After leaving the DA's Office, I never imagined that I'd find a rewarding journey so quickly, but the people at ABC News have made me feel like a part of the family. A huge thanks to Senior Editorial Producer Lisa Soloway, without whom I would never have had this experience, Executive Producers Colleen Halpin and Santina Leuci for their continued confidence in my ability to help tell a story, and Director Dave Hoffman and Post Production Editor Mitch Kress for somehow making me sound smart, and a special thanks to my friend Elizabeth Vargas, who has graciously allowed me to appear with her on NewsNation, where I am learning how to do live TV. I would also like to thank Ashleigh Banfield and Chris Cuomo for inviting me on their shows to discuss the latest cases of the day, and Dan Abrams of the Law and Crime Network.

It has been wonderful to work with Kelly McLear and Kevin Balfe at CrimeCon, where I've gotten to meet so many wonderful true crime fans and supporters. The CrimeCon universe has given me the chance to talk to a number of incredible podcasters who've brought out some of my best stories, including Heather McDonald and her awesome podcast *Juicy Scoop*, Susan Hendricks from *Headline Crime*, Melissa McCarty from *Killer Genes*, Angenette Levy from *Crime Fix*, and Joshua Ritter from *TCD Sidebar*.

A book is of course the product of many people's hard work. What you have in your hands wouldn't be possible without the superb effort of my agents, David Larabell, Mark McGrath, and Rachel Adler, along with their wonderful colleagues at CAA, who saw the potential of this project to speak to readers from the start. I could not have found a better partner than Adam Wilson at Hyperion Avenue to help me bring it to life, along with his team, including Alex Serrano, Kaitie Leary, Sara Liebling, Guy Cunningham, Sylvia Davis, Karen Krumpak, Christine Paik Choi, Amy King, and Charles Brock, who designed the amazing cover.

I also gratefully acknowledge and extend my heartfelt gratitude to the extraordinary work of my amazing writing partner, Jeremy Blachman, a true professional whose patience I'm certain I tested along the way. Thank you, Jeremy, for everything you have done. I hope we get to do many more books together.

Thanks to my legal assistant, Heather Rowland, who puts up with me and keeps my life running (semi) smoothly.

Thank you to Jessica, a brilliant writer and sweet soul, for inspiring me to write this book.

And, finally, thanks to all of you—for engaging on Instagram and elsewhere, for reminding me this work matters and that people truly do care, and for supporting my efforts to tell these stories and honor the victims and their families.